CW00556444

'Fighting Joshua'

A Study of the Career of
Sir Jonathan Trelawny, bart,
1650-1721
Bishop of Bristol, Exeter and Winchester

M.G. SMITH

DYLLANSOW TRURAN

First published 1985
Dyllansow Truran
Trewolsta, Trewirgie, Redruth, Cornwall.

1985 M.G. Smith

All rights reserved. No part of this publication
may be reproduced or transmitted in any form,
or by any means, electronic or mechanical,
including photocopying, recording, or any
information storage and retrieval system, without
permission in writing from the publisher.

The publication of this book has been assisted
by a grant from the
Twenty-Seven Foundation Awards

To the archivists of Great Britain
without whose courtesy,
helpfulness and suggestions,
many a scholarly reputation
would remain ill-formed,
this book is respectfully
dedicated.

Typeset in Times Series by Helston Printers Ltd.
Printed in Great Britain by A. Wheaton & Co. Ltd., Exeter.

PREFACE

The history of the Church of England from the Restoration of Charles II to the accession of George I has been ploughed and harrowed into a fine tilth by scholars on both sides of the Atlantic. So many biographies of bishops have appeared in this century that the academic world is weary of them. The writer can only plead that he began this present study many years ago when interest in the period was far from jaded, but that his duties have not afforded him either the time or the money to complete this book any faster. Apart from these handicaps, shared with most amateurs, the material out of which a biography of Sir Jonathan Trelawny, baronet, might readily be fashioned has not been plentiful. An early biography or an accessible accumulation of family papers is wanting. Frequently it has been necessary to sift, patiently, through mounds of routine diocesan administrative material in order to extract the occasional nugget of biographical evidence.

When Alfred J. Horwood travelled down to Trelawne on behalf of the newly formed Historical Manuscripts Commission, he discovered an accumulation of Trelawny family papers overwhelming in their number and range. In the days he stayed at Trelawne House as a guest of the baronet, he could do no more than skim the surface. In the Commission's *First Report* (1874) he included only occasional extracts from letters which caught his eye. When Trelawne House and estate were sold in 1921 there remained only the legal documents, leases, conveyances, court rolls and the like. All the letters and other papers, some dating from the fifteenth century, had disappeared. Extensive enquiries have not revealed the whereabouts of more than a handful of these. I am particularly indebted, therefore, to A.L. Rowse who alerted me to the existence of a manuscript volume containing a selection of papers and letters compiled by Sir William Salusbury-Trelawny, and to the late Mr. Francis Williams who generously placed the volume at my disposal.

There are many other people whom I wish to thank. H.R.H. the Prince of Wales, the Dukes of Marlborough and Rutland, and the Marquess of Bath for permission to consult the documents in their possession. I am grateful to Sir John Trelawny for letting me read one of the Bishop's sermons in manuscript and to Sir John Carew-Pole and Mrs. Rosemary Parker for permission to use the papers of the Buller family belonging to them. The staffs of the manuscript departments of the Cambridge University Library, the Bodleian Library, the British Library, Lambeth Palace, the University of Nottingham Library and Trinity College, Dublin, have all be most helpful: so too have been the archivists of the House of Lords, the Public Record Office, the county record offices of

Bristol, Cornwall, Devon, Dorset, Gloucester, Hampshire and Greater London, and of the cathedral chapters of Exeter and Winchester. The librarians of Christ Church and Corpus Christi, Oxford and of Magdalene College, Cambridge, the records officer of the Church Commissioners, and the librarians of Exeter City and Plymouth City have courteously allowed me access to the manuscripts in their charge. I am grateful to others who have answered queries by letter, notably members of the staff of the Royal Commission on Historical Manuscripts, the Royal Institution of Cornwall, the Royal Archives of Windsor, the Society for Promoting Christian Knowledge, the National Maritime Museum at Greenwich, James Derriman and the Reverend W.M.M. Picken.

Research has become an expensive business, so my thanks are due to the British Academy which gave me a grant from the Small Grants Research in the Humanities Fund. Without that financial help I doubt if I should have been able to complete the task.

I must record my deep personal thanks to Dr. Anne Whiteman who has encouraged me to persevere and who read these chapters as they were written. She has made many useful criticisms and corrections. Needless to say what appears here is entirely my responsibility. Finally, I wish to thank Miss Jane Newman for typing the chapters, and my wife and children for putting up, for so many years, with what has seemed to them a curious and amusing obsession with a man called, Trelawny.

Abbreviations

Add. MSS	Additional Manuscripts.
Administration	M.G. Smith, 'The administration of the diocese of Exeter during the episcopate of Sir Jonathan Trelawny, 1689-1707' (Oxford University unpublished B.D. thesis, 1964)
B.L.	Department of Manuscripts, British Library.
B.I.H.R.	*Bulletin of the Institute of Historical Research.*
Bodl.	Bodleian Library, Oxford.
B.R.O.	Bristol Record Office.
Buller	The Buller Papers at Antony House, Torpoint, Cornwall.
Cal. S.P. Dom.	*Calendar of State Papers Domestic.*
C.C.	Church Commissioners' Records, 1 Millbank, London.
Cooke Corresp.	Letters and Papers of the Cooke Family, Devon Record Office.
C.R.O.	Cornwall Record Office.
C.T.	**Collectanea Trelawniana:** a volume of transcripts made by Sir William Salusbury-Trelawny, bart., from papers at Trelawne House, Cornwall.
D.C.N. & Q.	*Devon and Cornwall Notes and Queries.*
D.C.O.	Duchy of Cornwall Office, Buckingham Palace Gate.
D.N.B.	*Dictionary of National Biography.*
D.R.O.	Devon Record Office.
E.C.	*The Epistolary Correspondence of the Right Reverend Francis Atterbury, D.D., Lord Bishop of Rochester* ed. J. Nichols (4 vols. second edn. 1789-90).
E.H.R.	*English Historical Review.*
G.R.O.	Gloucester Record Office.
Hearne	*'Remarks and Collections of Thomas Hearne'*, Oxford Historical Society (1885).
H.L.	House of Lords Record Office.

H.M.C.	Historical Manuscripts Commission.
H.R.O.	Hampshire Record Office.
J.R.I.C.	*Journal of the Royal Institution of Cornwall.*
Lamb. Libr.	The Library of the Archbishop of Canterbury, Lambeth Palace.
L.C.C.	London County Council Record Office.
Luttrell	Nacissus Luttrell, *A Brief Historical Relation of State Affairs* (6 vols. Oxford, 1859).
P.R.O.	Public Record Office.
Sermon... and charge...	*A Sermon on* [*1 Tim. iii, 1*] *by the Right Reverend Sir Jonathan Trelawny, Bishop of Winchester: and charge to the Clergy of that diocese, 1708,* ed. Sir John Salusbury-Trelawny, bart. (1876).
T.C.	Library of Trinity College, Dublin.
T.D.A.	*Transactions of the Devonshire Association for the Advancement of Science.*
U.N.L.	University of Nottingham Library.
Wake MSS	Christ Church, Oxford: the papers of William Wake as dean of Exeter, bishop of Lincoln and archbishop of Canterbury.

The portrait of Bishop Trelawny is
reproduced by kind permission of
Mrs. Rosemary Parker

The painting of Trelawne House is
reproduced by kind permission of
Lt. Col. P. M. S. Trelawny, M.C., D.L.

Contents

CHAPTER ONE

The Cornish Background

Bishop Sir Jonathan Trelawny is a man of whom many have heard but about whom very little is known. The work of recent historians of the Church of England has made the public aware of the formative period in which Jonathan lived and worked, yet, despite the spate of books on the period, he has received scant mention. In an age when a celebrity is a person who is well known for being well-known one would be tempted to conclude that Jonathan Trelawny has been ignored because he deserves to be; that if there was anything worth saying about him it would have been written long ago. The son of a vicar of Pelynt came to that very conclusion. 'The Trelawny name,' confessed Geoffrey Grigson, 'has been bruited about rather more than the services or the distinction of the clan deserve... look through the long pedigree and you will find...if the truth be told, [not] a great man among them all...I suppose the Lord Bishop is the only one whose life and personality could be reconstructed in detail, though would it have been worthwhile, humanly?' [1] Presumably Grigson would have answered his own question with a negative, but he wrote just as Norman Sykes was bringing to light the value of a close study of the late seventeenth and early eighteenth century Church. To think that the way it is, is the way it has always been, is a trap easily sprung and we frequently find ourselves caught in it. Rewriting history, either by re-telling it, or suppressing it has ever been the perogative of the victors. Historical truth, however, is not eradicated so easily. Eventually a later generation will ask, What was it really like? Was it always this way? And then a different version may receive a hearing. The ethos of the Church of England in which Jonathan had been nurtured was on the way to becoming a very different one when he died. Throughout much of his life he was a champion of attitudes and practices which were dying. Stubbornly or resolutely, whichever description the observer prefers, he adhered to the attitudes and practices of his younger days so that when the institutions that upheld them crumbled, his memory and reputation were buried among their ruins.

1

This history of the Church of England in which Sir Jonathan lived and died has been extensively researched and mapped out by two generations of historians. To repeat all that they have written would be tedious and unnecessary. The reader is referred to other books for detailed accounts of political and ecclesiastical events which here receive mention sufficient only to place Sir Jonathan's career in its context. However, where that career touches on certain aspects of the history of the Church of England which have been neglected, then some background explanation is given which the reader will not find easily elsewhere. The neglect by the professional historian of the pastoral relationship between parish clergy and the laity has largely passed unnoticed and lends some colour to Charles Smyth's bold assertion in his Birbeck Lectures that 'no one can write Church History who is not a parish priest or at least a person who has some understanding of the problems of a parish priest'.[2]

The way in which the Church touched the lives of English and Welsh people was changing. This point will be made clearer in a later chapter; suffice it to say, at this stage, that the reformed Church that Cranmer shaped, and that Hooker and the Caroline divines justified, was intended to be a strongly paternalistic and disciplined institution - a discipline that extended to laity as well as to clergy. Theory and practice were frequently at variance but churchmen returned to the idea again and again. The Church of England had its own courts and its own lawyers drawing fully on the rich tradition of medieval canon law and jurisprudence. These courts reached down to affect the lives of the most humble and obscure. Men might observe sourly that is was usually the humble and obscure rather than the wealthy and famous who were affected, and frequently they were correct; but the belief that a man's religion and morals were his own private affair only began to gain wider acceptance after 1688. After that date many still cared passionately that private morality be the concern of all, but the belief gained ground that a morally healthy society could only be achieved through statute law and magistrates, not through canon law and ecclesiastical judges; by educating the young in schools, not by pastoral discipline exercised by parish priests. By and large the Church of England has forgotten that it had once so paternalistic, indeed so authoritarian, an image of itself. One should no more read the writings of the theologians of the *via media* without this in mind than one would read the *Politics* of Aristotle without a knowledge of the ancient Greek city state. Whether or not a biography of Sir Jonathan Trelawny is humanly worthwhile is a judgement each reader must make for himself. If an outline of his career may help to rescue a reputation from under the rubble of a fallen system and illuminate something of this earlier Anglicanism, then one is justified in writing the life of the only one of the

Seven Bishops in the Tower yet to be honoured in this way.

Thoughout his life Jonathan Trelawny was moved by three great loves; Cornwall, the honour of his ancient family and the Protestant Religion, by which he meant the Church of England. He was swayed by other loyalties like the royal house of Stuart and Christ Church, Oxford, but they had ultimately to coincide with the first three if they were to receive his support. He could never clearly differentiate between his first three loves still less grade them in order of priority. Cornish folk are possibly more conscious of their entanglement with the past than the people of any county in England, and when a Trelawny was brought up to believe that he could trace his line back to before the foundation of Rome, then the history of Cornwall and the history of the family were as one. Like all Cornishmen Jonathan had a strong love for his local community with the security of close family ties and good fellowship. Outside Cornwall, Cornishmen feel themselves to be exiles and long 'to go down home along'. Canon Hervey preserved a story that when Bishop of Bristol, Trelawny would announce once he crossed the Tamar, 'Now I am no longer Bishop of Bristol, I am Sir Jonathan Trelawny'.[3] A later age misinterpreted this remark. It was thought to smack of worldliness, of an attempt to divest himself of the indelible character of episcopal order. It meant nothing of the sort. It expressed the keen enjoyment of a Cornishman aware that he had come home.

'A Cornishman will try the law for the wagging of a straw' wrote one old writer and that has remained a characteristic of the Cornish. The complicated sub-division of fishermen's and of tinners' shares and the intricate system of land tenure were fertile sources for litigation, but family honour was itself sufficient to cause many of the gentry to go to law. Jonathan's grandfather had threatened to sue Camden for omitting all reference to his family in his *Britannica*. Law suits punctuated the Bishop's career at regular intervals.

Jonathan shared other characteristics with his Cornish con-temporaries. When he told Archbishop Wake that 'gentlemen may be won but can't be frightened', or when he remarked to his registrar, 'you can be sure I love to be huffed' one can almost hear the old Cornish saying 'people will be slocked [i.e. persuaded] but won't be drove'. The Cornish tend to be abnormally sensitive, more deeply hurt by slights and injuries than others. They were also given to brooding more deeply over wrongs. This sensitiveness means that outside the close circle of family and friends they do not like to be blunt in speech: qualification and ambiguity is their preference. The old Cornish language never had words to express a plain yes, or no. What to the Celtic way of thinking is delicacy of speech can easily be construed by others as deviousness - even obsequiousness. A

3

sensitivity in themselves leads the Cornish to recognize it quickly in others: they have considerable gifts of empathy. It may seem strange to historians that Sidney, Lord Godolphin, who so disliked clergymen, should have got on so well with Bishop Trelawny. Considering they were both Cornish and understood each others' feelings it is not at all strange. In one respect Jonathan Trelawny differed from his fellow Cornishmen. They tended to brood on wrongs and take revenge. Godolphin, for example, remarked at a general election that 'he believed that he could influence one hundred voters in the county, but that Admiral Boscawen should not have one for he or the family had once refused him a trifling service and that too in an ungracious manner'.[4] Jonathan seldom allowed his resentment to ripen into revenge. It was a triumph of the 'life of the Spirit' over the 'life of the flesh'.

News of the birth of another son on 24 March 1650, must have been an occasion for muted joy in the household at Trelawne. Relief at the safe delivery of Mary Trelawny of a healthy boy who was baptised in Pelynt parish church on 26 April, and named Jonathan in honour of his father and in memory of a second son who had lived only a few months, must have been tempered by the knowledge that the family's fortunes were at a low ebb. The boy's grandfather, Sir John, the first baronet, and his father had both fought for the King in the Civil War. Sir John had raised, at his own expense, a regiment of that redoubtable Cornish infantry which worsted the Parliamentary forces at Stratton and Lansdown. His son, Jonathan, abandoning his studies at Exeter College, Oxford, when war broke out, fought with distinction and was a member of the garrison of Pendennis Castle when that royalist stronghold was the last in England to surrender. Both men compounded for their estates and managed to pay off the sum demanded, £629 11s. 4d., in the months before young Jonathan was born. That sum was for delinquency to the Parliament. In March 1651, Sir John paid a further fine of £18 7s. for delinquency to the Commonwealth.[5] In company with other Cornish royalists like the Vyvyans and the Rashleighs these were not the only financial exactions. In the early years of the Civil War, the Prince of Wales' council in Cornwall raised money by sequestering the estates of the gentry sympathetic to Parliament. Sir John Trelawny recieved £699 9s. 1d. from this source to disburse in the Prince's service. He had spent £631 7s. 6d. when the fortunes of war enabled the other side to seek revenge. Much of the money had been taken from the estates of the Bullers, a family who had long been a rival of the Trelawnys in south east Cornwall. In 1647 and 1648, John Buller successfully sued, arrested and imprisoned Sir John until he and Jonathan agreed to give security for the full amount of £699 9s. 1d. The Trelawnys were forced to repay a sum which, together with interest and

4

legal fees, came to over £1,200.[6] These fines and awards alone absorbed the total income from the rents for the next six years. Many Trelawnys must have wondered how the family honour could survive.

There is no doubt that the importance of family was one of the earliest lessons any young Trelawny received.

Trelawne, Trelask, Trelay,
Ashleighcross, little Bell Hay,
And Trendaway.[7]

is a mnemonic which, although is does not correspond to the family manors in the seventeenth century, clearly is designed to help children remember the family possessions. Jonathan saw little of his father during his first ten years of life. A defiant and active royalist throughout the period of the Commonwealth, he corresponded regularly with the King in exile and suffered several periods of imprisonment. Nevertheless, under the eye of his grandfather and a group of doting unmarried aunts and cousins, many of whom appear to have been strong characters in their own right, Jonathan, together with his brothers and sisters, absorbed the principles and responsibilities that went with birth into a family that claimed to trace its descent back to the fall of Troy. Jonathan never forgot this early lesson. Throughout his life, whether he was preparing to face the worst eventuality in his defiance of James II, or whether he was placing in stone the wolf hounds of the Trelawny arms at the entrance to Wolversey Palace, he was conscious of the loyalty he owed to the family. It is important, therefore, to know something of the history of the Trelawnys because it was a past kept fresh in the minds of the living and it helps to explain some of the motives which governed the career, especially the political career, of Jonathan the Bishop. Rivalries between Cornish landed families could be carried on for generations and crystallized very often in the plotting and manoeuring that accompanied elections of mayors and burgesses in the twenty-one parliamentary boroughs.

For landed families making their way up the social ladder in the late Middle Ages success could come through participation in a profitable war or, more securely, through a profitable marriage. Marriage to a co-heiress was a prize: birth of daughters only was a disaster. Sir John Trelawny, knight, of Altarnum, distinguished himself at the battle of Agincourt and had a modest share in the rewards that followed victory. Henry V granted Sir John an annual pension of twenty marks and the governorship of a French town. John left two sons. Richard, his heir, fathered two daughters and both married. His second son, John Trelawny of Menheniot, and all subsequent Trelawnys, never acknowledged that the two daughters born to Richard by Agnes Kenwood were legitimate. On Richard's death, John his brother began a series of lawsuits against the husbands, Richard Wace

5

and John Arundel, who swiftly occupied their wives' inheritance. In 1457 a court declared both daughters legitimate and much property passed out of the Trelawny family. Over a century later the loss was still keenly felt. In a manuscript book compiled by Edward Trelawny in 1593 he recorded:

    'and with these daughters went from this
House the Manors of Trelawny (In Altarnum)
Tregarricke, Tregenylke, Tregrill,
Folemore, Penhanger, and Wolstone
      Ecce hic flagellatio Dei'[8]

This dissension in the family which resulted in so grievous a loss of land seems to have taught a lesson which was passed on from generation to generation. Younger sons must learn to sacrifice their personal aggrandizement for the good of the family. The Edward Trelawny mentioned above was a younger son who devoted himself to the family estates while the head of the family, another John, concerned himself with politics. It was Edward who negotiated purchase of the manor of Trelawne in Pelynt from the Crown in 1601. It would be another Edward, the Bishop's fourth son, who, in November 1735, put up £5,000 of his own money to help pay his eldest brother's debts and who struggled successfully to clear all mortgages on the estates out of his salary as governor of Jamaica. No head of family acted alone. When it came to affairs that touched on the honour of the family, therefore, the Bishop consulted his brothers Charles and Henry. Their opinions and their interests had a bearing on any decision.

The Trelawnys were not unusual in this passionate attachment to the family. It was part of the inheritance of all Cornish families except perhaps the very poor. When William Hazlitt in his conversations with Northcote the painter, who was a Plymouth man, asked why west country folk did not more readily come to London, Northcote replied:

    'You are to consider it almost as a peninsula, so that there
is no thoroughfare, and people are more stationary in one
spot. It is for this reason they necessarily intermarry
among themselves, and you can trace the genealogies of
their families for centuries back; whereas in other places,
or particularly here in London, where everything of that
kind is jumbled together, you never know who any man's
grandfather was.'[9]

A local patriotism born of racial difference and geographical isolation knit together in a common unity Cornishmen who might differ in political and religious opinions. Rivalries there were, sometimes bitter ones, but they were quarrels within a greater family. Some quarrels might continue for several generations as, for example, between the Arundels and the

Trelawnys. Alternatively, as an older generation died out, friendships were renewed, as between the Boscawens, the Bullers and the Trelawnys. 'All Cornish gentlemen are cousins' went an old saying and Carew records the hectic social life they all enjoyed:

> 'A gentleman and his wife will ride to make merry with his next neighbour, and after a day or twain these couples go to a third, in which progress they increase like snowballs till through their burdensome weight they break again.' [10]

This local patriotism helps to explain the innate conservatism of the south west, a social conservatism which the industrial revolution in the mining industry in the late seventeenth century seems to have affected little. The Cornwall observed by Carew is immediately recognisable in the Cornwall described by Borlase. In economic terms the inhabitants grew steadily wealthier throughout the century and pauperism was not serious. Cornwall was spared drastic social upheaval and on all fronts of the economy many minor improvements served in place of any large scale advance.[11]

Economic gradualism went hand in hand with a social stability from which the gentry greatly benefited. 'To their gentlemen they carry a very dutiful regard,' wrote Carew, 'holding them as Roytelets (little Kings) because they know no greater.' This respect for the gentry remained true throughout the seventeenth century. The townsfolk, especially in east Cornwall, tended to become less amenable to control as their economic position improved, nevertheless, Cornishmen looked with affection upon their gentry, preserving old sayings about them such as

A Godolphin was never known to lack wit

A Trelawny courage

Or an Granville loyalty.

This affection was an expression of shared concern. Throughout the century agriculture remained the principal activity and many of the gentry farmed their demesne lands. Sir Jonathan Trelawny, the second baronet, did so and his son, Bishop Jonathan, continued the practice throughout his life, a fact which explains, in large measure, his frequent sojourns at Trelawne whatever diocese he happened to hold.[12] When gentry and peasantry both gained their livelihood from the soil they could not remain wholly indifferent to each others' lives. The almost universal form of tenure was by lease for three named lives. A new life could be inserted upon payment of a fine. This custom gave considerable security to the lease holder. Toward the end of the century, landowners were less likely to insist on suit of court from new tenants, but the manorial courts continued to function. In a letter to Robert Harley, earl of Oxford, in 1713, Bishop

Trelawny remarked that he would like to have given a burgesship at East Looe to the Lord Treasurer's son, but that he was well satisfied with the excuse offered

> 'since the interest of your family required Lord Harley
> should receive the respects of [New Radnor] which hath
> ever been servant to it'.[13]

This remark betrays a feudal attitude of mutual obligation which was still a living force in Cornwall even though it may have become an anachronism elsewhere.

The period of the Civil War, and its aftermath, had little effect on the social structure of Cornwall. After 1660 the loyalty of the royalist gentry to the House of Stuart became the more intense the greater the anticipation of royal reward. The plaster coat of arms of Charles II which still dominates with its colourful vulgarity the nave of the parish church of St. Ive near to Trelawne, is a reminder of the exaggerated loyalty of those early years of the Restoration. The Bishop's father inherited the baronetcy in 1664, together with the lawsuits his father had begun against the Arundels and the Bullers in order to recover the money they had got from the Trelawnys ten years earlier.

The second baronet received one immediate mark of royal favour. By a warrant dated 5 June 1660, he was appointed a gentleman of the Privy Chamber. Such a post brought honour, but no profit. So Jonathan sought in June 1660, and, after some delay, seems to have been granted a farm on a part of the Excise. In 1677 and subsequent years he received payments from the French subsidy, which Professor Browning considers was a pension which originated as compensation for some loss in connection with the excise farm. Certainly contemporaries do not appear to have looked upon it as a bribe.[14] It would seem, therefore, that Sir Jonathan was in receipt of £400 a year from the Crown. As early as 1688 he is listed as having some dependence on the Duke of York and from 1670-1674 he was comptroller of the Duke's household.[15] But £400 a year, although a welcome addition to the average income of £300 he received each year from the family estates, was small beer when compared with the rewards given to others. Furthermore, the costs he incurred out of his own pocket in serving the King as a deputy lieutenant, justice of the peace, and vice-admiral of the coast easily swallowed up that sum. At the end of his life, in order to forestall an arrest for debt, Sir Jonathan had to petition the Council to instruct the Treasury to pay him arrears of £503 4s. 10d. outstanding since the disbanding of the Duke of York's regiment of horse at the end of the proposed French War of 1678-1679. He had been lieutenant colonel of the regiment and, at five shillings and sixpence a day, his military pay came to less than one hundred pounds.

Sir Jonathan had several sons to provide for. John, the eldest, could take his father's place and was already being groomed for that responsibility. He had taken over the management of the demense lands and he was elected steward of East Looe in 1679. Then there were Jonathan, William, Charles, Henry and Chichester. Sir Jonathan's uncle Edward and his brother John had both chosen a military career, and Jonathan steered his sons in the same direction. William, who died in 1678, went into the Royal Navy. Charles was a captain in Skelton's regiment in the French Brigade from 1674 to 1678, and went to Tangier in December 1680 as Percy Kirke's lieutenant-colonel. Henry was commissioned in the Admiral's Regiment in January 1678: Chichester became an ensign in Kirke's Regiment in January 1681.[17]

There were three types of officer in the army of Charles II. Part-time garrison officers drawn from the local gentry; gentleman officers serving in the regiments in England and professional soldiers who learnt their craft on active service abroad. This last group was made up largely of the younger sons of impoverished gentry like the Churchills, the Kirkes and the Trelawnys. They formed a new type of military family virtually unknown in England before 1660. They were the butt of a certain amount of condescending amusement among an English aristocracy not noted for military bearing. Trelawnys served in Ireland, Portugal, France and Africa. To have so many sons fighting in foreign wars was tantamount to a public admission of failure in the socially acceptable fields of advancement. Outside their own county the Trelawnys suffered, if not a social stigma, then at least the handicap of being social oddities. This certainly did not mean exclusion from Court. It is remarkable that a non-noble family should provide a gentleman of the Privy Chamber, a lady-in-waiting to Princess Mary when she lived in Holland, and a groom of the Bedchamber to William III. Nevertheless the Trelawnys were never fully accepted in polite society and never really felt at ease far beyond the Tamar. Later the Whig gutter press was to seize gleefully on the Bishop's military connection and lampooned him viciously as 'fighting Joshua the son of Nun' in the *Tribe of Levi,*

'Though he to men of sense is a buffoon
He serves to make a spiritual dragoon'.[18]

In this family of military men, the Bishop was the only male to follow a different career. His elder brother died without an heir in October 1680. His father died in March of the following year. In a final clause to his will his father dictated, 'I do bard and forgive my son Jonathan'.[19] It was a curious choice of words; an example of that sardonic sense of humour which was a family trait. Jonathan could not mistake the meaning. Clergyman or no he was to be saddled with all the obligations of head of the family. Dutifully, he obeyed, even to the extent of laying aside his cassock and leading onto the field of inspection that troop of horse which had been his father's command in the county militia.

County militia officer was not the only post the Reverend Jonathan Trelawny was to hold. He was also appointed a vice-admiral of the coast. Vice-admirals of the coast were a part of the machinery of local government and stood alongside the justices of the peace in those counties of England, Wales and Ireland bordering the sea. Very little has been written about their work and what follows is by way of an excursus to demonstrate that the Trelawnys tended to be of above average ability among the gentry.

The work of vice-admirals meshed with that of the justices at some points. A vice-admiral would be included on the Commission of the Peace and three local justices sat with the vice-admiral on any commission of piracy which the High Court of Admiralty might issue from time to time. In all other respects vice-admirals were a class apart. Their authority derived not from a commission issued under the Great Seal, but from letters patent issued by the Lord High Admiral under the seal of the High Court of Admiralty.[20] They had cognizance of a limited range of cases and persons within a clearly defined territory. The practice and jurisprudence of their courts was derived from Roman Law; their officers were trained in Civil Law and, not infrequently, were the same men as those working in the ecclesiastical courts. John Anstis, junior, was registrar both of the court of the archdeacon and of the vice-admiral of South Cornwall. Vice-admirals could fine and imprison for non-payment without seeking a process from the Court of Exchequer. Their actions and legal decisions might have international repercussions because of the number of foreign ships and merchants whose affairs they might have to examine. They assisted the Royal Navy, especially in time of war, when they were employed in recruiting seamen and commandeering vessels.

The post of vice-admiral was not one to be entrusted lightly to any country gentleman with acceptable political views. It required a measure of ability, command and dedication well above average. As influential a politician as Sir Edward Seymour considered it an honour to be vice-admiral of Devon during the reign of James II. Each vice-admiral could appoint a deputy and he was assisted by a judge, a registrar and a marshall, all three appointed by letters patent. No vice-admiral was allowed to shelter behind the actions of his subordinates. He was held personally responsible for all that occurred in his jurisdiction over which the judge of the High Court of Admiralty exercised strict supervision. Each vice-admiral had to submit annually a written report between 29 September and 1 November. His letters patent included the proviso that failure to submit the report incurred automatic dismissal from office. It is a cause for much regret that none of these reports appear to have survived, but there is

10

evidence to suggest that, at this period at least, no laxity was connived at. Sir Leoline Jenkins, judge of the High Court of Admiralty, sent so stinging a letter of rebuke to Sir John Tredenham, vice-admiral of North Cornwall, concerning a contract made by one of Tredenham's agents with the master of a ship in distress, that Samuel Pepys had it copied into his letter book for future reference. The incompetence of Sir Robert Holmes, vice-admiral of Southampton and the Isle of Wight, earned him an abrupt dismissal in 1692.[21]

The jurisdiction of a vice-admiral included all merchants and seamen 'beyond the sea or within the floodmark', but he had power to arrest and seize goods on land. In addition to determining cases between parties and trying those charged with piracy, a vice-admiral enquired into all wrecks in order to prevent embezzlement of goods, and to assist all survivors of shipwreck. He ensured that those going to the aid of a ship in distress received only reasonable recompense and he quashed all bargains or contracts made by shipwrecked persons at times of danger or distress. He took into custody all flotsam and jetsam, sold it at auction and transmitted the proceeds to the Admiralty in London. He had power to arrest or release any vessel, he determined all matters of anchorage, lastage, and ballast. He was responsible for the maintenance of streams, rivers and ports within the floodmark and up to the first bridge. He checked the size of the mesh of fishing nets and regulated the methods of fishing. He might take a census of all seamen and ships within his jurisdiction. In addition to the ordinary courts of instance over which the judge presided, a vice-admiral was required to hold two, sometimes four, courts of enquiry each year. Using a jury presentment, similar to the sheriff's tourn, he enquired into all breaches of maritime law and custom, proceeding against offenders by fine or imprisonment. Of all the seaboard counties of England, only Cornwall had two vice-admirals, but as so many were employed in the seasonal pilchard fishing, probably more Cornishmen came under the jurisdiction of a vice-admiral sometime in their lives than the men of any other county in England. The holder of the office was accorded considerable honour and wielded no little influence.

The Bishop's father was appointed vice-admiral of South Cornwall in 1671, having served for ten years for North Cornwall. He wished to keep the office in the family, but the death of his eldest son jeopardized that desire. His younger sons were on active service abroad and there was doubt in official minds if a clergyman was eligible. Sir Leoline Jenkins pointed out that much though he respected Mr. Jonathan Trelawny, clergy were debarred from acting as judges in capital cases and a vice-admiral might have to sentence a pirate to death.[22] Jonathan's uncle John was appointed interim vice-admiral until Sir Leoline's objections were set aside. Sir

Jonathan's letters patent were sealed on 14 February 1682, and he served a vice-admiral of South Cornwall until 1693.[23]

Records are scanty but such as do survive show that the Bishop was an efficient and energetic vice-admiral. He can claim credit for averting what might have been an international embarrassment for the English government. In the autumn of 1687, a ship from Ostend bound for Spain with a rich cargo was wrecked on the Cornish coast. The cargo included presents from Germany to the king of Spain. Trelawny recovered the goods, forcing the local people to disgorge whatever they had rifled.[24] War with France after 1689 brought additional duties. He arrested a Danish vessel *en route* for Nantes; commandeered all ocean going vessels for transport duties to Northern Ireland or the Baltic and recruited seamen for the Royal Navy.[25] Despite the assistance of an able deputy, Nicholas Saunders, the war-time demands of the office were too burdensome for a bishop of a large diocese. In the autumn of 1693 he relinquished the post in favour of his brother, Henry, who held it until his death in 1701.

There can be little doubt that the office of vice-admiral of the coast held by a succession of Trelawnys (Henry was succeeded by his brother, Charles, and Charles by his nephew, John) contributed much to the prestige and authority of the family in the eyes of local men and it helps to explain the influence of the Trelawnys in parliamentary elections. Next to the office of sheriff the post of vice-admiral must have been the most expensive in local government. The Basset family who had suffered such heavy financial loss during the Civil War, were forced to relinquish the post. Sir John Tredenham had complained bitterly of the expense involved and Sir Leoline Jenkins, while remaining totally unsympathetic, acknowledged that he was correct. Within a year of taking office Trelawny was complaining of the cost.[26] The office of vice-admiral must have made a significant early contribution to the Bishop's financial difficulties, and cost may have been another reason why he relinquished the task in 1693. After his death Jonathan was remembered as one who possessed 'an uncommon knowledge of the world'. Certainly few clergymen acquired as much experience in local government as he was compelled to do once he succeeded to the baronetcy.

1. Geoffrey Grigson, *Freedom of the Parish* (1954), p.59.

2. C. Smyth, *Simeon and Church Order* (Cambridge, 1940), p.9.

3. C.T., p.227.

4. Buller, BO/23/63 (1).

5. Rutland MSS., QZ 29, f.43a; QZ 30, f.38a; QZ 31, f.34.

6. Rutland MSS., unlisted MSS. 1600-1700, ii, earl of Clarendon to Charles II, 23 April, 1663.

7. A.E. (Stothard) Bray, *Trelawny of Trelawne* (1837), p.65.

8. C.T., pp.201-13 passim.

9. Quoted in A.K. Hamilton Jenkin, *Cornwall and the Cornish* (1933), Introduction.

10. *Ibid.,* p.7.

11. For the economic history of Cornwall at this period see James Whetter, *Cornwall in the 17th Century: an economic survey of Kernow* (Truro, 1974).

12. See the inventory attached to the will of John Trelawny in C.R.O. proved 18 April, 1681, also B.L. Add. MSS. 38507, f.150, Charles Trelawny to Bishop Trelawny, 18 August, 1719.

13. H.M.C., *Portland MSS.,* v.329, T to Oxford, 11 September, 1713.

14. Andrew Browning, *Thomas Osborne, earl of Danby* (Glasgow, 1951), iii. 45, 55 note.

15. *Ibid.,* 36; C.T., pp.201-13.

16. *Cal. S.P. Dom.,* Jan. 1679 - Aug. 1680, p.403, Whitehall, 28 February.

17. *Cal. S.P. Dom., passim;* see also John Childs, *The Army of Charles II* (1976), pp.30-6. Dr. Childs in the first to draw attention to the importance of the Trelawnys as initiators of a new kind of English professional family. Unfortunately he confuses the family relationships by failing to distinguish between the sons of the second baronet and Sir Jonathan's uncle, Edward, and his brother, John.

18. 'The Tribe of Levi', quoted in Agnes Strickland, *Lives of the Seven Bishops* (1896), p.393.

19. C.R.O., Will of Sir Jonathan Trelawny.

20. Sir George Sherston Baker, *The Office of Vice-Admiral of the Coast* (1884), *passim.*

21. Magdalene Coll., Pepys MSS. 2872, f.216; Baker, *op. cit.,* pp.65-6.

13

22. William Wynne, *Life of Sir Leoline Jenkins* (1724), ii. 717.

23. P.R.O., High Court of Admiralty, 50.

24. H.M.C., *Downshire MSS.,* i, pt.i. 274, Newsletter, 7 November, 1687.

25. H.M.C., *Finch MSS.,* iii. 279; Baker, *op.cit.,* p.107; U.N.L., Portland MSS., PwHy 463.

26. B.L. Add. MSS. 28875, f.224, T to Ellis, 28 August, 1682.

CHAPTER TWO

The Ladder of Preferment

Jonathan Trelawny clearly had some academic ability, sufficient at least for his father to deem it worth the expense of good schooling to develop. In 1663, Jonathan was sent to Westminster School under the legendary Dr. Busby and from there he went as a student to Christ Church, Oxford. The eminence of both these institutions in the years following the Restoration has been full acknowledged.[1] Old boys of Westminster who also found themselves members of Christ Church formed an 'undoubted elite, a confident and superior group of clever young men who kept their own select company'.[2] This fraternity long outlasted the respective sojourns of its members in Oxford. Henry Aldrich and the Regius Professor of Theology, William Jane, had helped to make Christ Church a seminary for High Anglican doctrine and fiercely loyal monarchical principle. In such a place a royalist Cornish gentleman could feel completely at home. Westminster School, and Christ Church always exerted a claim on Trelawny's affections. He was one of the contributors to the cost of Wren's Tom Tower built between June 1681 and November 1682, and his arms are among the others in the gate house.[3] Toward the end of his life he paid Grinling Gibbons one hundred guineas for a stone statue of Cardinal Wolsey which is still to be seen as one goes towards the great hall. The theology he learnt at Christ Church remained his guide for the rest of his life and he liked nothing better than to surround himself with House men. Dr. Jane, his old tutor, always enjoyed his favour. Two of his chaplains, Launcelot Blackburne and Thomas Newey, were younger Christ Church contemporaries. Had he not chosen to decline the offer, George Smalridge could have enjoyed a similar position. Later Francis Atterbury was given an archdeaconry and a prebendal stall.

Trelawny took his B.A. on 22 June, 1672 and deacon's orders on 4 September, 1673. He received his M.A. on 29 April, 1675 and he was ordained a priest on 24 December, 1676. He was now qualified to pursue an ecclesiastical career. It was probably his father who persuaded Charles II to appoint him a royal chaplain extraordinary in 1677.[4] This had two great advantages.

15

In the short term it qualified Trelawny to hold two livings in plurality: in the long term it was the acknowledged first step to high office in the Church of England. As Bishop Morley of Winchester recalled in 1680, royal chaplains 'were woont in my Memorie (caeteri[s] paribus at least) to be preferred before those that were not'.[5] Trelawny's father also exerted himself to secure a suitable living for his son. The crown living of Calstock in Cornwall fell vacant just as Charles II was visiting Plymouth in August 1677, so Sir Jonathan begged it for his son and the King good-naturedly granted the request.[6] Nothing came of it, however, because Calstock was already promised to someone else. The Trelawnys promptly petitioned for the less lucrative rectory of St. Ive and an embarrassed king revoked a presentation already made and gave it to Trelawny on 22 September.[7] The previous incumbent had also held the Trelawny family living of South Hill so Sir Jonathan presented his son to Bishop Lamplugh who instituted him on 4 October. Within a year Trelawny was asking Bishop Lamplugh for the living of Dartington much to his diocesan's annoyance,[8] but he had to be content with the two livings of South Hill and St. Ive until his elevation to the episcopate.

Trelawny's request for the vicarage of Dartington was motivated not by worldly greed but by financial desperation. Charles Fotherby, the previous incumbent of St. Ive and South Hill had held the livings since the Civil War. He had suffered deprivation during the Commonwealth and he never recovered financially. When Trelawny was inducted into his livings in December he discovered to his dismay that both parsonages were in ruins. The following April he arranged with Thomas Kelly, the family's land agent, to have contractors view both houses and submit estimates for repair. They announced that all would have to be rebuilt at a total cost of £706 6s. 0d!⁹ So in addition to the charges of institution together with the taxes of first fruits and tenths, Trelawny was liable to face a bill for dilapidations amounting to over double the annual value of the tithe of both livings. Trelawny sued Fotherby's executor in the consistory court and lost. He appealed to the Court of Arches and settled out of court, thus adding the expenses of two law suits to his other debts.

There was no way he could have raised the money to rebuild the parsonage houses. The rural dean presented him for the ruin of both at the triennial visitation in 1680.[10] The only Trelawny who might have had any ready cash was his elder brother John, who had taken over management of the demesne lands, but when he died in October, 1680, he left a thousand pounds to his father and all Jonathan received was a annuity of twenty pounds a year and the task of administering the will. The second baronet's pension from the Crown died with him, so in March, 1681, Jonathan inherited his father's debts along with the family estates. Trelawny was launched on the long losing struggle against bankruptcy on which he was to engage for the rest

16

of his life.

A year later Trelawny was complaining to a friend of his lack of preferment. At the age of thirty his financial obligations far exceeded his income and looked like growing heavier. Unfortunately, at this stage in his career, Trelawny was unlikely to commend himself for higher ecclesiastical office on grounds of piety, pastoral care or academic distinction. He did not fit the image of the kind of parson Archbishop Sancroft needed for his grand scheme of Anglican reform. Trelawny was what a later age would call 'a hearty Christian'. He enjoyed good wine, good tobacco and boisterous company. He was a frequent and dedicated user of bad language and later used to explain to any who ventured to express disapproval of his profane swearing that he swore not as a bishop, but as Sir Jonathan Trelawny.[11] A bosom companion of Christ Church days was the Irish baronet, Sir John Perceval. Both friends were fanatical royalists and Trelawny was vociferously so. One Christ Church tutor and fellow Cornishman found him an embarrassment. 'Our regius professor [William Jane] is returned from his northern progress with his two baronets with him', wrote Humphrey Prideaux. 'I am afraid we shall hear more of one of them than we care for, I mean my fellow-countryman. He talks so madly I know not whom to compare him with but [Titus] Oates.' [12]

There is no hard evidence to indicate how well Trelawny cared for his two parishes. Certainly he resided in neither. Any correspondence from this period is always dated from Trelawne which is fifteen or twenty miles away from the nearer parish of St. Ive. However he continued to employ his predecessor's curate who resided at South Hill. To judge from the surviving archdeaconry act book, the parishioners were not at all troublesome. The churchwardens of St. Ive failed to appear at the archdeacon's visitation court in 1675 and one man refused to pay his church rate. At South Hill one man failed to attend church in 1675 and another man and a widow were presented for the same reason in 1676. The only parish register to survive from the period was purchased by the churchwardens of St. Ive in 1685. In it, two baptisms were recorded for 1683, which casts doubt on the efficiency of the rector's supervision. In 1686 nine baptisms were recorded together with fifteen burials, but no weddings.[13] There would not have been a great deal to occupy Trelawny's time had he been resident, but it is probably true to say that his estates, his local government work, his trips to Oxford and his chaplaincy to Lord Conway, meant that his parishioners saw little of him. He may have left his mark at St. Ive in the shape of a large wooden pulpit. It is carved in Jacobean style but Pevsner assigns it to the late seventeenth century. It is sited to that its occupant can see all parts of the nave and north chapel. It is the kind of gift Trelawny often liked to make to those parishes with which he was associated. One of the Pelynt church bells bears the date 1683 and the name Sir

17

Jonathan Trelawny.[14] The Pelynt churchwardens were in trouble with the archdeacon's court from 1674 to 1676 for the lack of church bells and the ruinous condition of the nave floor and seating. The present granite arcade with Tuscan doric capitals is dated about 1680 and may owe something to Trelawny's help and advice.

As for academic ability, Trelawny was intelligent but lazy. The polished latinity, which was a hallmark of an old Westminster, stayed with him throughout his life. He read widely, to judge from the books in his library, and he took a keen interest in local history. William Wake was later to acknowledge that he had a gift for composing public addresses.[15] But he could never bring himself to master any subject completely and he had no desire to be an author. The occasional sermon is all he ever had printed.

If Bishop Morley was right in thinking that a royal chaplain had a head start in the race for lucrative preferment, then the appointment of the Commission for Ecclesiastical Promotions on 27 February, 1681 must have greatly raised Trelawny's hopes. There were favourable auspices on his side. The political complexion of the Commission was unmistakeable. 'They, without exception, represented the *avant-garde* of Tory reaction.'[16] It soon became clear that among the commissioners, Archbishop Sancroft, Bishop Compton of London and the Earls of Rochester and Claredon were the main disposers of crown preferments. The Hydes were devoted to the Duke of York. Trelawny's father had been comptroller of the Duke's household and the first Earl of Claredon had been a close family friend.[17] From 12 August John Robartes, earl of Radnor, was added to the Commission. Here was a fellow Cornishman able to provide first-hand attestation of the political reliability of the Trelawnys. The Commissioners were to appoint clerics of proven loyalty to the Stuart cause. It is small cause for wonder to learn that by the end of that summer Trelawny was extravagant in his verbal protestations of loyalty. He was prepared to do almost anything to get himself noticed.

Nothing came to Trelawny from the Commissioners. Five royal chaplains went on to deaneries. They were older and more distinguished men. However no lesser preferment by way of rectory or canonry came Trelawny's way either. His resentment showed in a letter he wrote in August, 1682. Defiantly he had stayed on the Commission of the Peace for Cornwall when others withdrew out of deference to the Buller family. Trelawny wrote, 'without any arrogance to myselfe & with grief I doe assure you that the King hath not a gentleman he can entirely confide in but myself, & yet he gives me neither money nor preferment to bear up with against my debts (contracted in the service of the crown).'[18]

Francis Buller, junior, of Shillingham, whom Bishop Ward

18

reckoned to be one of the three most powerful presbyterians in the county,[19] was also the wealthiest landowner in East Cornwall.[20] Faced with Buller's opposition, Trelawny felt isolated and vulnerable. In this mood he wrote to the Earl of Rochester in November, 1683, using language which has often been quoted as an example of nauseating obsequiousness:

> 'My lord, the church & the conventicle, the loyalist & the rebel are at you lordship's tribunal and myself at your feet as becomes, my lord, your lordship's most obedient servant'.[21]

Not only did Trelawny need to defend himself against the local customs officers because he had espoused the cause of some local merchants, he was also making a thinly veiled plea to Rochester to bring his name before the Commission for Ecclesiastical Promotions, having been assured that 'I am in your lordship's remembrance and under assurance of its patronage'. In September, 1684, the Commission was revoked and still Trelawny was without further preferment. It may well be that his later dislike of Rochester as a two-faced politician stems from the fair assurances but practical neglect of these years. The sudden death of Charles II on 6 February, 1685, and the smooth accession of his brother James improved Trelawny's chances of promotion. He was reckoned among James' principal supporters in Cornwall. As the remodelling of the boroughs continued, Trelawny's name appeared in several of the new charters. He was named a freeman of Liskeard, an alderman of Lostwithiel, a justice of the peace for Truro, and a justice and free burgess of Fowey.[22] In February he was one of twenty-two noblemen and gentry favoured with a personal letter from the Privy Council urging them actively to canvass and employ all their interest to secure a return to the new parliament of 'persons of approved loyalty and affection to the government'.[23] In fact Trelawny anticipated the request and had written already to Lord Chief Justice Jeffreys asking whom he should nominate as burgesses and, so desirous was he to appear as a willing cypher of the Government, he went personally to the Court in order to receive his instruction from the mouth of the Secretary of State himself.[24] Several of the other recipients of this personal letter were already busy obeying the royal command and others replied with equally extravagant protestations of loyalty, but no other respondent was so painfully anxious to please as was Trelawny. Surely now such dog-like devotion would get him royal recognition.

For a clergyman, royal recognition, when it came first to Trelawny, took an unusual form. Parliament had assembled at Westminster in May. Three days after it met news reached London of the landing of the Earl of Argyle and that the Covenanters had risen against the King. Argyle's landing was part of a two-pronged invasion in support of the claim of the

19

Duke of Monmouth to the throne. Spies in Holland kept the Government informed of Monmouth's activities and by the beginning of June it was known in London that Monmouth had purchased two ships with which to carry men and arms to England.

Precautions were taken immediately. Samuel Pepys, secretary to the Admiralty, alerted naval vessels in the Channel in an attempt to intercept a ship known to be heading for a landing somewhere on the south coast. As a further precaution the militia needed to be called to arms in the southern maritime counties. Then it was realised at Whitehall that, as far as Cornwall was concerned, very few deputy lieutenants were in the county. Trelawny was in London attending Convocation as a proctor for the diocese, but he was despatched immediately to the west country.[25] It is tempting to see Pepys' hand in this for he was a shrewd judge of men. When he accompanied Lord Dartmouth to Tangier in 1684 he would have made the acquaintance of Charles Trelawny and he had had a hand in the appointment of Jonathan as vice-admiral.

Trelawny received his orders on 8 June and three days later Monmouth landed at Lyme Regis. It was no part of Monmouth's plan to march further west so the mobilization and defensive deployment of the Cornish militia which Trelawny carried out with great efficiency contributed nothing to the final outcome of the rebellion. The Government was very pleased with Trelawny's conduct, nonetheless. Just before the battle of Sedgemoor, the Earl of Sunderland sent a letter of congratulation.[26] Within days of Monmouth's defeat, it was rumoured in Oxford that Trelawny would be made a bishop.[27] James II had decided upon Trelawny's promotion by the end of April at the latest. The King had intended to translate Thomas Lamplugh to the vacant see of Peterborough and replace him with Trelawny. This proposal was thwarted by Lamplugh's refusal to move.[28] There was talk of moving Dr. Bathurst to Peterborough so that Trelawny could have his deanery of Bath and Wells but that suggestion did not meet with much favour. Finally, towards the end of June, the King decided to translate John Lake to Peterborough and offer the bishopric of Bristol to Trelawny.[29] Trelawny received the news of his intended preferment with abject dismay. He wrote to the Earl of Rochester on 10 July imploring him to get the King to change his mind. Could he have Peterborough or even Chichester, now that too was vacant? Lamplugh had hinted that he might move to Chichester if it fell vacant so could the King offer Lamplugh that alternative? 'Let me beseech your lordship to fix him there and to advance your creature to Exeter.' The financial burden terrifed him. 'I hear his majesty designed me for Bristol', he continued incoherently, 'which I should decline was I not already under such pressure by my father's debts as must necessarily break my estate to pieces if I find no better prop than the income of Bristol, not greater than £300 p.a. and the expense in consecration, first-fruits and settlement will require £200.' If the King was determined to offer him Bristol he would not refuse 'though my ruin goes with it' but he hoped that the King might have 'more tender compassions on his slave'.[30] Neither James nor his lord treasurer were impressed by this outburst and Archbishop Sancroft, when he learnt of it, was unsympathetic and irritable. Himself an abstemious recluse, Sancroft could never understand any cleric who was eager to lay up treasures on earth. Nor did he approve of the elevation to the episcopate of a man whose services to date had been to the State rather than to the Church. Any scruples Sancroft entertained either went unvoiced in the Privy Council or were brushed aside. As North observed, the Earl of Rochester was 'for perferring loyalists, which were such as ran about drinking and huzzaing, as deserving men, and to encourage the King's friends'.[31] On 17 October the Secretary of State informed Trelawny that his congé d'élire had passed the Dean and Chapter. Nine days later, the University of Oxford conferred on him a doctorate of divinity. He was consecrated at Lambeth on 8 November by two archbishops and six bishops all in London for the new session of parliament, and he took his seat in the Lords the following day.

After he had learnt that the die was cast, Trelawny wrote to Sir William Trumbull shortly before the latter's departure to take up the post of English ambassador at Versailles,

'I am just now entering into the world of business; the only qualification I carry with me is an honest heart to do the king the best service I am capable of. If I can miscarry in his interest, it shall be the fault of the public ministers for not vouchsafing positive commands in every particular debate and voice, for I am and will be always all obedience.' [32]

He had written in similar vein to the Secretary of State eight months earlier and there is no doubt that he meant it. In his own vocation, Trelawny was ready to serve the Stuarts with the same sacrificial loyalty displayed by his father and his grandfather. But Trelawny, at thirty-five years of age, was still comparatively inexperienced and impressionable. Futhermore, local Cornish politics aside, he was still politically naive. Now he was about to join in the discussions with, and come under the influence of, an exclusive fraternity of men select even in the days of a small ruling class. In 1685 the bench of bishops included some of the most forceful as well as some of the most saintly men who have ever led the Church of England. One cannot tell if James II knew anything of the life of Thomas Becket, and, even if he did, whether he would have acknowledged the analogy, but he was shortly to experience from Trelawny a redefinition of loyalties not dissimilar to that with which Becket treated Henry II.

1. See G.V. Bennett, *The Tory Crisis in Church and State 1688-1730* (Oxford, 1975), pp.24-6.

2. *Ibid.,* p.27.

3. Anthony Wood, *History and Antiquities of the University of Oxford* (1786), pp.449-51.

4 P.R.O., Lord Chamberlain's Papers 3, 28 (76).

5. Bodl. MS. Tanner xxxvii, f.66, Morley to Sancroft, 14 July, 1680.

6. B.L. Add. MSS 32095, f.30, Earl of Bath to Secretary Coventry, 19 August, 1677.

7. *Cal. S.P. Dom.,* 1677-78, pp.370-1.

8. *Cal. S.P. Dom.,* Mar.-Dec. 1678, p.425, Sir John Williamson to Bishop of Exeter, 30 September.

9. Lamb. Libr., Court of the Arches Depositions, Bbb 445/3.

10. D.R.O., Visitation Book 218.

11. C.T., pp.201-13.

12. *Letters of Humphrey Prideaux, sometime dean of Norwich, to John Ellis, sometime Under-Secretary of State, 1674-1722,* ed., E.M. Thompson (Camden Society, 1875), p.94, 22 September, 1681.

13. C.R.O., Archdeaconry Act Book, *ex officio,* 1674-76; St. Ive parish register.

14. E.T. Davies-Freme, *A Guide to Pelynt Parish Church* (Liskeard, 1960), unpaginated.

15. C.T., p.257, Wake to T, 19 September, 1704.

16. R. Beddard, 'The Commission for Ecclesiastical Promotions 1681-84', *Historical Journal,* x (1967), p.17.

17. C.T., p.209.

18. B.L. Add. MSS. 28875, f.224, T to John Ellis, 28 August 1682.

19. D.R. Lacy, *Dissent and Parliamentary Politics in England 1661-1689* (Rutgers, 1969), p.386.

20. See N.H.G. Pounds, 'Barton Farming in Eighteenth Century Cornwall', *J.R.I.C.* (New Series), viii, pt.i (1973), pp.55-6.

21. B.L. Add. MSS. 15892, f.161, T to Earl of Rochester, 18 November, 1683.

22. *Cal. S.P. Dom.,* Feb.-Dec., 1685, pp.304, 318, 357.

23. *Ibid.,* p.93, Sunderland to T, 17 February.

24. *Ibid.,* p.36, T to Sunderland, 22 February.

25. *Ibid.,* p.185, Sunderland to T, 8 June.

26. *Ibid.,* p.1135, same to same, 4 July.

27. *Letters of Humphrey Prideaux,* p.143, 9 July, 1685.

28. Bodl. MS. Tanner xxxi, f.117, Bishop Lloyd to Dean Patrick, 20 June, 1685. C.E. Whiting asserts that James II promoted Trelawny on the recommendation of the Bishop of Durham: see *Nathaniel, Lord Crewe, Bishop of Durham 1674-1721* (1940), p.144. Whiting cites no evidence. James II knew the Trelawny family well enough not to need any reminder from Lord Crewe.

29. Finally, Lake was translated to the diocese of Chichester.

30. *Correspondence of Clarendon and Rochester,* ed. S.W. Singer (1828), i.146, T to Rochester, 10 July, 1685.

31. A. Jessop (ed.), *Lives of the Norths* (1890), i.237.

32. H.M.C. *Downshire MSS.,* i, pt.i. 149, T to Sir William Trumbull, 19 October, 1685.

CHAPTER THREE

The Apprentice Years

In a letter to his old friend William Wake, Maurice Wheeler once fell to discussing the qualifications to look for in a good candidate for the episcopate. 'I remember when after a visitation,' he wrote, 'I and three or four of the graver Ministers of the Diocese met at a tavern together, it was the common wish of the company, that Dean Fell had first known what it was to be a Parson of a parish before he had been made a Bishop'. [1] The point Wheeler wanted to make was that sound scholarship and good intentions were insufficient. The role of a bishop at this period was a demanding one for which practical parochial experience was essential. Society looked for much more in a bishop than it does today. Government ministers expected regular attendance in parliament; fellow peers assumed bishops would be represented on committees of the Lords. Society in the late seventeenth century had none of the modern stereotype of a bishop offering soothing platitudes with engaging garden-party manners. In his diocese a bishop was accorded deference and respect. He enjoyed power and an income often far in excess of his clergy not for his personal benefit, but in order that he should govern both clergy and laity. Caroline theologians and their successors never tired of pointing out that the Apostolic Succession included not only the power to administer all the sacraments, but also the power of correction in the Church,an authority given mediately through the laws, but derived ultimately from the commission of Jesus Christ Himself. The Church of England was intensely conservative in its definition of the relationship between a bishop and his people. At every licensing and institution a clergyman took, and still takes, an oath of canonical obedience to his bishop 'in all things lawful and honest.' This canonical oath had feudal overtones. A bishop had the right to expect his clergy's obedience. In their turn, they had a right to expect their bishop to use his jursditional power in defence of the Church and in support of their pastoral authority over their parishioners. [2] In later years, Trelawny gave to a correspondent some of the reasons why he and the other bishops had presented the King with the petition against reading the

24

Declaration of Indulgence, the petition which resulted in their being sent to the Tower and being catapulted into fame:

> 'What we did was perfectly from the obligation of duty to God, our Church and character, for the protection of our clergy & in defence of the Act of Uniformity; to keep up our reputation with the Nobility, Gentry & all the people of our Communion who might have been tempted to foresake us and our Communion had we by a base complience with the King's arbitrary command encouraged him to have gone further.' [3]

In setting down these reasons Trelawny encapsulated much of what he understood to be the obligation of a bishop and this he must have heard in discussion with his brother bishops when he was learning the role.

The sacrament of confirmation, the administration of which takes up to much of a modern bishop's time and energy, was performed fairly frequently but was not accorded the same significance as it is today. In some parts of England it was never administered at all. Few if any archbishops of York ever went to Hexhamshire: no bishop of Winchester before Sumner stepped ashore on the Channel Islands. Ordination was taken more seriously because only a bishop stood between an unworthy candidate and the indelible character of holy orders. The ideal bishop of the seventeenth century was expected to combine several incompatible virtues. On the one hand he was expected to eschew secular matters, on the other to bargain shrewdly with his tenants for renewal of a lease. He was expected to be an example of humility but at the same time an authoritarian. He was to be gentle with the sinner, but rigorous with the criminal. The ideal bishop needed to be tough physically and mentally. Physically tough to withstand the rigours and perils of constant travel: mentally tough to stand up to frequent confrontations with groups and individuals.[4]

This was the ideal, but the reality was often very different. The reality was affected by the personal strengths and weaknesses of the men who made up the episcopal bench; also it was cut into as many facets as there were dioceses for one simple and obvious reason. No bishop ever entered a diocese with a completely free hand. He faced clergy and court officials who were there before him and had to work through an existing machinery of government moulded through the centuries by all the local history of the area.

This theme of continuity in the Church of England with its mediaeval past is well known. The effect that it had upon the effectiveness of a given bishop has not always been given adequate attention. It was not impossible for the same man to be an ineffective bishop in one diocese, but an effective bishop after his translation elsewhere. Much diocesan adminstration depended not on the activity of the bishop, but upon the activity, or lack of it, of his officials. To accord great significance to episcopal triennial visitations is a temptation that the historian must resist. Sir Thomas Lee pointed out in a debate in the House of Commons in 1672, 'The Ecclesiastical Courts in some things have too much power; in others, too little and the Bishops usually the least' and he was not alone in holding that opinion. Whereas the secular government by the end of the seventeenth century was beginning to evolve an administrative machinery which, if not yet separate from the old judicial forms, had a more tenuous connection with them, the Church of England still employed the old legal machinery for administration. This meant that every bishop was compelled to take into account the network of jurisdictions within his diocese and the nature and powers of his court officers.

Governing a diocese with many exempt jurisdictions (peculiars) was always a headache. Exempt from episcopal or archidiaconal visitation, the ordinaries of these peculiars held their own correction courts and issued their own licences. If they chose they could neglect their duties for years at a time and little could be done to remedy the neglect. Above all, the clergy licensed to such peculiars might cause trouble within the diocese but the bishop had no jurisdiction over them and so could do nothing to correct them or remove them. Even within his own jurisdiction a bishop had limited power over the officers of the church courts because most had security of tenure. In the course of the sixteenth century the letters patent appointing a chancellor of a diocese or a judge or registrar of an ecclesiastical court came to be regarded as conferring the office for life. It was as difficult to remove an incompetent or obstructive registrar as it was to deprive an archdeacon of his dignity (office). It was impossible to remove the most important officer, the chancellor, who generally combined in his letters patent the offices of vicar general and of official principal. In running a diocese much depended on the kind of man who had been given the office of chancellor and the relationship he established with his bishop. One obvious factor in such a relationship was its duration. A bishop's experience and confidence increased the longer he stayed in one diocese, and the less dependent he became on the advice of a chancellor who might know more than he about local conditions. Few bishops of Bristol ever stayed long enough to affect the relationship with the chancellor in this way.

It has been asserted that Henry VIII promised Bristol a bishopric and the status of a city on a visit to Thornbury in 1534.[7] When the promise was honoured on 4 June, 1542, it was a hasty and ill-considered project from the Church's point of view. Whatever the expressed priority in the letters patent, the townsfolk gained more than the clergy. It is true that the plum among the local monastic houses, the abbey of St. Augustine, became the new cathedral of The Holy Trinity and the abbot's lodging was reserved for the new bishop, but the city had the satisfaction of seeing all ancient abbatial claims to exemption from the jurisdiction of Bristol magistrates extinguished for ever.[8]

The bishops of Brisol never secured sufficient authority over the city. Even the militant Guy Carleston (1671-1679) was tempted to give up[9] and his successor, William Gulston (1679-1684), tended to reside in Bristol only when ordered to do so.[10] His request to be included in the commission of the peace in the new city charter of 1684 was ignored.[11] He complained to Sancroft at intervals throughout 1683 of a wood-wharf which the Dean and Chapter had allowed some merchants to establish just below the palace. The constant noise made the place uninhabitable.[12] Nothing illustrates better the low status of the bishop than the appointment of a new dean in 1684. Young John Knight, author of the new city charter, canvassed successfully for Richard Thompson, a creature of the Duke of Beaufort, despite the bitter opposition of both bishop and chancellor.[13] Yet the bishop of the day was expected to exert his influence on behalf of the government in city council politics.[14] The government regarded control of Bristol to be a matter of paramount importance. Bristol was the second richest corporation in the kingdom: although out-paced rapidly by London, her merchants still included wealthy men. Sea-borne and ocean-borne trade brought profits to the merchants and vital customs and excise duty to the crown. It was also potentially a turbulent city: its mob had a formidable reputation for rioting. Government agents and spies blamed Dissenters and exaggerated both their numbers and their nostalgia for the Commonwealth. In 1675 and 1677 government informers estimated that Dissenters numbered two-thirds of Bristol's population.[15] The returns of the Ecclesiastical Census of 1676 show us today how wildly inaccurate this estimate was. Of those sixteen years old and above in a total population of 6,169, there were only 620 dissenters and 5 papists, a figure that better accords with Terrill's claim that there were only six dissenting congregations in the city in the period from 1660 to 1687.[16] It was not so much this godly minority that required such a degree of government vigilance as that unknown fluctuating population of criminals and vagrants from the surrounding counties attracted to the port of Bristol who might easily provide the raw material for others to work on. The merchant magistrates did not entirely discourage the presence of such people. They provided a source for slaves, for the source became exclusively black only later. A local annualist in the early eighteenth century wrote 'there is not a brick in Bristol but what is cemented with the

27

blood of a slave'.[17] Therefore from 1660 to 1688 'The militia was used quite frankly as a counter-revolutionary army, often called out to enforce the laws against dissenters and even, on occasion, to influence the votes of the Council.' [18]

Bristol had its exclusionists in 1679 to 1681 and many of them were implicated in the Rye House Plot. When the opportunity offered itself, *quo warranto* proceedings against the City were initiated in King's Bench in the Hilary Term of 1683. The Crown got its way only with a struggle, but the charter issued in June, 1684 gave the Crown 'all the control over the corporation that despotism could wish for'.[19] It was a hollow victory. The Council created by this charter passed not a single ordinance. The merchants adopted an attitude of sullen non-cooperation. James II had to order dismissal after dismissal and, eventually, had to nominate councillors by privy council warrant. In January 1688 James was forced to use Nathaniel Wade, who had fought for Monmouth less than three years before, to purge the Council completely and reconstitute it with Whigs and Dissenters. This was the last straw for that staunch high church man, Edward Colston, who, in disgust, emigrated to Surrey calling in a loan of £4,000 which plunged the City Council deeper into debt, a debt already considerable as a result of the cost of defending the city during Monmouth's rebellion and the extravagant royal entertainment in August, 1686.[20] Indicative of the decline in civic pride was the fate of the mayor's barge. When the Council were taking desperate petty economies, the barge was put up for auction. There were no takers so it was broken up and sold for scrap.[21]

There were seventeen parish churches and chapels in Bristol and all of them miserably endowed. St. Mary Redcliffe was not technically a parish church but a chapel annexed, together with St. Thomas, to the vicarage of Bedminster in the diocese of Bath and Wells. Fourteen parish churches in Gloucestershire were also included in the bishop's jurisdiction and eight of them were impropriated. This meant that they were served by curates on pitifully small stipends. The wealthiest of the other six was reputed to be worth no more than £140 a year.[22] The parishes of Bristol were unlikely to attract many able clergy. The bishop was patron of Littleton and impropriator of Almondsbury and Herfield. That was the extent of his patronage. A large part of the county of Dorset was transferred to Bristol from the diocese of Salisbury and formed the only archdeaconry, quite separate from the city of Bristol. The bishop had a residence in Dorset at his manor house of Symondsbury. The Dorset livings were better endowed and more numerous than those of Bristol. There were two hundred and four parishes and nineteen chapelries. However Dorset was riddled with peculiar jurisdictions. The dean of

Salisbury had twenty-eight parishes: thirteen more belonged to prebends of Salisbury. Then there was the royal peculiar of Gillingham and the Sarum dean and chapter's peculiar of Stourpaine. All these peculiars bordered the archdeaconry of Dorset but within it were the peculiars of Canford Magna and Poole, Corfe Castle, Sturminster Marshall, and Wimborne Minster.

With an episcopal income estimated to be £350 a year Bristol was often only a stepping stone to a more lucrative diocese. Guy Carlton was translated to Chichester in January, 1679 and John Lake in October, 1685. Short tenure of the see made continuity of administration difficult. Much depended on the chancellor in Bristol and the archdeacon in Dorset. By the terms of his letters patent the chancellor might visit the deanery of Bristol annually. He was expressly inhibited during a triennial visitation year and the bishop reserved to himself all institutions, all licences to preach and teach and all letters dismissory. He also reserved the right to sit in his own consistory court.[23] In Henry Jones, LL.D., the diocese possessed a modest, reasonably competent, chancellor who must have been adept at guiding new bishops, for in this respect the smallness of the diocese made it a good training ground. Fate has not dealt kindly with diocesan records. Those belonging to the archdeaconry court and the Dorset division of the consistory court were stored at Blandford Forum. Many appear to have perished in a great fire in 1731. In October, 1831 during election riots in Bristol, the mob, having set fire to the bishop's palace, wanted to extend the blaze to the neighbouring cathedral chapter house. The stone vault of the roof resisted the heat but the court records piled up on the floor to start the fire were almost all destroyed. However, a bundle of citations and one cause book *ex officio* survive from the time of Bishops Lake and Trelawny to show a consistory court despatching business equivalent in range and volume to that of an archdeaconry of modest size. Henry Jones was personally involved in correction work; the court seldom sat with a surrogate presiding.

Trelawny entered upon his duties at Bristol at a fortunate moment. The mood of the city was sullen but quiet and Richard Thompson, the dean, was dead! In a letter of thanks to Sancroft for his impending translation, John Lake expressed his profound relief 'to be freed from the impertinence and insolence of our Dean'.[24] At his death Thompson was still fighting a stubborn rearguard action against Lake's visitation of the cathedral despite the direct intervention of the Commissioners for Ecclesiastical Promotions in April of the previous year.[25] Trelawny had also managed to make his peace with Archbishop Sancroft. Using the good offices of Francis Turner, bishop of Ely, he pledged himself 'by prayers and earnest application' to discharge the duties of 'that sacred and weighty order of a bishop' to which he hoped that God

29

himself had called him. He had even raised enough cash to cover his confirmation and consecration expenses.[26]

As soon as parliament was prorogued that autumn, he travelled to Bristol to make the acquaintance of his officers. The visitation of the cathedral was a piece of unfinished business which he decided to tackle first. A mandate to the Dean and Chapter was issued on 19 December and he held his court in the chapter house on Tuesday, 19 January, 1686. Articles of enquiry were delivered and returned on 26 January. Trelawny probably used the articles prepared by Lake. Trelawny concluded his visitation on 19 February with the issue of a set of injunctions. In contrast to the animosity and bickering of previous years all passed off quietly and smoothly. A year later William Lovett, the dean, told the Archbishop how much he valued the kindness and support Trelawny had given him in getting work done in and around the cathedral and, above all, in discharging all the debts contracted and unpaid during the mismanagement of previous deans. 'There have of late alsoe in this place beene very undutifull misbehaviours towards former Bishops. I hope we shall now all contain ourselves in due Bounds'.[27] For the first time in years there was a happy relationship between dean and bishop.

After February Trelawny began to make preparations for his primary visitation of Dorset which he held after Easter. His printed articles of enquiry under eleven heads were drawn up no doubt after consultation with his chancellor, but the order of priority may show something of Trelawny's particular concerns. The state of the church and churchyard, the conduct of divine service and the administration of the sacraments cover the first three headings. Certainly the injunctions he issued on 13 June, 1686 suggest that he had been particularly concerned to extract answers to the questions on these topics. Churchwardens were ordered to place the communion table against the east wall of the church and have it railed in with a central door. They were to provide all ornaments and books of the Church's use 'required by the laws and canons now in force'. Too many clergy, he discovered, were omitting whole services or parts of services. Services were to be read 'in the order as enjoined by the rubrics on all Sundays and their Eves, Holy Days and their Eves'. Trelawny also wanted the litany to be read every Wednesday and Friday in church in all market towns and large villages. This was a practice he was used to in his home diocese of Exeter and he was shocked to find that in Dorset the practice had been allowed to lapse. Ante-communion was to be read at the communion table, not at the reading desk and the prayers following the sermon or homily were not to be omitted. The order for the visitation of the sick was to be confined to its proper use and the duty of visiting and praying by the sick was urged upon all the parish clergy. Rubrics governing the baptism and catechising of children were to be strictly adhered to and no minister was to be allowed to preach unless the churchwardens were satisfied of his loyalty to the Church of England and that he had been duly licensed. The names of all visiting preachers were to be registered in the church book.

At this stage Trelawny was still very much a creature of the King. He had received his instructions about his visitation both from his archbishop and the Secretary of State. His visitation ended, he returned to Bristol on 24 April and then went down to Cornwall. He took care to report first to the Secretary of State emphasising his tender regard for the King's Roman Catholicism. At Cerne in Dorset, the churchwardens presented twelve Roman Catholics for not coming to church. Dr. Jones enquired what he should do about them and Trelawny ordered that they be dismissed. A clergyman at Dorchester who preached an impudent sermon with anti-popish 'innuendos' was threatened with suspension, but Sir Winston Churchill interceded with the Bishop on his behalf. In his visitation charge Trelawny acted as an ardent apologist for royal policy, strongly emphasising the ill consequences of preaching anti-popish sermons.[28] In the meantime he had been drafting his injunctions. He despatched a copy to Sancroft for his approval together with a covering letter explaining the principal neglects he had found. After reading the letter and persuing the injunctions, Sancroft was impressed and delighted. 'To such an account as your lordship sends me of your late visitation an *Euge, Bone et Fidelis!* is a proper & most just acclamation...your Injunctions...so pertinent & significant, that I shall only say *Quo pede capisti ec.* Go but on as you have begun & your diocese will soon be in beautiful order.' [29] Trelawny was delighted to receive so fulsome a congratulation from a man held so much in awe. Sancroft's letter must have played a part in weaning him away from the Court.

Sancroft mentioned to Trelawny that he had encountered members of Bristol Corporation at Hampton Court summoned thither by the Council, and that local gentry were to be added to the Bristol magistracy 'to teach them to govern that great Citie more wisely.' The aldermen and councillors were before the Council to answer for several days and nights of rioting between 18 and 24 May, which began with the mob staging a profane and indecent parody of a Corpus Christi procession with the Virgin Mary represented by a buffoon, and ended with pitched battles in the streets between mob and the soldiers of the Queen Consort's Regiment of Foot Guards called out to disperse them. The rioting had been sparked off by the knowledge that there was a priest saying Mass in the city. The Bishop had been told about it on 25 April but shifted responsibility to the Mayor, who carefully timed his arrival at the house after the Mass had ended and the congregation had dispersed. A fortnight later an exasperated crowd threatened to lynch the priest whereupon one of the prominent local gentry, Sir John Knight, having tried in vain to get Bishop and mayor to act, took matters into his own hands and arrested the priest. When ordered by the Privy Council to account for his actions, Knight sought to implicate the Bishop, among others, claiming that Trelawny, (in the course of delivering a charge to the Bristol clergy) had particularly impressed on the Mayor the duty of preventing the celebration of Masses.[30] James was very upset on learning this, so Trelawny was forced to exonerate himself at length.[31] In doing so he revealed the lengths he was prepared to go, at this juncture, to obey all royal commands. He had upset public opinion in Bristol by visiting John Romsey, the town clerk, before calling on the Mayor. Romsey was the principal royal agent in the city and the Bishop was complying to the letter with the Lord Chancellor's instructions. The cathedral clergy were ordered to have nothing to do with Sir John Knight, and Trelawny preached on the virtue of passive obedience and studiously refrained from any adverse comment on Roman Catholicism. No bishop since the Restoration had entered Bristol with so poor a public image. Several influential men assumed he was a crypto-papist. It was chance that the garrison consisted of the Queen's Regiment commanded by the Bishop's brother, Charles; in fact it was transferred to Portsmouth the following summer.[32] Unfortunately, the Queen Consort's, comrades of 'Kirke's Lambs', was a seasoned but violent band from Tangiers.[33] The population resented the presence of regular troops in the first place. Trelawny's open hospitality to his brother and the officers of his regiment at the palace only increased dislike for the Bishop and seemed to confirm suspicions that he was a papist

In the face of such active hostility it speaks much for Trelawny's courage that he should have stuck to his high church standards of order and decency in public worship and that he should face his people and visit the Bristol deanery parochially in 1687 and 1688. When he was in his diocese he resided at Bristol. This was a residence dictated more by financial necessity than by choice. He could not afford to maintain two residences in the diocese.[34] An indication of the strain he was under in February, 1686 is the frequency with which he rode out to Kings Weston to relax with old Sir Robert Southwell, a former secretary of state to Charles II and related to Trelawny's old friend from Christ Church days, Sir John Perceval. Another indication is that his health was far from good. Like so many of his rank at this period he suffered agony from gall stones. The first onset of the disease came in January.[35] By 1688 he was forced to seek relief from the waters at Bath, where the King's Messenger found him on 30 May and served him with the warrant to appear before the Privy Council with

32

the other six bishops, an appearance which led to his imprisonment in the Tower.[36]

To judge from the practices he unearthed in the course of the parochial visitations of 1687 and 1688, Trelawny's predecessors since the Restoration had never carried out a similar exercise. The Chancellor's annual visitation could have been no more than mere form. The orders published early in 1688 reveal city parishes barely recognisable as anglican. Trelawny's natural sociability and conviviality made him desire to know his people and break down the barrier of dislike and suspicion. An item in the churchwarden's accounts of St. John's parish indicates the tactics he used. '6 February 1687 spent with vestry at Bell tavern when my Lord Bishop visited this church - 13s.' [37] If any were tempted to confuse conviviality with laxity the order dated 6 January, 1688 soon disabused them:

> 'Whereas we are given to understand that it is a frequent practice of this City to lend out the plate which is sett apart and ought only to be made use of in the celebration of the Holy Sacrament of the Lord's Supper to be fraudulently employed at funerals and on other occasions, we therefore being heartily troubled at such an irregular and indecent practice doe require all Church-wardens that for the future they doe not presume to use themselves or to lend out to others the Church plate or utensils upon any occasion or account whatever but to keep them in their proper chests that they may be reserved only to the use to which they were appropriated.'[38]

Laudian reform had made little headway in Bristol. The number of active Dissenters may have been small, but the ethos of the city was far from anglican. Funerals were conducted without prayer book office or even the presence of an anglican priest. Trelawny cited a recent example in the parish of St. Peter and added an injunction to all parish clerks and sextons that they were not to receive any corpse without the knowledge of their minister, or, in his absence, without first calling on a neighbouring lawfully ordained clergyman to read the burial office.

Early in 1688, Trelawny extended his parochial visitation to the country parishes of the deanery. In the parish of Littleton with its chapel of Elberton, he discovered more scandalous neglect. He sent his chancellor to Lambeth to seek Sancroft's advice and authority in dealing with the situation. 'In my life I never saw such ill churches or such ill parishioners,' he wrote, 'In one, Elberton, the sacrament has not been administered since

33

the Restoration, in the other very seldom, and all the plate is but a small silver bowl and that too kept in a Quaker's house, till my late orders to the contrary'.[39] Trelawny's order appears to have had some effect so perhaps the treatment of church plate was caused by ignorance more than by wilful contempt. The diocese was so small that it was not uncommon for an incumbent to hold two livings, reside in his other parish in the neighbouring diocese of Gloucester or Bath and Wells and neglect his Bristol parish with impunity. In disciplining such a clergyman, the Bristol consistory court would run up against all the problems of citing a person out of one diocese to another, a problem which was not insuperable but one subject to endless delay and legal expense.

The loss of records prevents any assessment of the effectiveness of the consistory court in Dorset, but the *ex officio* cause book for Bristol shows a chancellor struggling to maintain his authority but fighting a losing battle. If one takes the period August 1683 to July 1686, before the Declaration of Indulgence of April 1687 distorted the picture, the Chancellor cited a total of two hundred and thirteen persons. Five of them were cited twice. Tabulated, the offences for which they were cited appear as follows:.-

CLERGY	for canonical disobedience	2
	for no licence to serve a cure	2
	for performing clandestine marriages	2
LAITY	for not attending church	107
	for clandestine marriage	72
	for fornication	5
	for trading on Christmas Day	18
	for failing to have a child baptised	3
	for not producing a licence to practice surgery or midwifery	3
		Total 214

(one man was cited for different offences)

Nine persons were dismissed and only fifty-nine (28.9%) appeared in court. Of these, nine refused point blank to obey the court; ten were ordered to get a certificate to say they had attended their parish church but never produced one; two were enjoined a penance which they failed to perform. Out of all the persons cited to appear in court *ex officio* in the course of three years, the consistory court could claim credit for reforming only thirty-eight, a mere 17.8%. The Chancellor duly excommunicated the bulk of them and although the absence of any mention of significavits is no

34

evidence, it seems most unlikely that any of the excommunicates were imprisoned. Even if the Bishop was willing to incur the expense of obtaining a writ *de excommunicato capiendo* it was unlikely it would be served in a city like Bristol. An indication of Dr. Jones' despair at ever imposing his authority was his practice of requiring a bond from some of those who promised to attend church. Even then one merchant was prepared to forfeit his bond rather than obey.

Trelawny might bravely issue injunctions and orders but it is doubtful if his consistory court had the authority to ensure that he was obeyed. He never sat in court himself. In Dorset he was learning what effect peculiar jurisdictions could have on the morale of his clergy and the ethos of his diocese. He complained to Sancroft that the Dean of Salisbury never visited his peculiars so that those parishes had become havens for the ill-disciplined and rebellious clergy who were independents at heart. They served as an example and, in some cases, as an excuse for the behaviour of his own clergy.[40] Later he discovered that churchwardens with presbyterian sympathies might invite a clergyman of similar persuasion to preach in their church. If the clergyman resided in a peculiar the Bishop was powerless to proceed against him. He could admonish his churchwardens but as they changed each year a bishop could find himself back where he started.[41] The clergy of these peculiars knew perfectly well that they could thumb their nose at the local bishop. The Minister and Official of Sturminster Marshall never served the cure himself, but employed a curate, paying him as little as he could get a man to accept. Trelawny once sent a messenger with a letter to Watkinson, the minister, with the request that he should allow his curate thirty pounds a year. Trelawny received an insulting reply which, for a man of his uncertain temper, must have been hard to bear.[42] It is not surprising to discover that when he did have a clergyman of scandalous life within his jurisdiction he pursued him with implacable determination. Dr. Samuel Rich, rector of Stalbridge in Dorset, is an example of this. The churchwardens promoted the office of the judge in the Dorset division of the consistory court against their rector for neglect of his clerical duties, but especially for adultery with the wife of one of his parishioners. The case was heard toward the end of 1688 but went on appeal from an interlocutory sentence to the Court of Arches where the Dean retained the cause and pronounced a sentence of deprivation.[43] Trelawny continued his interest in the case after he had left the diocese for Exeter. In July, 1689 he entered a caveat that Rich receive no royal pardon until he had had an opportunity to be heard.[44] He had every intention of arguing against any pardon for Rich who, after a fruitless appeal to the Court of Delegates, was deprived in June, 1690.

Trelawny stayed at Bristol for little more than three years so his

35

impact on the diocese was not great. His most effective work had been to support his dean in restoring the cathedral finances. For him, personally, the experience was invaluable. He had mastered quickly the craft of a bishop. He was learning what a bishop could or could not achieve. In his concern for ornaments and worship and in his treatment of his clergy one can begin to discern the germ of a policy he was to make very effective by the time he left the diocese of Exeter.

1. Wake MSS. xxiii, f.131, Wheeler to Wake, 5 April, 1699.

2. For a further discussion, see M.G. Smith, *Pastoral Discipline and the Church Courts: the Hexham Court 1680-1730* (York, 1982)

3. C.T., p.211.

4. The death of Offspring Blackall, bishop of Exeter, in November 1716, was the result of a fall from his horse within hours of setting out for a visitation. Grangrene set in above the knee and the surgeons were afraid to operate.

5. Ed. Rosemary O'Day and Felicity Heal, *Continuity and Change: Personnel and Administration of the Church in England 1500-1542* (1976) p.15.

6. A. Grey, *Debates in the House of Commons 1667-1694* (1763), i. 110; ii. 72. See also A. Tindal-Hart, *William Lloyd 1627-1717* (1952), p.53.

7. G.F. Nichols and John Taylor, *Bristol Past and Present* (Bristol, 1882), i. 239.

8. The text is given in R.C. Latham, *Bristol Charters 1509-1899* (Bristol Record Society, 1947), pp.93-4.

9. H.M.C., *Portland MSS.*, iii. 348, T J to Sir Edward Harley, 4 January, 1675.

10. *Cal. S.P. Dom.*, 1680-81, pp.451-2.

11. *Cal. S.P. Dom.*, 1683-84, pp.85, 302.

12. MS. Tanner cxxix, ff.103, 108, 109, 113.

13. MS. Tanner cxxix, f.70, Henry Jones to Sancroft, 4 February, 1684; f.78, Gulston to Sancroft, 12 February, 1684.

14. Latham, *op. cit.*, pp.47, 49.

15. *Cal. S.P. Dom.*, 1675-76, pp.7-10; 1677-78, p.426.

16. E. Terrill, *Records of the Church of Christ, meeting in Broadmead, Bristol 1640-1687*, ed. E.B. Underhill (Hanserd Knollys Society, 1847), pp.213-4.

17. Nichols and Taylor, *op. cit.*, iii. 165.

18. Latham, *op. cit.*, p.44.

19. *Ibid.*, pp.46-51.

20. Nichols and Taylor, *op. cit.*, ii. 134, puts the cost of entertainment at £573 0s. 1d.

21. *Ibid.*, iii. 118.

22. MS. Tanner cxxix, f.1, List of parishes with valuations of the deanery of Bristol.

37

23. Text given in *Parliamentary Papers* (1883), ii.679.

24. MS. Tanner cxxix, f.148, Lake to Sancroft, 21 July, 1685.

25. MS. Tanner cxxix, f.46, Thompson's humble submission to the Commissioners.

26. MS. Tanner xxxi, f.207, T to Turner, 22 September [1685].

27. MS. Tanner xxx, f.173, Lovett to Sancroft, 7 January, 1687.

28. 'Trelawny Papers', ed. W.D. Cooper, *Camden Miscellany,* ii (1853), 19, T to Sunderland, 21 May, 1686.

29. C.T., p.262, Sancroft to T, 8 June, 1686.

30. *Cal. S.P. Dom.,* Jan. 1686-May 1687, p.159, Sir John Knight to [?earl of Sunderland], 7 June.

31. *Ibid.,* pp.184-5, T to Sunderland, 25 June.

32. *Ibid.*

33. Nichols and Taylor, *op. cit.,* i. 134, quoting Evans, p.241: the soldiers 'committed great disorders beating some and stabbing others.'

34. 'Trelawny Papers', *loc. cit.,* T to Sunderland, 21 May, 1686.

35. Add. MSS. 46962, f.202v, Sir Robert Southwell to Sir John Perceval, 8 February, 1686; f.212v, same to same, 18 February, 1686.

36. C.T., p.210.

37. Nichols and Taylor, *op. cit.,* i. 153.

38. B.R.O., Dioc. Misc. Papers, Bundle marked 'Draft Letters etc.'

39. H.M.C., *Ninth Report,* p.460a, T to Sancroft [undated].

40. MS. Tanner xxx, f.50, T to Sancroft, 1 June, 1686.

41. E.g., see MS. Tanner xxx, f.83, same to same, 19 July, 1686.

42. Lamb. Libr., Gibson MSS. 941 (13), f.75, copy of letter from an unknown writer, undated.

43. *English Law Reports* clxi. 763-4, 1 Hagg. Eccles. [App], pp.7-8.

44. *Cal. S.P. Dom.,* Feb. 1689-April 1690, p.205.

CHAPTER FOUR

A Towered Bishop

As Trelawny prepared for his consecration on 8 November news was reaching England, carried thither by refugee Huguenot clergy and their families, of the final act in the long drawn out persecution of the French protestants. On 22 October Louis XIV had formally revoked the Edict of Nantes and had ordered all Huguenot ministers to leave France within fifteen days. At the same time as this news reached England James II was sounding out individual opinions concerning repeal of the recusancy laws and the Test Act of 1678. The King assured those interviewed that he did not intend a general relaxation of all church discipline, just a fair deal for the small minority of his co-religionists. Then, on 9 November, at the opening of the new session, arrayed in his new episcopal habit, seated with his fellow bishops near the fireplace in the Lord's chamber, Trelawny heard James in his speech from the throne allude to the incompetent performance of the militia during Monmouth's rebellion; the need for an increased regular army and the inadvisability of his dismissing Roman Catholics in the army in case they might be needed 'if there should be another rebellion'.[1]

Many members of both Houses were growing suspicious and uneasy. The bishops had let James II know before the opening of the new session that they would not support any repeal of the Test Act and actually began to concert a campaign against him.[2] As the junior bishop Trelawny presumably listened and learned. He attended the Lords on 19 November when all the bishops stood up in order to demonstrate their concurrence with a speech by the Bishop of London in which he attacked the employment of catholic officers in the army and declared that repeal of the Tests would leave the Church of England defenceless. Trelawny was coming under the influence of the strong-minded Francis Turner, bishop of Ely, already tipped as Sancroft's successor, and two bishops whose dioceses bordered on his own, Frampton of Gloucester and, more especially, the saintly Thomas Ken of Bath and Wells. These three bishops were in the forefront of anti-papal pulpit propagandists.

39

Faced with such opposition from that section of the House of Lords who had so strongly supported him during the Exclusion Bill crisis, James prorogued parliament on 20 November and never called it again. It was dissolved on 2 July, 1687. Such an affront to royal authority as the bishops had offered could not go unanswered. James decided to fire a warning shot across their bow. He issued a general pardon on 10 March, 1686. It was cleverly timed. A general pardon would disrupt all correction business in the church courts where obdurate offenders were involved, but it would not wholly undermine ecclesiastical authority. During the previous autumn, the correction courts would have dealt with the bulk of those presented at the visitations of that year. Offenders who submitted would have taken the sacrament at Michaelmas or Christmas and certified their renewed attendance at worship to their respective ordinaries. Only the cases of the contumacious or excommunicate would still be before the courts in March.

Sancroft and his colleagues were not to be deterred. Four of them, Lake of Chichester, Lloyd of Norwich, Trelawny of Bristol and White of Peterborough, being newly consecrated or translated, could and did conduct primary visitations of their dioceses. In addition Sancroft ordered White of Peterborough and Sir Thomas Exton, a senior advocate of Doctor's Commons, to conduct a triennial visitation of the diocese of Lincoln where the senile Bishop Barlow was unable to act. That Sancroft was reacting to the general pardon can be gleaned from the behaviour of Sir Thomas Exton. Sancroft wanted the triennial visitation to be conducted without delay. Exton had legal work before the courts to attend to. He protested and got Sancroft to agree to postpone the visitation until the next law vacation.[3] The triennial visitation of Lincoln was a deliberate provocation on Sancroft's part. If James could make use of his royal prerogative to issue a general pardon, Sancroft could make use of his metropolitical prerogative to enforce church discipline over the vast diocese of Lincoln, where a bishop could only assert his authority over his commissaries at the time of an episcopal visitation.[4]

Renewed activity in the church courts after Easter 1686 was paralleled in the secular courts by a severe enforcement of the Conventicle Acts. James and his advisors were determined on retaliation and the Archbishop's action directed discussion to an attractive way of upping the stakes. If Sancroft could fall back on his metropolitical powers of visitation, why should the Temporal Head of the Church of England not exercise his visitatorial authority? In May, John Sharp, rector of St. Giles-in-the-Fields had preached two anti-papal sermons which offended the Court. Compton, his bishop, refused to suspend him when ordered to do so. James was advised to do to Compton what Sancroft had done in the diocese of Lincoln. Whoever it was who advised James in his dealings with the bishops was well versed in the ways of the ecclesiastical courts and of Canon Law. Modern historians tend to assume it was Jeffries. His prominence on the Ecclesiastical Commission points that way, but the timing both of the general pardon and of the first issue of the Declaration of Indulgence suggests the advice of a canon lawyer. The King's Proctor, Dr. Pinfold, is a likely candidate. He was an eminent advocate of Doctors' Commons and retained strong Jacobite sympathies after 1689. On 15 July James set up an ecclesiastical commission to exercise the visitatorial powers of the King.

The exact status of the Ecclesiastical Commission has been much debated among modern historians. In the Bill of Rights it is described as 'the Court of High Commission'. This was a deliberate use of emotive language, but it is difficult to see what other title could be given it in law. Macaulay assumed that the 'Court' referred to in the Bill of Rights was synonymous with the early Stuart Court of High Commission and he had no hesitation in concluding that the institution of the former was illegal by virtue of the statutes passed both by the Long Parliament of Charles I and the Cavalier Parliament of Charles II which abolished the latter. David Ogg pointed out, quite rightly, that the clause of the Elizabethan statute vesting all visitatorial power in the Crown had never been repealed and its confirmation was implied in the clause of the act restoring the church courts which affirmed that the King's supremacy in ecclesiastical affairs was unabridged.[5]

Unfortunately, Ogg looked at the Ecclesiastical Commission through common law spectacles and assumed that the hall marks of a court are the sanctions of fines and imprisonment. Such retributive sentences had been imposed in the past but were expressly abolished by statute and, in any case, were not in the mainstream of canon law sanctions. Furthermore too much attention has been paid to the wording of the Commission itself by taking it at its face value. There was more behind setting up the Commission than James' declared purpose of curbing anti-popish preaching, but it is a mistake to think that the Commission was concerned solely with persons of ecclesiastical or semi-ecclesiastical status. No records of the Commission's proceedings survive but three pieces of evidence prove that like any other visitation court, the Ecclesiastical Commission did exercise jurisdiction over the laity. Clandestine marriage was one of the frequent and widespread abuses of the Age. On 4 November, 1686 the Commission issued an injunction applicable to the entire Kingdom, forbidding for the future all clandestine marriages upon pain of suspension for the clergy involved and upon pain of contempt for the laity. The Commission ordered this injunction to be entered in all registers and published in all churches and chapels.[6] 'In pain of contempt' was the first stage in applying ecclesiastical sanctions. Failure by a layman to purge the contempt might lead to excommunication. This matrimonial injunction encouraged some noble ladies to hope that they could bypass the ordinary church courts and bring their marital difficulties before the Commissioners. In April, 1687, they heard the Duchess of Norfolk. The scandals surrounding her marriage were to be the talk of London society for years to come. On 10 Februray, 1688 Lord Coventry appeared before the Commission at the suit of his wife[7]

In short, the Ecclesiastical Commission was an ecclesiastical court. It was an extension of a jurisdiction residing in the Crown which was used from time to time in order to cope with some of the anomalies left over by the Henrician breach with Rome. There were certain peculiar jurisdictions which, before 1534, had been exempt from all ecclesiastical jurisdiction save that of the papal court in Rome. The King took the place of the Pope: therefore these peculiars could be visited ecclesiastically only by virtue of a royal commission. One such commission had been issued three or four years earlier to deal with the peculiar of Lyme in Dorset.[8] The advantage of a visitation court was well-known to any ecclesiastical lawyer.[9] The procedure was summary; licences could be revoked at pleasure; suspensions could be decreed on the spot and injunctions issued to regulate behaviour for the future. A visitation court was not confined to dealing with any particular class of ecclesiastical offence. It was not unprecedented for laymen to be included in such a royal commission. In fact only the absence of any canon lawyer makes the composition of James' ecclesiastical commission notably different from a court of delegates convened to hear an appeal from the Court of Arches. This Ecclesiastical Commission was stretching the prerogative power but not over-stepping it. It was violating the spirit of the law in one respect. No time ran against pope or king, but all other visitation courts had a limited life. For example, a bishop visited his diocese once every three years, but it was understood that the obligation to visit carried with it an inhibition from visiting more frequently.[10] The King's advisors were conscious of the problem. A new commission was issued in October, 1687 including new commissioners and excluding the Earl of Rochester.[11] It was its continuous existence until its abolition which encouraged some to think of it as a new court of first instance and which led the drafters of the Bill of Rights to call it 'the Court of High Commission'.

The Ecclesiastical Commission wasted no time in dealing with the refusal of Compton to dismiss Dr. Sharp. He was suspended on 6 September. In the meantime James continued to use his powers of dispensation and patronage, partly to undermine Sancroft's authority

42

among his suffragans. By the end of August it was taken for granted that all Dissenters who applied could have dispensations and by the end of November, a regular dispensation office was set up charging fifty shillings a time for the indemnification of an entire family.[12]

James hoped quickly and easily to undermine the solidarity of the episcopal bench. Lord Crewe of Durham was a courtier; Thomas Lamplugh of Exeter became less enthusiastic a Sancroftian as the months went by. The King assumed, not unreasonably, that he could count on Trelawny's support as well. With that curious rigidity he showed in his dealings with people, James never seems to have accepted that a Trelawny could ever be other than an obedient servant and that every display of obstructiveness was a temporary aberration. Professor Turner drew attention to the remarkable fact that during his reign James showed none of that vindictive spirit against personal enemies which was so marked a feature before and after his reign. He suspected that James was so confident of success that he could afford to postpone vengeance.[13] At the beginning of January, 1687 Trelawny had returned 'a smart answer' to some ineptly phrased question put to him by the King which made one of his friends realise that Trelawny was not made 'entirely of court clay'.[14] Then, on 4 April, came the King's final blow against the whole system of Anglican uniformity and discipline. James issued his Declaration of Indulgence. His supporters among the bishops were expected to follow this up with a propaganda set piece announcing Anglican support for the Declaration. Cartwright of Chester noted in his diary that he attended a meeting at the Lord Chancellor's lodgings together with Sunderland and the Bishops of Durham, Oxford, Rochester and, curiously, Peterborough to discuss the drawing up of an address of thanks to the King.[15] On 26 April Sunderland sent Trelawny a copy of the address, a list of those bishops who had signed it already and an express order from the King that he was to sign it too. Not only was he directed to canvass it among the clergy of his diocese but also to commend it to 'those of his acquaintance' - a hint that he was to talk to the bishops and leading laity in his part of the country.[16]

On receipt of the letter Trelawny promptly replied with a promise that he would present the address to his clergy. Then for three weeks he did nothing. This dilatoriness in contrast to his eagerness to obey royal commands in the preceding months strongly suggests that he had reached a personal crisis and that he needed time to think. In his anxieties over his family finances, and in his past desperate desire for promotion Trelawny had, metaphorically speaking, put a ring through his own nose. If the King and his advisors took Trelawny's extravagant protestations of loyalty at their face value and expected his conduct to match his words, it was difficult for him not be led down the path of unquestioning obedience. He could not have been happy in pursuing a policy so favourable to Roman Catholics. His persecution of Roman Catholics at the end of his life may well have been, in part, an unconscious act of expiation for his behaviour in 1686 and 1687, behaviour which must have sorely troubled his conscience. He could stifle his conscience for a time with the argument that gratitude to the King for his promotion and the obedience he owed to the Lord's Annointed demanded that he be an active supporter and not simply a passive well-wisher. Now James made it difficult for Trelawny to argue with himself this way. This Declaration of Indulgence was a direct assault on the Church he loved. There is no record of whose advice he sought, but one may hazard a guess that it included his old tutor Dr. Jane, dean of Gloucester and 'my good lord and friend the Bishop of Bath and Wells'. Trelawny was torn by three conflicting loyalties, his king, his Church and his family. If he placed his Church before his king what would be the effect on his family? He was less concerned for his personal fate than he was for the future of his family. He had had it drilled into him his duty to preserve and hand on to his descendants the Trelawny inheritance. This much is clear from the letter he sent to the family land agent quoted below. In this context he had much more to lose by defying the King than most of his brother bishops. Despite his current moderation, James had a formidable reputation for implacable hostility toward those whom he regarded as his personal enemies. All the leading men in England, even those engaged in correspondence with the Prince of Orange, were careful not to give James any opportunities for action against them. Lord Ailsbury alleged that the Earl of Shrewsbury hedged his bets by mortgaging his lands for thirty thousand pounds when he went over to Holland so that 'he might not want bread in case of failure' and that others took similar precautions.[17] Apparently few had any illusions about James' vindictiveness.

Trelawny came to his decision. He would not sign the address. He summoned his Bristol clergy, first letting them know privately by Dr. Jane that he would not sign. Trelawny recorded among his private papers 'This was necessary for several, as 'twas hinted to me, out of feare would otherwise have signed it altho' now they refus'd it to a man.'[18] Furnished with this precedent, Trelawny then ordered his archdeacon of Dorset to convene his clergy. Archdeacon Fielding politely refused, pointing out that he could not summon the clergy on his sole authority, his visitation for that year having been concluded. Four days later Fielding received a further order to do as he was told.[19] Trelawny would carry out his promise to put the address before the clergy but he was confident that with the example of their diocesan and of their Bristol brethren before them, the Dorset clergy would also refuse to sign. Only two broke ranks; Thomas Pelham, rector of Compton Valence, son of a Cromwellian major, who signed 'out of natural

44

hatred to the Church', and Robert Forsite, curate of Wimborne Abbas, whom Trelawny intended to dismiss if his employer did not save him the trouble.[20]

Trelawny then returned the address with its derisory two signatures to the Secretary of State with a covering letter. He drafted one reply, then had second thoughts and sent another. He preserved both drafts among his private papers and a comparison of the two is instructive for what they reveal about the man. In the first draft he explained to Sunderland that he had called together the clergy of Bristol and recommended the address to them. They refused to sign whereupon he asked for their reasons 'which were so convincing' that 'if I had considered them before I should not have troubled them with this affair.' He went on to say that he was fully satisfied that the address 'invincibly tends to the dishonour of this Church so it will be very prejudicial to his Majesty's interest in these parts.' He concluded with a paragraph expatiating on the loyalty of his ancestors and how he had tried always to be governed by their example. This reply is a fair example of Cornish deviousness. Trelawny did not tell an outright lie: he merely concealed the part he played in helping the clergy reach their decision and, without denying what he thought of the address, managed to convey the impression that he was the innocent mouthpiece of the opinions of others. Trelawny was not satisfied with this draft reply. His last paragraph hardly fitted with the rest of the letter. It was hypocritical to pledge obedience in the course of disobeying an express royal command. In the actual reply it was omitted. He had not explained his long delay. This he said, resulted from the time it took to convene the Dorset clergy and to learn of their response. Then he looked again at what he had written about his Bristol clergy. The phrase 'their refusal to sign' was too strong. It might be concluded to mean that all blame lay with them. He changed it to read 'there seemed a great uneasiness in them signing it'. Finally, he decided that his own opinion was expressed too bluntly, so he changed it to read that the reasons given by his clergy convinced him to such an extent 'that had I fully considered them before I should have begg'd leave of your lordship to have offer'd my humble opinion that it seemed not altogether for the advantage of his Majesty or the honour or interest of the Church of England'.[21]

James was furious when he learnt of Trelawny's refusal to sign. Determined not to retreat and fearing the worst, Trelawny made what prudent preparations he could to protect his family estates. He expected to have dragoons quartered at Trelawne at the very least and did not rule out the loss of his bishopric. He instructed Thomas Kelly, his land agent in Cornwall, to sell all his horses and cattle and rent out all the demense land and the glebe of his two rectories. 'The debts of the family are grievous to

45

me', he wrote, 'and of the greatest disturbance.....Could I bear up for a year or two the method and income would be so fixt by you, that I should then live without clamour by being able to be content in such half-yearly payments as would give the creditors great satisfaction, but me abundantly greater.' [22]

The mortgages on his lands were not the only family burden he had to carry at that time. The courage of the Trelawnys stemmed, in part, from a reckless temper which, in individual members of the family, might come close to insanity. The Bishop's youngest brother, Chichester, for some reason had developed a pathological hatred for him. Several times Chichester tried to murder his brother. The last attempt must have occurred about the middle of 1687 and landed him in jail. Trelawny mentioned to Sancroft that some persons were trying to get his 'unnatural brother' released from prison in the hope that his next attempt at murder might be more successful.[23] Chichester was tried at King's Bench and fined five hundred pounds. It was probably the good offices of Lord Godolphin that inclined the King to remit the fine but James ordered that Chichester either be sent to Bedlam or otherwise kept in custody and provided for out of his own estate by his relations.[24] Chichester was removed to the county jail at Launceston where he remained until his death in 1694.[25]

Trelawny followed his disobedience over the address of thanks with a deliberate defiance of the Ecclesiastical Commission in December. The Commissioners used the vacant presidency of Magdalen, Oxford to visit that college in June. The details of this long drawn out affair have often been described.[26] It concluded with the expulsion of Dr. Hough, the president elected by the college, together with twenty-six of the Fellows. On 10 December the Ecclesiastical Commissioners decreed that all the expelled Fellows were incapable of holding any dignity or benefice or of taking holy orders. Three days later Trelawny signed an instrument of presentation for one of the Fellows, Charles Penyston, to be vicar of Sandhurst, a living in the diocese of Gloucester in the gift of the bishops of Bristol. Frampton accepted the presentation and instituted Penyston on 17 December.[27] If challenged, Frampton might have defended himself on the grounds that refusal to institute laid him open to an action of *quare impedit* in the courts of Westminster Hall. Trelawny could offer no excuse at all. On 8 December Johnstone, the English spy working for the Dutch, reported to the Hague the rumour that if the Fellows of Magdalen College 'should be incapacitated they will be presented to livings' and that any bishop who collated 'would be suspended at least'.[28] If Johnstone is reporting brave coffee-house talk then one can only say that resolution evaporated in the face of the decree of 10 December. In the end only five of the twenty-six expelled fellows were given preferment in 1687. Four,

46

including Peynyston, were presented to livings and one was given a curacy in the diocese of Rochester. It is clear that Trelawny was now one of the leading opponents of the royal policy towards the Church.

No notice was taken of Penyston's preferment. From the King's point of view it was as significant an act of defiance as that of a small boy shouting rude words at a safe distance and he could afford to ignore it. All attention was fixed on a future parliament. By the spring of 1688 all was going well from James' point of view. The personnel of local government had been so re-arranged that it was thought safe to call a new parliament. Only the clergy continued to offer any open opposition. In January 1688 Trelawny went down to Cornwall to canvass opinion among the gentry and to advise them what answer to give to the Lord Lieutenant when he asked those who were deputy-lieutenants and justices of the peace whether or not they were prepared to vote for repeal of the Tests. Trelawny advised that they should not give an outright no but reply that, if chosen, they would be governed by conscience and reason. If they showed their hand there would be a positive command that they should not be elected.[29] James decided to break this continued clerical resistance by re-issuing the Declaration of Indulgence and ordering it to be read out in every parish church on two successive Sundays, in May for London and its environs, and in June for the rest of the country. Johnstone's informants seemed to think that the new Convocation when it assembled with the new parliament, would be required to make full acknowledgement of royal dispensing power under threat of *Praemunire*.[30] If so, then reading the Declaration would create a precedent the Convocation would find hard to resist. During the spring an inner group of bishops had been meeting at Lambeth to devise an effective opposition.[31] Trelawny did not attend the Lambeth discussions but he was included probably through his meetings with Ken of Bath and Wells.[32] Trelawny had a long argument with Lamplugh of Exeter in August in an attempt to put some backbone into him. Both Ken and Trelawny had written to him in May to urge him not to order his clergy to read the Declaration.[33] It would appear that the concerted clerical opposition to James at this juncture was managed by the skilful leadership of Turner of Ely. On 12 May he persuaded Sancroft to summon immediately to Lambeth seven bishops who could be relied upon. Trelawny was one of the five who responded. He attended the last crucial meeting on 18 May when the wording of the bishops' petition was agreed on and he accompanied Lloyd of St. Asaph, Turner of Ely, Lake of Chichester, Ken of Bath and Wells and White of Peterborough when they crossed the river to Whitehall that same evening, to present their petition against reading the Declaration to the King in his closet.

Their encounter with James has often been described. Taken

47

completely by surprise, James lost his temper. 'This is a great surprise to me,' he said, 'here are strange words. I did not expect this from you; especially from some of you.' Here he looked at Turner, one of his former chaplains, in particular. Then he went on, 'This writing is a trumpet of rebellion.' Mention of the word 'rebellion' shattered Trelawny's composure. He lost his temper. He fell again to his knees, 'Rebellion, Sir! I beseech your Majesty do not say so hard a thing of us, for God's sake! Do not believe we are or can be guilty of rebellion! It is impossible for me or my family to be guilty of rebellion! Your Majesty cannot but remember that you sent me to quell Monmouth's rebellion and I am as ready to do what I can to quell another. We will do our duty to your Majesty to our utmost in everything that does not interfere with our duty towards God.' [34] Trelawny's bodily posture belied his mood. The outburst did nothing to mollify the King. He replied, 'If I change my mind you shall hear from me, if not, I expect to be obeyed!' Later James recalled bitterly that of all the bishops, Trelawny had been 'the most saucy'.

Trelawny carefully preserved this recollection of what he had said to the King among his personal papers. It is interesting to speculate why. In challenging the King in this way, he was violating both his upbringing and all the canons of gratitude for his advancement. It was an incident charged with emotion. Was his outburst also prompted, in part, by a guilty conscience? He was careful to record another conversation he had had in late February, 1689 with John Robartes concerning the allegation by William Harbord (who had written the Prince of Orange's declaration published in October 1688) that the bishops had invited the Prince to come over. Trelawny told Robartes he believed the insinuation to be utterly false and, in reply, Robartes gave him Harbord's response to his own question on the same topic, 'no damn 'em they were not so honest'.[35] Thirty years later this issue was still a sensitive one with Trelawny when Echard published the third volume of his *History of England*.[36] In 1717 Trelawny wanted Lloyd of Worcester, then the only other surviving bishop from those days, to put his hand to a joint declaration that no bishop had sent a letter of invitation to the Prince of Orange.[37] He glossed over the fact the Compton of London had been one of the signatories of the invitation of 30 June 1688. On the other hand, Burnet was told by one of his relatives that on 8 June when the seven bishops were committed to the Tower, Trelawny stated that 'the Prince of Orange would soon come to get him out'. Burnet and Trelawny detested each other so any information from that quarter must be received with caution. Much depends on two extraneous factors: how much did Trelawny learn from his brothers about disaffection in the army? And how early had that disaffection begun? Colonel Charles Trelawny, together with General Percy Kirke and Lord Churchill, openly associated with the disaffected. If Ailesbury is to be trusted, on one occasion he begged the King to arrest all three.[38] He implies that it was after Bonrepas had been sent across from France to offer James military assistance. Bonrepas had his first audience of the King on 25 August. Ogg states 'the rot began in July' when James ordered a census of the army to discover how many were Roman Catholics.[39] Churchill was in communication with the Prince of Orange in July 1687. It is possible, therefore, that on the evening on 18 May 1688 although not involved personally, Trelawny knew more than he was prepared to say. The decision to prosecute the Seven Bishops for seditious libel; their imprisonment in the Tower and the events which followed their state trial and acquittal in Westminster Hall are one of the best documented incidents in English history. Trelawny played no significant part except during the preliminary hearing before the King's Bench on 15 June when William Blathwayt noted that his averment 'turned the main point'.[40] Cheerfully and characteristically, he over-contributed his share of the expense for the trial.[41] Trelawny preserved the following brief account of the trial and acquittal among his private papers:

'I was committed to the Tower and we were by Habeas Corpus brought to Westminster Hall on Friday June 15 where all our pleas being over ruled we were required by recognizances to appear Fryday fortnight the 29th. After a tryal from 9 in the morning to 7 at night we were ordered to attend Saturday the 30th. The Jury about 10 that morning brought us in not guilty. We went immediately to Lambeth in the Archbishop's barge. The Archbishop himself read Ps. 103 115 Te Deum with a prayer of Thanksgiving & some other prayers as his chaplain did the Litany.' [42]

News of the acquittal, as it spread throughout the Kingdom, produced scenes of wild joy. In Bristol 'all the bells rang, they gave very large expressions of joy and at night bonfires were made in many parts of this city.' [43] Miles away in the little fishing port of East Looe the news was received with equal joy. The bells of Pelynt rang out. The mayor fired the two town cannon 'with great solemnity'. The curate of St. Martins juxta Looe fired the first gun 'by Mr. Mayor's leave'. In the evening beer and sack flowed freely.[44]

The Bishops wasted no time in capitalising on their victory. Sancroft sent his suffragans back to their dioceses with instructions to hold confirmations partly in response to the remarkable confirmation tour taken by one of the vicars apostolic in England, and partly because such gatherings afforded an excellent opportunity to strengthen relations with

49

leading laity. They were also instructed to keep up a friendly correspondence with Dissenters. It was not until mid-September, however, when James learnt for certain that William of Orange intended to invade, were there any signs of a change in royal policy. The Bishops had several inconclusive interviews with the King who by now was showing all the signs of a man on the verge of a nervous breakdown. Various concessions followed: Compton's suspension was lifted; the Ecclesiastical Commission revoked, and its work at Magdalen College undone. James refused to budge on the question of his dispensing power and the Declaration of Indulgence was not rescinded. On 12 October the Bishops began to disperse to their dioceses. On 5 November William landed at Torbay.

The forty days from the arrival of William to James' second departure are the most extraordinary in modern English history. By December it became apparent, to the horror of many, that William had come not simply to restore the laws and the protestant religion, but to claim the throne. Despite the presence of a foreign army, William's appropriation of taxation to his own use and his performing acts of government in the area under his control, the government of James continued to function, including the advancement of ecclesiastical appointments. In these circumstances Trelawny found himself translated to Exeter!

James received in audience on Thursday, 15 November, both Thomas Lamplugh, who had retired to London ahead of William's advance on Exeter, and Trelawny. Lamplugh was informed that he was to be archbishop of York and Trelawny was told that he was to succeed Lamplugh at Exeter.[45] The following day James ordered the congé d'elire to be prepared for the Dean and Chapter of Exeter.[46] What James intended by these promotions at this particular time can only be guessed at. Danby and his supporters had risen in favour of William and had occupied York, so both dioceses were in rebel hands. Perhaps in some muddled way James recalled how the Bishops had saved him during the Exclusion Bill crisis of 1679 to 1681 and hoped that loyal bishops in these places would somehow help to restore the loyalty of the gentry. Only six months earlier Trelawny was being systematically stripped of his offices in Cornwall. On 23 June he was removed from his office of alderman in Lostwithiel and freeman of Liskeard. His brother Charles was removed from his office of freeman of Liskeard on 9 September.[47] In the west country the Earl of Bath had declared for the Prince. James may have remembered how useful a royal watchdog Trelawny had proved to be during the session of the Stannary Parliament of 1686. Perhaps he knew how the Granvilles and Trelawnys disliked each other and hoped in some way to counteract the influence in Cornwall of a pro-Orange Granville with a pro-Jacobite Trelawny. One

50

can only speculate on the reasons for James' remarkable *volte-face*. In any case the decision to translate Trelawny to Exeter was made by a man who no longer knew his own mind. After dithering for two days, James finally decided to join his army in Wiltshire on 16 November and he left Whitehall the following day.

The steps in appointing a new bishop are laid down clearly in the Henrician Statute (25 Hen.VIII, cap.20). The congé d'elire under the Great Seal is sent to the dean and chapter, together with a letter missive under the privy seal naming the person to be elected. Upon receipt of these documents the dean and chapter have twelve days in which to act. When that body has certified under their seal that the election has been duly performed, the bishop swears fealty to the king, who then certifies the election under letters patent under the Great Seal to the archbishop. A ceremony of confirmation in the Court of Arches follows. Then the archbishop consecrates him and the archdeacon of Canterbury inducts him. Legally, the candidate does not become bishop elect of his new diocese until the cathedral chapter has certified the election. Only then is his former diocese vacant. Lamplugh faced no delay in this respect. York had been left vacant for over a year. When Trelawny wrote anxiously to enquire of Turner of Ely what progress had been made, he was relieved to hear early in December that although the messenger carrying the documents for Lamplugh's election had been captured by those in arms somewhere north of the Trent, the black box with the instruments had been forwarded to York.[48] The Dean and Chapter of York acted promptly and their certification must have been returned because Trelawny knew that his congé d'élire had been sealed.[49] It would appear that the instruments for his election were sent to Exeter and a certification duly returned, because a pass issued in London to one of Trelawny's servants on Monday, 10 December, accords him his new title.[50] At this point events overtook the legal process.

James had reached Salisbury on 19 November and was confined to his tent for the next two days with continuous nose bleeds. At a council of war held on 22 November, James decided to order a retreat. In retrospect these four days decided James' fate, but Trelawny was concerned not with the fate of princes but with the state of his own finances. After three years at Bristol he was already £1,500 in debt and the income from his two small livings of St. Ive and South Hill were quite inadequate to meet the expenses of his translation. If, at this distance in time, his attitude appears mercenary it had the full and sympathetic consideration of Turner of Ely, who had undertaken to supervise all the legal steps in London while Trelawny remained at Bristol. Turner could see no reason why Trelawny should not continue to hold St. Ive and South Hill whilst acquiring the rich living of Shobrooke in Devon, which automatically went *in commendam* with the bishopric of Exeter. 'Your Lordship's expenses will be so considerable in your own Province that I for my part know no reflection it ought to bring upon you to hold both your Benefices.'[51] There was also the matter of the royal deanery of St. Buryan which Lamplugh had held in his *commendam.* Trelawny was pestering the Secretaries of State immediately after his appointment. Lord Middleton asked the King about it at Salisbury. With more weighty matters on his mind James understandably refused to decide one way or the other.[52] Trelawny was still pressing Lord Preston for a decision on 6 December.

Waiting in suspense over his translation and his *commendam,* Trelawny had to decide on his attitude toward the Prince of Orange. On, or shortly after, 25 November, Charles Trelawny deserted his regiment and went over to the Prince. On 27 November, probably after learning of his brother's decision, Trelawny wrote to Turner assuring him of his loyalty to James which Turner duly passed on to the King on 30 November. The King was pleased, which must have reduced Trelawny's apprehension. James knew of Charles Trelawny's desertion because a warrant for a new colonal was signed the following day. He could, vindictively, have put a stop to Trelawny's translation. On 21 November William had left Exeter and moved with his army toward London. On the afternoon of 5 December the Earl of Shewsbury and a regiment of infantry entered Bristol. The Earl had a letter for the Bishop from the Prince. Trelawny replied immediately, in cautious terms, announcing his approval of the steps being taken for the preservation of the protestant religion and of the laws and liberties of England.[53] By this date James was close to his final decision to flee the country. Decisions were still being taken, perhaps partly as a cover to conceal the King's true intention. One such decision was the announcement that John Chetwood was to be Trelawny's successor at Bristol. Then, at one o'clock on Tuesday morning, 11 December, James left Whitehall on his way to France. As he crossed the river to Lambeth he dropped the Great Seal of England into the water. His motive is generally thought to have been a desire to impede the calling of a new parliament, but a consequence was that Trelawny's election could not be certified to the Archbishop because there was no Great Seal available to attach to the letters patent.

It is given to few to recognise a revolution when they are living through one. Only after the King returned to London on 15 December, did William's intentions become clearer to most Englishmen. At first, his concern was to supervise the calling of a new parliament; now, it was clear that he aimed at the throne. James' departure from England, on 23 December, finally ended all hopes of completing the legal formalities of

Trelawny's translation. It was as bishop of Bristol and not of Exeter that he was summoned to the Convention the following January.

1. *Lords' Journals,* xiv, 9 November, 1685.

2. See G.V. Bennett, 'The Seven Bishops: a reconsideration', *Studies in Church History* xv (1979), 275, quoting Morrice MSS., f.491, 7 November, 1686.

3. *Downshire MSS.,* i, pt.ii. 151, Rupert Browne to Sir William Trumbull, 17 April [1685]; 177, same to same, 3 June, 1686.

4. N. Sykes, *William Wake* (Cambridge, 1957), i.201.

5. David Ogg, *England in the Reigns of James II and William III* (Oxford, 1957), p.177.

6. *An Order directed against Clandestine Marriages,* publ. by the Ecclesiastical Commission, London, 4 November, 1686.

7. Luttrell, i.399, 431.

8. MS. Tanner cxxix, ff.86, 87.

9. See Smith, Administration, pp.267-8.

10. E. Gibson, *Codex Juris Ecclesiastical Anglicani* (1761), i.958.

11. T. Harrison, *The History of King James' Ecclesiastical Commission* (1711), p.27.

12. G.V. Bennett, *loc. cit.,* p.278.

13. F.C. Turner, *James II* (1948), p.357.

14. *Ellis Correspondence,* ed. Lord Dover (1831), i.4, 5 January, 1687.

15. *The Diary of Dr. Thomas Cartwright* ed. J. Hunter (Camden Society 1st series xxii, 1843), p.47, entry for 20 April, 1687.

16. *Cal. S.P. Dom.,* 1687, p.371, Sunderland to T, 26 April, 1687.

17. *Memoirs of Thomas, earl of Ailesbury,* ed. W.E. Buckley, printed for the Roxburghe Club (Westminster, 1890), i.130.

18. C.T., p.216.

19. *Ibid.,* p.214, John Fielding to T, 24 May, 1687; T to Fielding, 28 May, 1687.

20. MS. Tanner xxix, f.47, T to Sancroft, 1 July, 1687.

21. C.T., p.216.

22. *E.C.,* iv. 328-32, T to Kelly, 20 June, 1687.

23. MS. Tanner ccix, f.47, T to Sancroft, 1 July 1687.

24. *Cal. Treasury Books,* viii, pt.iii, 1685-89, p.1484, secretary of the Treasury Commissioners to T, 28 July, 1687.

25. This appears to be the likeliest event. Sir William Salusbury-Trelawny noted, 'At Ham there is a sort of certificate receiving into custody the body of Christopher Trelawny at the County Gaol. *vide* letter from Miss Collins' (C.T., p.424). Christopher could easily be a misreading for Chichester.

26. See F.C. Turner, *op. cit.,* pp.336-44; David Ogg, *op. cit.,* pp.183-5.

27. G.R.O., G.D.R. D1/235.

28. U.N.L., Portland MSS., PwA 2112/2112a, Johnstone to Bentinck, 8 December 1687.

29. MS. Tanner xxviii, f.139, T to Sancroft, undated. This letter has been ascribed to the month of August, but the letter was written when it was known that the Lord Lieutenant was to be sent down to the county, but before he had arrived. The Earl of Bath went into Cornwall in mid-February 1688 (Luttrell, i.432).

30. U.N.L., PwA 2112d.

31. G.V. Bennett, *loc. cit.,* p.280.

32. Ken stayed with Trelawny in Bristol when he baptised his first child in the cathedral in March (C.T., p.411). It is just possible that Turner of Ely held a regional meeting with Trelawny and Ken in Bristol in the spring, but the evidence is flimsy. It rests solely on an extract from the churchwardens' accounts of St. Peter's Bristol: 'Paid the ringers when the Bishops of Ely and Wells came' (Nichols and Taylor, *op. cit.,* ii.134). The reference could easily have been a miscopying of Bath and Wells. Unhappily St. Peter's records were destroyed.

33. MS. Tanner xxv, f.158, T to Sancroft, 16 August, 1688.

34. *J.R.I.C.,* viii (1881-83), pp.218-9.

35. C.T., p.215.

36. *Gentleman's Magazine, lxxxviii, pt. 1 (1818), p.199.*

37. *C.T., pp.217-8, T to Lloyd, 25 January, 1717.*

38. *Memoirs, op. cit.,* i.184.

39. Ogg, *op. cit.,* p.202.

40. U.N.L. PwV53 [Phillips MSS., 8555, iii], Blathwayt to Sir Robert Southwell, 19 June 1688.

41. J. Gutch, ed. *Collectanea Curiosa,* (Oxford, 1781), ii.370. The bishops agreed to

share out the cost of just over £614 at the rate of six percent of their annual income. Trelawny's share of £350 was £21. He paid £37 12s. 6d.

42. C.T., p.211.

43. Nichols and Taylor, *op. cit.,* iii.134.

44. *Tre Pol and Pen Cornish Annual* (Truro, 1928), p.50.

45. *Original Letters of Ellis,* 2nd Series (1827), iv.151.

46. *Cal. S.P. Dom.,* June 1687-Feb. 1689, p.354.

47. P.R.O., PC/2/72, Privy Council Register, 4 April 1687-16 December 1688.

48. C.T., p.263, Francis Turner to T, 1 December, 1688.

49. H.M.C., *Seventh Report,* p.420, T to Lord Preston, 6 December, 1688.

50. *Cal. S.P. Dom., loc. cit.,* p.419.

51. C.T., p.264, Turner to T, 11 December, 1688.

52. *Cal. S.P. Dom., loc. cit.,* p.359, Middleton to Preston, 22 November, 1688.

53. *Ibid., p.374, T to Prince of Orange, 5 December, 1688.*

CHAPTER FIVE

Bishop of Exeter - The Wilderness Years

In his letter to the Prince of Orange dated 5 November, 1688 Trelawny welcomed the Prince's actions to preserve the laws and protestant religion, but he did not indicate support for William beyond that. Like many Englishmen, Trelawny did not realise the full extent of William's ambition until King James' second departure. It was one thing to protect the Church of England against the misguided policies of a legitimate king: it was quite another matter to support measures leading to the deposition of that king. The constitutional crisis that ensued and the debates whereby the Glorious Revolution was finally secured have been the subject of fresh investigation in recent years. The discovery of new evidence in the shape of voting lists for the House of Lords among the Ailesbury MSS makes it possible to have a clearer idea of Trelawny's position at this stage in his career.

The argument that the King's flight to France was a legal demise so that the crown devolved on the Princess of Orange commended itself neither to the loyalists nor to the supporters of William. After discussion with some of the peers, experienced former members of the Commons, and aldermen and councillors of the City of London, William agreed to summon a convention for 22 January. Various ideas were being canvassed ranging from proclamation of a republic to the recall of James. There was no visible political consensus when the members of the Convention assembled at Westminster. However, loyalists had realised that the composition of the Commons was more radical than that of the Lords and tried to delay debate in the Commons until the Lords had taken the initiative. William's supporters in the Lords cancelled out that tactic by adjourning until 29 January, the day after the one the members of the Commons fixed for their debate.

It was reported that the Bishops had agreed on a policy,[1] but Compton of London was not among them. He had already thrown in his lot with the Williamites. Trelawny was wavering. It was noted that when he read prayers in the Lords on Wednesday, 24 January, he 'skipped over' the prayer for the King.[2] At this stage he hesitated between two positions, clear as to what he did not want but uncertain of the way forward. He did not wish to see James return. Later in life he declared he had a real fear of James' vindictiveness. He did not want to abandon the doctrine of hereditary divine right. When Princess Anne made a tentative attempt to construct a party to support her pretensions to follow her sister Mary in the order of succession, Trelawny was among a group of Tory peers including three other Bishops who had a meeting with her in January. As late as 27 January, Prince George told Clarendon that neither he nor his wife would consent to alter the succession.[3] In a committee of the whole House with Hampden in the chair, Whig speakers dominated the Common's debate on 28 January and the House voted by acclamation that James had broken the original contract, abdicated the government and left the throne vacant.[4] The following day the Lords debated and voted on a motion for a regency in James' name during his life-time. The motion was supported by the loyalists, some out of conviction, others merely to gain time. The motion was narrowly defeated by 51 votes to 48 with 2 abstentions. Trelawny was one of the two who 'modestly withdrew' before the vote was taken.[5] It is possible that throughout January, Trelawny was influenced by his brother Charles and the Churchills. Lord Churchill retired to St. Albans in late January in order to avoid taking part in any vote in the Lords. Through their military connections the Trelawnys and the Churchills knew each other well. Many years later Sarah, duchess of Marlborough, and her husband were still on terms of intimacy with the Bishop.[6] The Churchills supported Anne and had already introduced Sidney Godolphin to the group of advisors surrounding the Princess. Godolphin was a fellow Cornishman with whom Trelawny had much in common. A comparison of their voting records over the next few years show both men holding similar opinions on the great issues of the day, even on the Place Bill of 1692 and 93 when Godolphin, although a minister, also voted to commit the Bill, but was absent on the day the Court just managed to defeat the second division.[7] It has been suggested that Trelawny belonged with Danby and a small group of six or eight peers who favoured the choice of Princess Mary as James' rightful successor, but his voting record in February scarcely bears this out.[8] It is more likely that once he realised that Anne was playing a double game with the Hydes, he moved back to supporting the loyalists. On 30 January, the feast day of King Charles the Martyr, a day full of emotional memories for royalists, Trelawny voted with the majority to substitute the word 'deserted' for the word 'abdicated' in the Commons' resolution. The next day in a committee of the whole House he voted with all the other bishops, except Compton, against declaring the Prince and Princess of Orange king and queen, and refused to agree with the clause declaring the throne to be vacant. The

Commons refused to accept the Lords' amendment. William made it clear that he expected to be offered the throne in his own right, but agreed that Anne's children should have precedence before any children of his by any wife other than Mary. When Anne agreed to give up her rights to William should Mary pre-decease him, the Lords had little room for manoeuvre. By the evening of 6 February majorities were mustered for accepting the words 'abdicated' and 'vacant', and for a motion to make William and Mary king and queen. On the first vote of the evening Trelawny voted against accepting the word 'abdicated' and recorded his formal dissent. Clarendon alleged that the victory of the Williamites was due, in part, to the departure of several lords before the division. He instanced, among others, Godolphin and Trelawny.[9] Recently discovered voting lists show that Clarendon was wrong. Both men voted with the loyalists in all three divisions that evening.

On Tuesday, 13 February, Trelawny appeared at a thinly attended House to agree that the King and Queen be proclaimed and he accompanied the other lords to present the declaration to William and Mary in the Banqueting Hall at Whitehall. He was present at all stages of the act legitimising the Convention and took the oath of fealty with the Bishops of London and Lincoln on Saturday, 2 March. Despite their tendency to flamboyant parades of loyalty, the Trelawnys always had a strong vein of grainy granite common-sense in any situation where they were convinced that the outcome was inevitable. The Bishop's son, Edward Trelawny, for example, was to recognise that the Maroons of Jamaica could not be defeated and concluded a treaty with their leader within a year of becoming governor. A more distant descendant was to grasp the nettle of the compulsory church rate in the nineteenth century and sponsor the 1868 Act which abolished it. Once it was obvious that William and Mary were to be offered the throne, then there was no point in continuing to oppose them. Years later Trelawny still recalled the sense of inevitability about the revolution settlement. he reminded Lloyd of Worcester 'we thought ourselves obliged to accept of the deliverance brought us', a comment which resembles the advice the Churchills were giving Anne at the time.[10] Like so many Tory gentlemen, Trelawny had no wish to go forward in the path indicated by the Whigs; but he had an even stronger desire not to go back to the despotism from which the nation had just escaped. Above all, he had no desire to go back to a situation which threatened the Protestant Religion. He assured his Cornish clergy in the General Election of 1690, 'I have no other concern but the support of our Religion and in the defence of that no person either could or shall fright me'.[11] Unlike Frampton, Ken, and Turner, his close associates among bishops, Trelawny had no scruples about taking the oaths of allegiance to

58

the new monarchs. Ailesbury recorded that James had asked the bishops before his departure to take part in public affairs in order to protect the future rights of the Prince of Wales, and that some bishops used this as an excuse to keep their bishoprics. It is not likely that Trelawny used this excuse. Support of the Church of England was his main motive. In his opinion bishops should no more desert their flocks in the face of danger than officers their troops on the field of battle. Yet there must have been another, equally powerful, motive. His obligation to ensure the survival of the ancient house of Trelawny could not be ignored. Apart from the pecuniary disincentive of double fines on all who failed to take the new oaths, his family had suffered enough loss for the sake of the Stuarts for him to want to destroy the family fortunes completely. His estates were already burdened with mortgages. He depended on his episcopal income if he was going to have any success at all in keeping the family credit afloat. Through the centuries the ancient Cornish families had watched rulers come and go. They had survived by accommodating themselves to new masters. Godolphin's remark to some close friends as he left the Lord's Chamber on the evening of 6 February, after having voted three times against the Williamites, that 'he was to attend the Prince of Orange at the Treasury' displays a realism his fellow countrymen understood and approved of. Trelawny's translation to Exeter might appear a reward for changing sides but it was nothing of the sort. Bishop Ward of Salisbury died 9 January and Trelawny had great hopes of succeeding him. The annual income of Salisbury was four times that of Bristol and needed no *commendam* to maintain it. William gave it to his close advisor, Gilbert Burnet. In later years Trelawny attributed his failure to be given Salisbury to the direct result of his voting record in February. At the beginning of the next reign he reminded the Earl of Nottingham that the loss had been the direct result of following him through the opposition lobby on that fateful evening.[12] Unlike poor Mr. Chetwood whose nomination by James II to the see of Bristol had not even proceeded as far as the issue of a congé d'élire, Trelawny's translation to Exeter had been well advanced before the King's flight. It was important for the new monarchs to be punctilious in strengthening the legitimacy and continuity of their succession to the throne. Accordingly William and Mary renewed the offer of Exeter together with the royal deanery of St. Buryan and the rectory of Shobrooke *in commendam,* shortly after their coronation.

The warrants were issued at Whitehall on 16 March 1689. The Dean and Chapter of Exeter acted quickly on this second congé d'élire and royal assent was given on 4 April. The *commendam* was widened to include any two dignities in the Bishop's gift which fell vacant. On 13 April Trelawny was formally translated to Exeter and on 15 April he was granted

59

restitution of temporalities from the day of his translation from Bristol.[13]

William depended on the votes of the Bishops in the Lords as time went by but he could never count on the votes of either Compton, Sprat or Trelawny. William was not unaware of the ability of the Bishop, or of his two military brothers for that matter, but the Bishop was never *persona grata* at Court. The past connections of his family with the exiled James had been too close for the Bishop's anti-Jacobite stance to be believed by everybody. William's episcopal appointments have been re-assessed in recent years.[14] Many were Nottingham's recommendations. The new bishops belonged to high church circles and were not as latitudinarian as was once thought. They were men of ability and learning and their appointment was intended to reconcile the parish clergy to the new régime. One cannot ignore, however, the very real difference of approach between the old bishops and the new. The old bishops were still adherents of Sancroft's ideal of a godly anglican discipline imposed on the nation and supervised by an apostolic episcopate. They accepted the Act of Toleration; they acknowledged the supremacy of Parliament, but they still adhered to the belief that the Church of England had a divine right, derived from the Apostolic Succession of bishops, to administer the discipline of Christ to all its members. They saw no justification in acquiescing in the recent shift in public opinion which wanted to see the church courts powerless to deal with many routine lapses of discipline among the laity and they strongly resented the tendency of Whig lawyers to obstruct or ignore the church courts. When Peter King, a rising young Whig lawyer from Exeter, argued 'that he thought all honest men should endeavour to advance the Law above the power of the Church' Trelawny was outraged. He considered that no bishop ever asked anything for the Church which the Law did not already give her.[15] The new bishops, on the other hand, were prepared to accept the new mood of rebellion among the laity. The party line between old and new bishops was clearly drawn as early as January 1692, when the Duke of Norfolk first tried to introduce his divorce bill into the Lords. The bill was committed by 46 votes to 38, 'All the new bishops present went one way, all the old the other', Sprat reported to Trelawny. The old bishops resisted this attempt to bypass the church courts where all marriage cases properly belonged.[16]

This stand by the old bishops on the question of a divorce petition which had not been brought before any ecclesiastical tribunal conceals an issue of fundamental importance. In the late seventeenth century few considered morality to be a private matter. Men and women divided on whether morality was a matter for the State or for the Church. If it was a matter for the State then it was for Parliament to define the offence and fix the penalty, and for the magistrate to enforce the law. If it was a matter for the Church then it was for the parish clergy to supervise the lives of their flock in accordance with Canon Law derived from Scripture and from the decisions of the Church, and, where necessary, calling upon the church courts with their sanctions of admonition, penance and excommunication to enforce pastoral discipline. The State employed the sanctions of fines and imprisonment which were swiftly imposed, therefore considered by many people to be more effective as a deterrent. However, the magistrate's interest in the offender ceased with his imposition of the punishment. The approach to the individual was negative and detached. The attitude of the Church was very different. Canonical punishment was designed not so much to deter as to bring about a change of heart in the offender. Penance before a Sunday morning congregation brought a more direct personal influence to bear on an individual than did the payment of a fine. A parish priest who would continue to be concerned with the penitent's spiritual health long after the offence, was felt to be more likely to effect a reformation of behaviour than would a bench of magistrates encountering the offender briefly in the course of a busy session. Edmund Gibson put his finger on the main issue when he complained about the baleful affects produced by the number of parliamentary statues passed after 1689 regulating public morals:

> 'The Clergy as well as People, slide into a general opinion
> that this or that crime is punishable nowhere but in the
> Temporal Courts.....and the punishment of Vice and care
> of Spiritual Matters are by degrees, transferred to the
> Laity, who have neither at heart.' [17]

It was the attitude of mind described by Gibson that the old bishops wanted to resist. The new bishops did not see how this new tendency could be stopped. In the years following 1688 the clergy of the Church of England had to go through an agonizing reappraisal of all that they had stood for theologically, morally and pastorally. 'Could Anglican divines disavow their preaching for a generation? If they shifted their allegiance where stood now the religious view of society and social obligation?' [18] The parish clergy were particularly unhappy. They had to come to terms with a new pastoral situation which had arisen almost overnight. First, they were faced with the partial collapse of the pastoral discipline of the Church of England. Persuading the English nation to worship regularly in their parish churches on Sundays and major Holy Days had become an increasingly difficult task since the Reformation. The legal demise of the Church of England during the Commonwealth period had done nothing to make that task easier, so the restoration of the church courts in 1661 was important for the parish clergy. Toward the end of the reign of Charles II, with the help of the courts, the parish clergy seem to have made some

61

headway in enforcing discipline among the laity in many parts of the country, if surviving evidence for the number of communicants is any guide. There is little doubt that enforcement was resented, but, with the passing of time, habit and custom would have strengthened it. However, this policy was thrown into complete disarray by James II's determination to win support for his co-religionists by a sweeping, indiscriminate, use of the royal prerogative. His Declaration of Indulgence halted all the *ex officio* business of the ecclesiastical courts which concerned non-attendance at church, failure to send children to be catechised and neglect of baptism. After the passing of the Act of Toleration in 1689 public opinion interpreted the Act not in the light of the situation preceding the first issue of James' Declaration, but in the light of the previous two years when pastoral discipline in matters of church attendance had to all intents and purposes ceased. Stillingfleet of Worcester put the problem to Archbishop Tillotson in 1694 with his usual clarity. He told his primate that the King might well be advised to include a strongly worded injunction reminding the parish clergy of their duty to catechize regularly:

> 'But what if the People will not send their Children?
> Suspension and Excommunication doth but drive them
> out of the Church; and they care very little for coming to
> it. And the best Ministers in my Diocese complain most
> of this, either that Parents or Masters will not send their
> Children and Servants; or if they do, that they will not
> go.'

Stillingfleet could ask the question, but he had no answer.[19] Secondly, this partial collapse in pastoral discipline was compounded by the Toleration Act itself which gave many parsons the spectacle of a local congregation of Dissenters meeting openly for worship in a legally licensed meeting house with a lawful minister of their own. This meeting house offered an alterative place of worship to a digruntled parishioner which the passage of time would make respectable as Parliament had made it legitimate.

Thirdly, the parish clergy had to face an extraordinary expansion of Nonconformist education. The sector most affected was what a later age would call 'higher' or 'adult' education. The Dissenting Academies were institutions of university standard intended in the first place for candidates for the ministry, but favoured even by Anglican parents who baulked at the conservative politics and heavy expense of Oxford and Cambridge. The new Societies for the Reformation of Manners included among their activities, an element of adult education which, like the Academies, lay outside the supervision of the Church of England.

Finally, the parish clergy had to watch the development of a practice known as Occasional Conformity whereby Dissenters paid a single visit to their parish churches in order to receive the Sacrament of Holy Communion once and so qualify for public office under Test and Corporation Acts.

Even if ecclesiastical ordinaries and their officers still wanted to support the parish clergy they were obstructed by the open partiality shown by the the judges of the Courts of Westminster Hall who granted prohibitions against trials in the church courts for the flimsiest of excuses. Relations between common lawyers and ecclesiastical lawyers had always been strained. The jurisprudence of the latter had always lent itself more to the upholding of prerogative government, of which James II's late Ecclesiastical Commission was an unpleasant reminder. Until 1688 the animosity of the common lawyers had been restrained by the Crown. After 1702 judges again became more circumspect in their attitude, but between 1688 and 1702, the King made no attempt to check his common law judges. Ecclesiastical lawyers were not in favour. In September, 1693 the suspected Jacobite sympathies of many of them seemed to be proved when two leading advocates of Doctors' Commons declared their opinion that captured privateers holding a commission from King James could not be tried as pirates because James had a right under international law to try to regain his throne by force.[20] The prompt dismissal of both men from government posts was quickly followed by a writ of *mandamus* removing the registrar of the Consistory Court of Hereford for refusing to take the oaths of allegiance.

For a bishop it was a particularly difficult time in which to be a church leader. His clergy still looked to him for support in dealing with their more recalcitrant parishioners. Anglican laity still expected him to uphold the privileges of the Church of England, only now he was expected to uphold only those aspects of church discipline approved by his critics. The Anglican laity now expected to be exempted from discipline in matters of church attendance and compulsory Christian education by way of catechism classes, but still expected the full rigour of Canon Law to be applied to the parish clergy. In 1689, and again in 1694, parliament agreed to an Act of General Pardon. In the lists of exemptions 'adultery and other Enormous Crimes committed by any person in Holy Orders punishable in any Ecclesiastical Court' were specifically excluded from the scope of the pardon. A bishop, and an archdeacon too for that matter, had to defend his role as upholder of 'the discipline of Christ' on two fronts. Opposition came not only from those who regarded much of the Church's discipline as archaic, but also from the Societies for the Reformation of Manners whose members regarded the discipline as irrelevant. The attitude of these Societies, which began in and around London in 1690 and spread rapidly thereafter, was that moral correction was a matter for the secular courts;

63

nothing could be looked for from the church courts with their cumbrous procedures and ineffective sanctions.[21] In the aftermath of the Toleration Act a bishop faced a new challenge to his authority. Before 1689 a layman might defy his bishop but in doing so stood purely on the defensive. After 1689 a layman might threaten to desert the Church and join the Dissenters if his wishes were ignored or any attempt made to discipline him. The congregation of Merther chapel in Cornwall, used this form of blackmail and forced Trelawny to licence their candidate as curate.[22]

A further difficulty in 1689 was that the bishops themselves were temporarily without a leader. Archbishop Sancroft had withdrawn from public life but was not replaced until 1691. The new archbishop, John Tillotson, did not relish his task and gave no clear lead. Only with the succession of Thomas Tenison in 1695 do signs emerge of a renewed sense of direction in the Church of England. Trelawny felt this absence of leadership keenly. He was urged in 1691 by John Buller to instruct all his clergy to read from the pulpit a declaration of the Cornish magistrates dealing with the statutes against vice. He replied that it was too serious a matter for him to decide by himself and that when he had an opportunity he would consult with 'several bishops', by which he usually meant Compton of London and Sprat of Rochester.[23] The Government was also aware of the leadership vacuum. William supplied the deficiency by issuing a short set of injunctions to Compton for despatch to the bishops of both provinces. The King promised to support the church courts in their prosecution of sexual offences but only because there was no statute law dealing with such matters. The injunctions show plainly that, in William's opinion, the role of the bishops was to keep a strict watch on the clergy: the sins and vice of the laity were the concern of the magistrates. When Tenison took up his duties in January, 1695, William had an archbishop who shared his mind in these matters. The King issued a second, more comprehensive, set of injunctions largely to do with the conduct of the clergy. Tenison followed this in the summer with a set of his own and required all his suffragans to give him a full account of what they had been doing in their dioceses when they next attended parliament. Later that summer the King ordered the Archbishop to render an account by Christmas all commutation money collected and disbursed.[24] Clearly the new Archbishop· intended to assert his authority from the start. Proceedings were continued against Watson of St. Davids.[25] Thomas Watson was another of James II's appointments who made little secret of his Jacobitism. His tendency to single out his Whig clergy for pastoral discipline lead to charges of extortion, simony and *crimen falsi* being brought against him. Archbishop Tillotson suspended him in July, 1694 pending a full investigation. What both King and Archbishop looked for among the Bishops was aceptance of the fact that any increase in spiritual effectiveness would have to come from the hard work of the clergy. Crown patronage was entrusted to a small commission of five bishops who were 'to seek out the best and worthiest men they could find that such only might be promoted'. The task of a bishop was to discipline the clergy in such a way as to ensure that they continued at all times to be diligent in their pastoral duties. Tenison was an enthusiastic supporter of the whole voluntary movement involving devout lay folk. The Society for promoting Christian Knowledge and the Society for the Propagation of the Gospel became leading voluntary societies in a movement which included Charity Schools and the Societies for the Reformation of Manners. Under Tenison's guidance some of the most vital work of the Church came to be done by voluntary assocations outside the legal establishment. Tenison used the well-established custom of the bishops to meet with the archbishop at Lambeth after Easter for mutual support, advice and discussion, to guide and instruct his suffragans.

How effective a leader was Trelawny, and what attitude did he take toward the new policy? It is significant that he wasted no time in conducting his primary visitation. Contrary to what some have written he visited the whole diocese in August and September 1689. No articles of enquiry or charges have survived for any of his visitations for Exeter but surviving records show that the clergy were left in no doubt as to his policy. He would not tolerate non-residence, scandalous behaviour, performance of clandestine marriages or defiance of lawful admonitions. After his primary visitation two Devonshire clergy were prosecuted for refusing to take the oath as rural dean; the vicars of Wendron and West Alvington and the rector of St. Martins juxta Looe were suspended for failing to find curates for their chapels. Three more clergy were brought to book for performing clandestine marriages. The pages of the act book of the Court of Audience show a concern throughout Trelawny's episcopate to punish any clergyman not servicing a cure, preaching without a licence, neglecting pastoral duty or performing clandestine marriages[26]. In doing this Trelawny was continuing a policy he had begun while Bishop of Bristol and, in this respect, he found no difficulty in conforming to royal and metropolitical expectations. In fact he told his archdeacons that he had already included the gist of the archbishop's injunctions of 1695 in his visitation charge three years earlier. Trelawny's relations with Tenison were outwardly correct and respectful. He always passed on orders from Lambeth to his officers. But the disagreement on a fundamental matter of policy became obvious in 1699.

After discussion with some of the bishops, Tenison issued a pastoral letter on 4 April to be communicated to all the clergy. Its theme was 'the sensible growth of Vice and Prophaneness'. In addition to urging the clergy to be diligent in piety and in study, the work of the Societies for the Reformation of Manners was cautiously commended. Tenison mentioned the church courts, but laid greater emphasis on the clergy informing the civil magistrates. He concluded that since Parliament had provided this statutory assistance 'it would be a great failing in us not to make use of them when all other Methods have been tried to little or no Effect.' [27] Trelawny and his episcopal allies could not look on such advice as this as anything other than a craven capitulation to the wishes of a calvinist king. Agitation for a revival of Convocation had been gathering strength for the previous two years. Tenison steadfastly refused to support such agitation. His settled policy was not to put 'any avoidable hardships upon our good master the king'.[28] The godly magistrate had ever been a calvinist ideal: to urge this ideal upon the clergy at this stage was to deny that a sitting Convocation was necessary. Trelawny dared not defy his metropolitan by refusing to transmit the letter: the treatment of Watson of St. David's, who was currently fighting Tenison's sentence of deprivation, had been a profound shock to the older bishops and they feared to give any excuse for proceedings to be started against them. Instead Trelawny forwarded copies of the archbishop's letter with a printed pastoral letter of his own. This letter is a fine example of that passive obstruction in which the Cornish excel. Despite its respectful language there is no mistaking the intention in the first paragraph of cutting the ground from under the archbishop's feet. Having first pointed out that most of the duties enjoined on the clergy by the Archbishop had been dealt with by him and his arch-deacons years ago, he concluded 'that where *our* Advice may prove *ineffectual,* His Grace's great authority supervening will be fully *prevalent.'* He then proceeded to cast doubt on the willingness of the civil magistrates to enforce the statutes against vice and to question whether any progress in that direction was possible until a form of censorship was re-imposed on religious publications. As Trelawny made no secret of his desire to see a sitting Convocation take strict measures to put a stop to the writings of Atheists and Deists he neatly contrived to oppose his archbishop in the guise of supporting him.[29]

Trelawny was not prepared to relinquish his authority over the laity. Immediately after his primary visitation the churchwardens of Honiton were summoned to the Palace at Exeter to be admonished that their chapel was no place in which Dissenters might hold services. Several inhabitants of Saltash discovered that the Bishop would not allow them to keep the communion cup in their houses or take a crop of hay from the churchyard. A schoolmaster in Moretonhamstead was ordered to stop teaching until he had obtained the Bishop's licence to do so. This persistence in enforcing discipline over the laity must have irriated the Government. In 1693 when a church-warden of Plymouth presented the master shipwright and several workmen in the naval dockyard for working on a fast day in July, it was Trelawny who received the Queen's order to put a stop to the proceedings even though they were being conducted in the archdeacon's court.[30] During the middle years of the reign the Bishop restrained himself. Once he detected a softening of attitude he initiated the prosecution of unlicensed schoolmasters, and in Anne's reign, prepared and began a policy of requiring the laity to maintain and repair the fabric of churches. Trelawny was an effective leader in his diocese but one out of sympathy with official policy. He forbade his clergy to join the Societies for the Reformation of Manners and was totally opposed to the Charity School Movement. Trelawny did not approve of the Movement for several reasons. Many people who were keen on Charity Schools were also supporters of the Societies: some were Dissenters. In any case, support for Charity Schools was tantamount to an admission that the traditional method of education by means of catechism classes conducted by the parish clergy had decayed beyond hope of recall.[31] He was not prepared to abdicate all responsibility for discipline over the laity, but he recognised that such a discipline had to be tempered with realism. It could not be otherwise in a county like Devon with such a high number of licensed dissenting preachers and meeting houses, and an influential general assembly of nonconformist clergy with high academic and professional standards.[32] However, if his clergy could not look to him for support in areas of pastoral ministry like attendance at worship or bringing children to be catechised, they could still look to him for support in other ways.

Once a clergyman earned his bishop's strong disapproval he found Trelawny to be an implacable opponent, but if a clergyman found himself in trouble through no fault of his own, he found his Bishop a ready champion. Robert Hancock, rector of St. Martins juxta Looe, had been in trouble with Bishop Lamplugh and was well known to the Trelawny family. He did nothing to discharge his pastoral responsibilities either at St. Martins or in the town of East Looe, refused to repair the chancel roof and let his parsonage go to ruin. Proceedings against him were begun in the bishop's court 31 October, 1689. He was suspended in January, 1691 and his living sequestered. Hancock appealed to the Court of Arches. While that appeal was pending, the Bishop ordered a further prosecution in his court in October, 1691 for dilapidations of chancel and parsonage, the judge being instructed to accept no certificates that repairs had been carried out until the Bishop was satisfied of the truth. In December a third prosecution was started, this time for Hancock's failure to wear a surplice. This case was left pending until Hancock's death in 1694. The court act

67

books provide other examples. Trelawny was even prepared to risk stirring up a hornets' nest in Tavistock, a centre notorious for its strict covenanting presbyterianism. Most land in Devon was owned by families of small local gentry but Tavistock was the centre of the Devon estates of the dukes of Bedford, a family with presbyterian sympathies. A new method of singing metrical psalms was making headway in the diocese with the active support and encouragement of the Bishop who issued orders to several parishes, at the request of the incumbents, designed to quash the opposition of conservatives in the congregations. Playford's version of the psalms was introduced into Tavistock parish church in 1698. With the encouragement of John Reynell, the vicar, a number of people learnt to sing the new versions. One Sunday afternoon in late autumn, Reynell interrupted the singing of Psalm 148 on the grounds that the *Gloria Patri* was blasphemous and, after a brief prayer, dismissed the congregation. This lead to uproar in the parish and, from the depositions of the witnesses in Reynell's prosecution, it seems that the conservatives took heart and resumed singing in the old way. The Bishop was brought into the affair straightaway when two parishioners rode to Trelawne to seek his opinion on the offending *Gloria Patri*. He saw nothing blasphemous in it and told them to continue singing Playford. The disturbances continued and this led to Reynell and several of the congregation being summoned to Trelawne. After listening to both sides, Trelawny drew up a list of twenty metrical psalsm with tunes and got both sides to agree to sing them successively for the next six months. He learnt that Reynell was not saying morning and evening prayer in church and ordered him to do so for the future. Having, as he thought, restored peace, the Bishop sent them home, urging them all to receive the Sacrament together next Sunday to seal their reconciliation. Reynell's continuing refusal to obey led to his prosecution. He had influential supporters, notably Sir Francis Drake and Ryder, the local agent of the Duke of Bedford, but after consulting with his episcopal allies while attending parliament in the winter of 1699, and encouraged by the attempt to impeach the Lord Chancellor Somers, in which he took an active part, Trelawny began the case in May 1700. He expected a lengthy struggle but fortunately the old Duke of Bedford died and in his correspondence with the new Duke and his mother, Trelawny persuaded them to withdraw support for Reynell. The Bishop wrote to his deputy-registrar,

> 'The business of Tavistock will now come to a speedy issue. The duke of Bedford and his Grace's Mother by letters I received this morning tell me that they will not encourage Reynell in his contumacy; since those great persons have been so just to the right of my see I am

68

resolved on the fellow's asking me pardon and paying the
fees, for the future to forget his stubbornness and pass by
all the affronts Sir Francis Drake and Ryder by him put
on me and the episcopal jurisdiction, both which they
hop'd to have lessened and in time to have destroyed.'

The prosecution was dropped on 16 November: Reynell died shortly
after.[33]

    The Reynell affair shows Trelawny not only as a disciplinarian but
also as a peacemaker, a role in which he seems to have been just as active.
Disputes over church seats were serious matters in an age acutely
conscious of social distinctions and family honour. The Bishop's policy
was to leave such matters to the consistory court, but he often took a
personal interest. Trelawny was the target of petitions on seating and other
matters from many people from all walks of life. Once a petition was
received it was never ignored. Each one was referred to an appropriate
officer for information and, if he thought it necessary, the Bishop would
intervene. For example, in October, 1705 two letters went from Penzance
to the Bishop giving him both sides of a dispute involving the mayor of
Penzance and the vicar of Madron. John Carveth, the mayor, claimed to
appoint the curate to St. Mary's Chapel without reference to Thomas
Rowe, the vicar. Trelawny dealt with the claim humourously but firmly:

'I never heard that the Mayor of Penzance was Vicar
General, and had a superintendency given him over all
the Bishops; till he can produce such a power over me, I
shall approve of and establish Mr. Rowe's curate as soon
as I know his name, unless I have any objection to his
manners or learning, as I believe I shan't, confident Mr.
Rowe won't present such a one to me.'

When the Mayor retaliated by locking the chapel door and refusing to give
Mr. Rowe the keys, the Bishop let it be known that if the Vicar did not get
the keys, he would prosecute Carveth 'to the extremity of the law'. The
Mayor capitulated and gave no further trouble.[34]

    Trelawny was a stern disciplinarian of his clergy. Even after his
translation he was seeking the names of clergy involved with others in
plundering the wreck of an East Indiaman off Polperro.[35] He earned the
dislike of some and the fear of many. His aristocratic hauteur irritated at
least one other, yet Rowe was not the only clergyman to receive his
bishop's unstinting support. When a Grenadier Guards officer accused the
minister of Calverleigh of being an enemy of the Government, the Bishop
took steps immediately to learn who it was so that he might attack him.
The registrar was told to assure the clergyman concerned

'That as I never will fail of punishing an ill clergyman I

69

am always ready to support a good one, and will stand
close by him against all the powers and factions on
earth'.[36]

Trelawny was always anxious to promote a good clergyman and regretted
that the paucity of his patronage seldom gave him opportunity to do so.
Futhermore, he was never vindictive. Reynell was let of lightly; the
poverty-stricken Adam Sleeman, rector of Holacombe, was given a
penance and ordered to pay nominal costs for performing clandestine
marriages, instead of being suspended. Trelawny was aware of the poverty
of many of his clergy. He tried to persuade impropriators to pay their
curates more, and set them an example at West Looe by paying a curate
forty pounds a year out of his own pocket. The diocese of Exeter was one of
the largest payers of tenths in the Church. Exeter paid 9.3% of the total:
only Lincoln diocese paid more.[37] Atterbury alleged that Trelawny
petitioned William III to discharge all arrears of tenths and first fruits on
all the poorer livings throughout England. Atterbury's memory was never
very good when it came to detail and he may have been recalling a petition
on behalf of the diocese of Exeter. What is certain is that when several
bishops were petitioning Anne on behalf of their own poor clergy,
Trelawny urged the Lord Treasurer to discharge all arrears on all livings of
thirty pounds a year or less on the queen's books throughout England and
Wales. At one stage, he actually got Godolphin to agree. He was bitterly
disappointed when Godolphin went back on his word and proposed to
reduce the offer to livings worth thirty pounds a year in real terms, and that
on condition that the livings were first filled.[38] The credit for persuading
the Queen and the Lord Treasurer to take this step has been given to
Archbishop Sharp, but, at the very least, the credit should be divided
equally between him and Trelawny. Both men deserve honourable
mention in the moves which preceded the setting up of Queen Anne's
Bounty in 1704. Trelawny's activities behind the scenes would help to
explain why his address of thanks was the first to be presented to Anne.[39]
Defoe compared the attitude of the clergy of Devon favourably with that
of the clergy of Wiltshire in the summer of 1705 and attributed the
difference to the even-handed way with which their bishop treated them.[40]
Trelawny had done his best to help his parish clergy adapt to their
changing role in society.

The clergy of Wiltshire were on bad terms with their bishop, Gilbert
Burnet, and so was Trelawny. This dislike of the two bishops for each other
was not simply a matter of rivalry, first for the diocese of Salisbury and
later for that of Winchester. The pair clashed on fundamental questions to
do with the doctrine and discipline of the Church of England. That Burnet
was also a favourite, some thought a creature, of the Whig Junto, doubled

Trelawny's dislike of him. Burnet did not retaliate openly, but he did intrigue against Trelawny when and where he could. The waspish comment about Trelawny in his *History* has been repeated too often to need repetition and, once the Whig Bishop's interpretation of events had gained ground, this was sufficient to exclude all credit to Trelawny.[41] It is by not means inconceivable that Burnet magnified his part in the events leading to the establishment of Queen Anne's Bounty and deliberately suppressed all mention of Trelawny's activity. On his part, Trelawny was concerned not so much to mount a witch-hunt against Burnet as to breathe some life into his fellow bishops by encouraging them to re-assert discipline over their flocks. If Burnet's understanding of episcopacy became norm then any theological justification for the system of discipline in the Church of England was cut down at a stroke. This theological dispute is explained later in the chapter on the Convocation Controversy.

It was very much easier for Trelawny to discipline his flock in Devon and Cornwall than it had been for him in Bristol and Dorset, despite all that happened between 1686 and 1689. The factors which made for weak administration were not present in the diocese of Exeter. There were fewer peculiar jurisdictions, the bishop's courts continued to wield considerable authority and the rural deans continued to conduct annual visitations. Four hundred and seventy-four parishes were divided into four archdeaconries. Those of Exeter, Barnstaple and Totnes divided Devon between them. The archdeaconry of Cornwall took up the whole of that county and three parishes in west Devon. Thirty-seven scattered parishes made up the peculiar jurisdiction of the bishop; a further thirty equally scattered, belonged to the dean and chapter. By a determination of Bishop Ward in 1663 the jurisdiction of the capitular peculiars was vested in the dean for the time being and not in the prebendaries as well. The dean alone had jurisdiction over the Cathedral Close and the parish of Braunton. The custos and vicars choral had the parish of Woodbury. Uffculme, in east Devon, belonged to the dean of Sarum and the last three parishes of Land's End made up the royal peculiar of St. Buryan. A very small proportion of parishes were outside the bishop's supervision and only two peculiars, Uffculme and St. Buryan managed to be wholly outside the jurisdiction of the bishop's courts. The relationships between the various jurisdictions was governed by a remarkable agreement drawn up in 1616, conceding to the bishop and his chancellor powers over the peculiar jurisdictions which ran clean contrary to practice elsewhere in the country. This, together with other local factors, increased the activity of the bishop's courts at the expense of the inferior jurisdictions.[42]

An equally remarkable feature of Exeter administration was the

71

survival of the bishop's Court of Audience. As happened elsewhere in England and Wales the two offices of official principal and vicar general had merged in the post of chancellor of the diocese, but, unlike the rest of the country, these two sides of the chancellor's work were not handled in one consistory court. In other dioceses a situation could and did arise where bishop and chancellor were deadlocked in opposition to each other, where the bishop could not use his own consistory court because the chancellor would not let him. This situation could never happen in the diocese of Exeter. The bishop's Court of Audience was immediately responsive to his control. He could intervene and cut short proceedings without running the risk of a legal dispute concerning the terms of the letters by which a chancellor was appointed for life. The lack of definition in the cognizance of the consistory court and the court of audience meant that the work of the latter court could be streamlined by handing over to the consistory court any cases unconnected with a particular line of policy. One use Trelawny made of his court of audience will be looked at in the next chapter, when the role of the twenty-four rural deans is considered.

Trelawny was also able to do something many bishops could only dream of doing: he was given the opportunity to appoint his own chancellor. Old Dr. Masters died in 1692 and his post was offered to Dr. John Edisbury. Edisbury was four years older than Trelawny, a Master in Chancery, as well as an advocate of Doctors' Commons. He was reputed to be a staunch high churchman. Trelawny may have offered Edisbury the chancellorship because he had been passed over for the post of ambassador to Spain. The new ambassador was Lord Lansdown, one of Trelawny's sworn enemies. It may have been one way of appointing a chancellor who shared his bishop's feelings about the Granvilles.[43] The two men always got on well with each other and Edisbury was a frequent guest at Trelawne. He did little routine administration, however, and seldom presided over the courts in Exeter, but his advice was frequently sought, even though the Bishop did not always take it. Much use was made of his legal position and contacts in London.[44] Trelawny was doubly blessed in having as his deputy registrar, Francis Cooke, junior. Three generations of the Cooke family served the diocese as registrars from 1660 to 1730. Industrious and discreet, experienced and of unimpeachable integrity, the Cookes shouldered most of the daily routine administration of Church affairs with great efficiency. Seth Ward appreciated the work of Francis Cooke, senior and Trelawny thought so highly of the family that when Francis junior's son, John, was ordained, he appointed him one of his domestic chaplains.

• Insufficient correspondence survives to give a clear picture of the Bishop's relations with his archdeacons. He remained bishop of Exeter long enough to replace three out of the four. In 1694 he collated George

Snell to the archdeaconry of Totnes, and, in 1703, Richard Burscough was rewarded with Barnstaple. In this choice of local men Trelawny was observing the king's injunctions that archdeacons should live in their own jurisdictions. His other appointments were dictated by other considerations. In 1701 he gave the archdeaconry of Totnes to Francis Atterbury in order to secure him a seat *ex officio* in the Lower House of Convocation. This preferment was unsolicited and effected with a speed which took everyone by surprise. In 1704 Trelawny made himself archdeacon of Exeter and held it *in commendam* until his translation. His motive was probably political and concerned control of the city of Exeter.[45] The one archdeaconry unaffected was Cornwall. This archdeaconry differed from the others in that some of the powers of an episcopal commissary was attached to the court. Rural deans in Cornwall made their annual presentments to the archdeacon's official and not to be principal registry in Exeter. Once the breach between Edward Drewe and his bishop had widened after 1704, the archdeacon pursued a deliberate policy of non-cooperation until his death in 1714. The only correspondence to survive between Trelawny and an archdeacon of the diocese is to be found in the letters sent by Atterbury. They reveal an archdeacon of Totnes working very closely with his bishop, seeking direction in all important disputes and receiving a steady stream of instructions in return.[46]

Edward Drewe's dispute with Trelawny arose partly out of national politics, partly out of the need to reform the cathedral chapter. Drew did not approve of his bishop's support for Marlborough and Godolphin at the expense of the Earl of Rochester and other high flying Tories. Learning a lesson from his predecessor, Trelawny had never attempted a visitation of the cathedral. He used his power of patronage and persuasion to place his own supporters in key position in the inner chapter of residentiary canons. These men tightened up the procedure whereby the cathedral was financed and the worship maintained. When Wake became dean he sided with the reforming canons and pursued Trelawny's wishes that residence be enforced and disorderly behaviour in the cathedral be checked. All this reforming zeal left the 'old guard' in the chapter, Drew and George Hooper, the precentor, isolated and resentful. The pair intrigued recklessly against the Bishop on every issue which presented itself but met with defeat on every occasion.[47] It must have given Trelawny some satisfaction to know that by 1707, the cathedral debts were reduced and the standard of music improved. Only his personality, however, imposed unity and harmony on the rest of the chapter. The canons promptly broke into factions the moment he was translated to Winchester.

Thomas Hearne had no love for Trelawny at all, yet even he

admitted that he had 'done some good offices' for the Church while bishop of Exeter.[48] There is little doubt that Anne was completely satisfied that he deserved the diocese of Winchester. She applied two criteria: was the candidate physically fit and was he a man of quality. Merit and service were two additional recommendations.[49] As bishop of Exeter, Trelawny served the Church well. It is time now to look at his most important and enduring services.

1. *Portland MSS.,* iii. 423, Sir Edward Harley to Rober Harley, 26 January, 1689.

2. *Ibid.*

3. Edward Gregg, *Queen Anne* (1980), pp.69-71.

4. Lois G. Schwoerer, 'Journal of the Convention at Westminster', *B.I.H.R.,* xlix (1976), pp.142-3.

5. Bodl. MS. Ballard 45, f.25 [Robert Woodward to George Smalridge?]

6. C.T., pp.218-9, Duchess of Marlborough to T, 31 December, 1715.

7. Eveline Cruickshanks and David Hay to Clyve Jones, 'Divisions in the House of Lords.....Ten new Lists', *B.I.H.R.,* liii (1980), pp.56-87.

8. Henry Horwitz, 'Parliament and the Glorious Revolution', *B.H.I.R.* xlvii (1974), pp.36-49.

9. Alan Simpson, 'Notes of a Noble Lord', *E.H.R.,* lii (1937), p.95.

10. C.T., p.218, T to Lloyd, 25 January, 1717; Gregg, *op. cit.,* p.70.

11. C.T., p.268, Letter to Clergy about choosing Knights of the shire.

12. B.L. Add. MSS. 29584, f.109, T to Erl of Nottingham, 7 February, 1703.

13. *Cal. S.P. Dom.,* Feb. 1689-April 1690, pp.25-6, 58, 64.

14. G.V. Bennett, 'King William III and the Episcopate', *Essays in Modern Church History in Memory of Norman Sykes,* eds. G.V. Bennett and J.D. Walsh (1966), pp.104-131.

15. D.R.O., Cooke Corresp., 30 November, 1700.

16. C.T., p.271, Sprat to T, undated [January 1692].

17. Wake MSS. xvii, f.239.

18. Bennett, *The Tory Crisis in Church and State,* p.10.

19. Edward Stillingfleet, 'Letter to the Archbishop about the King's Injunction, *Miscellaneous Discourses.....*ed. James Stillingfleet (1735), p.377. For further discussion, see M.G. Smith, 'Toleration and the Pastoral Ministry: the long-term effect of James II's religious policy', *Churchman,* xcvii (1983), pp.141-53.

20. Luttrell iii. 183, 229.

21. For further discussion, see M.G. Smith, *Pastoral Discipline and the Church Courts.....,* pp.2-10.

75

22. D.R.O., P.R. Bundle 16, no. 19.

23. C.R.O., Buller records, Bundle 405, T to Buller, 28 December, 1691.

24. E. Cardwell, *Documentary Annuals of the Reformed Church of England* (Oxford, 1839), ii. clxvi, 13 February, 1690, clxvii, 15 February, 1695, clxviii, 16 July, 1695; D.R.O., P.R. 57, Patent Book, pp.154-6, 168.

25. E. Carpenter, *The Protestant Bishop* (1956), p.183.

26. Smith, Administration, pp.185-91.

27. Thomas Tenison, *Circular Letter to the Bishops of his Province [on the growth of vice and prophaneness in the Nation]*, 4 April, 1699.

28. T.C., Lyons Collection 621, Tenison to King, 17 August, 1699.

29. Sir J. Trelawny, *Letter of the Bishop of Exon to the Archdeacon of Exon,* 14 April, 1699.

30. *Cal. S.P. Dom.,* 1693, p.260, 10 August.

31. F.L. Harris 'Education by Charity in Eighteenth Century Cornwall', *J.R.I.C., new series,* ix, pt.i, p.33.

32. Alan A. Brockett, *Nonconformity in Exeter 1650-1875* (Manchester, 1962), pp.49-73; H.P.R. Finberg, *West-Country Historical Studies* (Newton Abbot, 1969), pp.196-210.

33. D.R.O., P.R. Letters on Unusual Subjects no. 102; P.R. 57, Patent Book, p.167; C.C. Act Book 757, 827A; C.C. Bundle 181 (157); Cooke Corresp., 14 March, 1700, 26 June, 1700, 17 September, 1700, 11 November, 1700. For prosecution of another clergyman, see M.G. Smith, 'Bishop Trelawny and the Office of Rural Dean', *T.D.A.,* cxi (1979), pp.26-7.

34. P.A.S. Poole, *The History of the Town and Borough of Penzance,* 1974, pp.65-6.

35. India Office Libr., E/1/198, pp.99-101, 30 December, 1708.

36. D.R.O., Cooke Corresp., 2 December [1700].

37. H.M.C., *MSS. of the House of Lords* (NS) v.558.

38. *E.C.,* iv. 403, Atterbury to T. 23 March, 1703; iii. 16, T to Spray, 20 July, 1703; iv. 430, Atterbury to T, 24 July, 1703.

39. C.T., p.280, T to Godolphin, undated; p.281, T to Wake, undated; *Cal S.P. Dom.* 1703-4, p.550; *Cal Treasury Books* Jan. 1704-Mar. 1705, p.378, Lowndes to T, 17 October, 1704.

40. *Portland MSS.,* iv. 213-4, Defoe to Harley.

41. *E.C.,* iii. 30, 87; G. Burnet, *History of My Own Time* (1823), v.337.

42. Smith, Administration, pp.104-19.

44. Smith, Administration, pp.148-50.

45. Smith, Administration, pp.139-141.

46. Smith, Administration, pp.144-6.

47. For a full discussion, see M.G. Smith, 'The Cathedral Chapter of Exeter and the Election of 1705: a reconsideration', *T.D.A.* cxvi (1984), pp.109-126.

48. Hearne, i. 94.

49. Gregg, *op. cit.,* pp.135, 146.

CHAPTER SIX

Fighting Joshua the Son of Nun

The writer of the *Tribe of Levi* who lampooned Trelawny as a spiritual dragoon could not have known how prophetic his words might sound twenty years later if given not a military but a legal connotation. Trelawny sublimated into legal battles that pugnacity and courage which his brothers took on active military service. The Exeter College case and the case of Hele *versus* the Bishop clarified and determined the law respecting episcopal powers in two areas of importance in the life of the Church of England. Furthermore, policies carried out by his courts had much influence on Church life in the south west.

The Exeter College Case was occasioned by one of those sordid scandals that is liable to afflict involuntary celibate communities from time to time. That it grew into a national *cause célèbre* leading to an important legal judgement affecting the whole University of Oxford was largely the fault of one man, Dr. Arthur Bury, the rector of Exeter College. Bury held opinions and behaved in a way which would have earned him notoriety even in a more sexually permissive, pluralist society. He appears to have had one of those personalities about which others find it hard to be neutral. He enjoyed flouting conventions: collegiate statutes, liturgical posture, trinitarian theology and sexual morality were all grist to the mill of a dedicated nonconformist. Wood's description of Bury as a 'Presbyterian double-married' was factually wrong but captured the essence of the man.

Born in 1624, son of John Bury of Heavitree, near Exeter, nicknamed 'Blackbury' from the colour of his skin, Arthur was elected a fellow of Exeter College at the age of nineteen. Expelled from his fellowship in 1648 upon his refusal to take the Covenant he was restored in 1662 and elected Rector in 1666 on the special instructions of Charles II. Within two years of his installation he became embroiled in a long-standing dispute with the college body about the proper number of Cornishmen on the foundation. He supported the candidature of a fellow Devonian by suspending Cornish Fellows, thus disqualifying them from voting. They appealed to the Vice-Chancellor of the University who quashed their suspensions. Bury resorted to the King, who admitted his candidate by royal warrant 'not withstanding any statute to the contrary.' [1]

Bury was not prejudiced against all Cornish Fellows. The incident does demonstrate, however, Bury's obstinate determination to have his own way. When James Colmar was elected to a Cornish fellowship in 1683 he was on very friendly terms with his Rector. In the course of 1688, Anne Aris and Anne Sparrow, two servant girls in the college, both gave birth to bastards and, by the following summer, it became obvious that Anne Sparrow was pregnant again. There was a fair amount of college gossip, much of it being passed on to the Rector by his wife. Circumstantial evidence pointed to James Colmar as the culprit in both Anne Sparrow's pregnancies. Dr. Bury privately interviewed Colmar accusing him of the deed, but Colmar insisted he was innocent. Bury laid a charge before the court of the vice-chancellor who dismissed the case on the grounds of insufficient evidence. The only deposition taken was that of Colmar's servant, Ferdinand Smith, who testified to Colmar's innocence. Bury now became convinced that there was a college conspiracy to conceal the truth from him. On 10 October, 1689 he called a college meeting with seven senior fellows present. Using the admissions he himself claimed to have extracted from Ferdinand Smith in the course of a lengthy interview in his study, Bury pronounced Colmar guilty of incontinence and expelled him from the college on 16 October. [2]

The statutes regulating Oxford and Cambridge colleges usually included provisions for an appeal to the visitor in such cases. A college visitor was usually a bishop, especially if the college had been an episcopal foundation. Walter de Stapledon had founded Exeter College, hence the bishop of Exeter was visitor. Bury could not abide the thought of having any of his decisions scrutinised. He informed Colmar that his sentence of deprivation was definitive, and that his oath as a fellow debarred him from making an appeal to the visitor. Colmar and his friends among the junior Fellows consulted first the college statutes, then Dr. Bouchier, the professor of Civil Law, whose advice agreed with their interpretation of the statutes, that a fellow's oath to the Rector in no way prevented him from making an appeal. Accordingly Colmar lodged his appeal with Bishop Trelawny on 24 October.

Bury's reputation for high handedness was not unknown. For him to prounounce sentence in a case the Vice-Chancellor had dismissed was sufficient grounds for the Bishop to review the decision. Exeter College had close connections with Exeter diocese. Over half the men Trelawny was to ordain as Bishop of Exeter matriculated from the College. [3] When so many of his future clergy came from there, a bishop was bound to feel some responbility for the life of that establishment. On the other hand, the level of responsibility was not clearly defined. Was a visitor similar to a trustee or landlord who entered the college periodically in order to satisfy himself that the intentions of the founder were being carried out? Was a visitor similar to an ecclesiastical ordinary who had the right to enquire into, and regulate the personal lives, of the college community? Not all visitors were ecclesiastical persons. The earls of Pembroke visited Jesus College, Oxford, and the Lord Chancellor, who was no longer likely to be a bishop, visited Gloucester Hall. The sovereign was a visitor of three more colleges, though whether in his capacity as head of the state or temporal head of the Church of England had never been clearly determined. College statutes frequently laid down that disputes within a college might be taken to the visitor, but again it was not clear whether he acted as an independent arbiter or as judge of a court of appeal. The Oxford colleges had created the university: not the university the colleges. They were fiercely jealous of their autonomy. Despite Bury's reputation, members of other colleges sympathized with the attitude he adopted even though they would not have gone to the lengths he was prepared to go.

Trelawny was attending parliament when the appeal reached him. His first act was to issue the Rector and Fellows with an inhibition order suspending proceedings against Colmar together with an order to the Rector and Fellows to send two of their number to London with a copy of the proceedings. Later it was alleged that, at this stage, had the Bishop agreed with the evidence, he intended to confirm the Rector's sentence. Bury knew perfectly well that he had circumstantial evidence against Colmar but no legal proof. He would not subsequently have followed up the evidence on Anne Aris if he had been certain that the charge concerning Anne Sparrow was convincing. He deeply resented the Bishop's interference. As far as he was concerned, it was a matter of internal discipline and no business of outsiders. He refused point-blank to cooperate. He took the line that the Bishop's inhibition was irrelevant because the statues gave a visitor no such authority. Colmar was no longer a member of the college in any case. No copy of the proceedings was available because, in accordance with the statutes, the procedure followed had been summary, not plenary, so there was no written record. As the Bishop had had no experience of being a visitor, Bury thoughtfully had the whole statute transcribed and sent him a copy.

Trelawny was not at all sure how to proceed next. The bishops whose advice he would have sought were now non-jurors and absent from parliament. Some months elapsed before he made his next move. He returned to Exeter in late December and moved on to Trelawne for Christmas.[4] Presumably he took the advice of his chancellor, old Dr. Masters, and sent him with a commission to Oxford in March, 1690 to hear

80

Colmar's appeal. Dr. Masters went to Oxford and called on Dr. Bury in his lodgings on Thursday, 20 March, to tell him that he would execute the commission the following Saturday morning. The Rector and the senior Fellows duly appeared at the time appointed and a series of procedural wrangles began. Dr. Masters wanted to adjourn until the following Wednesday. Dr. Bury pointed out that the Statute of Visitation allowed only three days *proxime sequentes* for business. Caught off guard, Dr. Masters agreed to reconvene that afternoon. When they returned, Dr. Masters kept the chapel doors open for anyone to attend. The Rector and senior Fellows entered a protest against any proceedings in Colmar's case. After some debate, Dr. Bury asked for a further adjournment because two Fellows were absent. Dr. Masters granted the request and adjourned to the following Tuesday. On that day the Rector and senior Fellows submitted another protest, this time against the doors being open. Dr. Masters accepted the protest but proceeded to restore Colmar to his fellowship and awarded him £13 6s. 8d. for costs. As Dr. Masters left the college, Dr. Bury tried to give him the visitation fee of twenty shillings, which he refused. These procedural wrangles, trivial in themselves, were aimed at establishing a legal point of great importance. As far as Dr. Masters was concerned, he was hearing an appeal, *not* conducting a visitation. Dr. Bury wanted to establish that it was a visitation, because the statutes debarred a visitor from visiting more than once every five years. By accepting the argument that he could not adjourn to Wednesday, Dr. Masters had allowed himself to be out-manoeuvred. His keeping the doors open was his attempt to retrieve the advantage because it meant treating the session as an appeal court. He had been forced to limit the proceedings to three days so he had to accept both protests in order to save time. The offer of the twenty shillings was an obvious manoeuvre which Dr. Masters easily saw through.

In the meantime, Dr. Bury obtained proof of Colmar's fornication with the other serving maid, Anne Aris. At the time of her delivery it was assumed that Colmar's servant, Ferdinand Smith, was the father. Anne Aris's mother had persuaded her to name only Smith and suppress the fact that she had also had intercourse with Colmar, because she was afraid that she might lose her job as a college bedmaker. After the Colmar affair had arisen, Anne's mother developed scruples and took her daughter before Sir William Walker, one of the Oxford justices, to swear an affadavit that she had had intercourse with both Smith and Colmar. This affidavit was taken on 11 January, 1690 and Bury must have known about it and kept it in reserve, because the day after Dr. Masters restored Colmar to his fellowship, both the mother and the sister of Anne Aris swore affadavits that what Anne Aris had said was true. Bury then called a meeting of senior

81

Fellows, summoned Colmar, together with a notary public, to record and attest the proceedings, presented the legal proofs and again expelled the pretended fellow. In February, Bury published his version of Colmar's expulsion.

Up to the end of March, 1690 the whole affair had been confined to Exeter College. There was a number of tensions within the college. In December, 1688, Colmar, with other Fellows had opposed the Rector's candidate for the vacant post of chaplain because he would have voted exactly as Dr. Bury wished and so helped secure for the Rector complete control over the College. Nevertheless it could have remained an Oxford affair had not Bury chosen this moment to publish his new book, *The Naked Gospel.* The ideas in this brief book were to receive wider currency under the pen of John Locke and were a variation on the perennial theme of the simple gospel. Christianity can be reduced to two simple notions: Jesus is the Messiah; faith is a duty which leads to personal penitence before God. Questions to do with grace or predestination and above all, speculation on the nature of Jesus and his relationship to God the Father are unnecessary complications introduced in the Patristic Age. Arthur Bury belonged to the theological school of Chillingworth, Hale and Falkland, who were convinced that all Scripture could and should be brought into harmony with natural reason. If by Revelation was meant belief in certain teachings on the bare authority either of the word of Scripture or of the credal formulations of the universal church, then Dr. Bury rejected the idea. 'So plain it is that the Faith which the Gospel requireth had its foundation in Natural Religion, and while Abraham is proposed as the *Father of the Faithful,* Natural Faith is also proposed as the mother of the Evangelical.' [5] Christianity should be commended only by the rigorous employment of the methodology of euclidean geometry.[6]

In his treatment of the Person of Christ, Bury revealed the difficulty faced by all who relied solely on natural reason. He could not bring himself to talk about God the Son. He argued that Jesus was the son of God only in terms of his mission. He tried to take refuge in the mystery of the Messiah, but in language not differing greatly from that of Paul of Samosata. 'These [titles of Jesus] and the like high characters speak of him as a Person of Supereminent and unmeasurable greatness; a Person like (his emblem) the light, so glorious that by our most intent view we cannot discover anything of it but this, that we cannot discover'. His Divinity 'maketh the Dignity of his person unintelligible.' All those who deviate from orthodox christology have eventually to contend with certain Johannine passages and Bury was no exception. Commenting on John 10 verses 31-39, which states the complete identification of God the Son with God the Father, Bury betrays his socininian belief. Christ 'speaketh nothing of what he had been from

Eternity in Himself but what he was in Relation to the World and in comparison with all other messengers of God to it.' [7]

The *Naked Gospel* was written originally for private circulation among members of the Convocation which first sat on 21 November, 1689 and continued, bogged down by problems of procedure, until prorogued on 25 June, 1690. Convocation was in a mood antagonistic to any form of change. Opposition to the proposals of the Commissioners appointed by William and Mary with the task of revising the Liturgy to enable dissenters to enter a new comprehensive church, had been whipped up already in a pamphlet war by William Jane and Thomas Long. These two men played an important part in the subsequent fate of *The Naked Gospel.* They were two of the leading theologians of the High Church group which was beginning to emerge in the Church of England, and Trelawny was numbered among the bishops of that group. Thomas Long, a prebendary of Exeter, was an acute, learned, and redoubtable controversialist who had the distinction of being one of the few clergy in his generation who had refused a bishopric. His pamphlet, *Vox Cleri,* had set the tone for most of the debate over revision of the Prayer Book. William Jane's election as prolocutor of the Lower House of Convocation effactually ensured that the Commissioners' proposals would come to nothing. He was elected by a large majority who had no desire to sit at all and who had no time for novelty of any kind. [8] Yet it was among this audience Bury chose to circulate his book. Most of those who perused *The Naked Gospel* were unsympathetic to its thesis. Bury did not help his cause by the provocative way he introduced it. With that not infrequent academic indifference to practical politics, Bury asserted that the present poor state of the Christian Religion was the direct result of neglect of the simple gospel. For men who had just lived through the trauma of James II's religious policy and a revolutionary settlement, such an assertion of academic omniscience must have irritated them beyond bearing.

Unaware of the mood of the bulk of the clergy or perhaps unconcerned, Bury decided to publish *The Naked Gospel.* Using his power of licensing as a pro-vice-chancellor, the book appeared anonymously in Oxford on 1 April, 1690. [9] The book was withdrawn 'before twenty copies were dispersed' on the advice of some friends who persuaded him to interpolate two chapters, one on the Trinity and another on the Incarnation. The amended version went on sale speedily, but the following month, unamended copies were also freely available; reproduced in London, so Bury claimed later 'by Certain Persons to him unknown'.

Bury did not launch *The Naked Gospel* on an unsuspecting academic public. Its circulation in manuscript among the proctors of Convocation ensued that its contents were known. On publication day Dr.

Bernard informed a friend '*The Naked Gospel* is industriously concealed & without hope of procuring a loan of a copy.' Eight days later, still without having read the book, Bernard could offer as his opinion that the book would do more to lose Bury his rectorship than would his defiance of the visitor in the matter of James Colmar.[10]

Trelawny could not have ignored Bury's deliberate defiance of his authority as visitor, but with the publication of *The Naked Gospel* the punishment of contumacy took on the nature of a crusade against heresy. Thomas Long could easily have acquainted his Bishop with the theological dangers and later in the year he began writing a counter attack. By April Trelawny was already threatening to expel the Rector. Later that month Colmar went down to Exeter and had an interview with Trelawny[11] but the affair had now gone beyond a matter of his guilt or innocence. He would be restored because Bury must be expelled.

On 16 May Trelawny forwarded a citation to the College announcing that he would conduct a visitation in person on 16 June. He arrived in Oxford on 13 or 14 June and stayed with Dr. Jane at Christ Church. The day following his arrival, the Fellows of Exeter college waited on him in two parties: the Rector with his supporters and Colmar with his. Bury asked the Bishop not to carry out a visitation. It would be contrary to the college statutes because Dr. Masters had visited the previous year and another visitation could not be held until 1694 at the earliest. A protestation under the common seal had been prepared against it. Ignoring the request, Trelawny, habited in rochet and chimere walked from Christ Church to the Turl on the morning of 16 June. The college gates were open. The Bishop entered, crossed the main quadrangle to the chapel doors, banged on the door but could gain no admittance. The Rector and some senior Fellows then approached him as he stood in the quadrangle and presented him with the protestation. The Bishop refused to take it, saying that if they had anything to offer it should be done in the chapel whither they had been cited. Ignoring that remark Bury ordered a notary public to start reading the protestation. Trelawny promptly lost his temper, snatched the document and threw it on the ground. Bury and the twelve Fellows who supported him walked off, leaving the Bishop standing there with the other eight Fellows. The Bishop then tried to enter the hall but found that too was locked, and a brief search revealed no butler with a key. Trelawny then went into a staircase doorway still attended by a rump of the Fellows and got some of them to declare on oath that the citation had been duly affixed to the chapel door. Then, after treating any in earshot to some pithy and unprintable comments about the senior Fellows, the Bishop returned, still fuming, to Christ Church.[12]

Trelawny wrote immediately to the Secretary of State, the Earl of

Nottingham, for his advice. Nottingham was a strictly orthodox high churchman who would surely have some sympathy with the case. He was also an acknowledged legal expert. Nottingham advised a petition to the Council to request an inhibition to prevent the College proceeding to elect a successor to Colmar. Trelawny submitted the petition and travelled up to London in July to be on hand when the Council discussed it. The Council debated the affair at a meeting in Whitehall on 5 July and, having heard counsel on both sides, refused the petition and advised the Bishop to seek a remedy at Common Law. In the meantime Bury was consolidating his position within the College. The statutes provided the penalty of expulsion on any who failed to vote at an election of a new fellow. Some had boycotted the election held to fill Colmar's place. Bury registered a suspended sentence against them, declaring that he would expel them if their future behaviour ceased to be acceptable. Faced with the prospect of living under that form of arbitrary government Bury's opponents in the college realised that they would have to cease being passive well-wishers of their visitor and become his active supporters. For his part Trelawny had come to a decision. He stayed in London for several days after the council meeting in order to consult his legal advisors. The Council had referred him to Common Law. He would force his opponents to sue him in the courts of Westminster Hall.[13]

His second appearance in Exeter College was planned along the lines of a military exercise. He returned to Oxford, but let it be known that he had no intention of appearing as visitor. While his opponents were lulled into relaxing their guard he quietly organised the opposition within the College. Suddenly, on Tuesday, 24 July, Trelawny served a citation announcing he would hold a visitation on the following Thursday. He refused to see a deputation of three senior Fellows bearing a letter asking him not to come. Instead he sent them a message by one of his servants that he expected all possible opposition but he was determined to visit. On Wednesday night the Rector order the college gates to be locked and nailed up. Around dawn, before the Bishop was expected, his supporters inside the College went into action. After 'broken heads, loss of periwigs and some blood' the gates were opened and shortly afterward Trelawny, accompanied by Dr. Masters and Dr. Bouchier, made his way through a crowd of excited onlookers straight into the Hall and opened the proceedings. Caught off guard the Rector and senior Fellows elbowed their way through the crowd only just in time to answer their names. Prevented from reading a protestation Bury and his supporters withdrew and the Bishop with his two assessors got down to business. Nine senior Fellows were suspended for three months and the Fellows who remained were ordered to submit in writing all they knew about the mismanagement of the College. Trelawny stayed in Exeter College in Mr. Hutchin's rooms on the Thursday and Friday evening. Mr. Kingston, the chaplain, conducted prayers in chapel that evening despite his suspension. He was excommunicated the following morning, but most of Friday was taken up with collecting evidence concerning the sale of college offices by the Rector, and his sexual behaviour with maids in his lodgings. On Saturday, Mr. Vivian, who had been elected in Colmar's place, was expelled and Colmar, his own misbehaviour now completely forgotten, was restored. Dr. Hearne was expelled for taking a living incompatible with the terms of his fellowship and Dr. Bury was expelled from his rectorship for heresy, bribery and incontinence. Furthermore he was ordered to quit the rector's lodgings by 1 August on pain of excommunication. All the proceedings were conducted 'with episcopal gravity' although as one don observed, 'some say Sir Jonathan spoke now and then as well as his lordship.' The visitation concluded, Trelawny left Oxford immediately for Exeter leaving the University beside itself with excitement.[14]

Bury had been expelled for heresy on the judgement of one bishop who did no more than establish from the printer the identity of the author. Aldrich and Jane wanted a more authoritative condemnation than that. They egged on some of the masters of the arts to petition the Vice-chancellor to have *The Naked Gospel* formally condemned as heretical by the University.[15] The Vice-chancellor resisted at first but gave way in the face of their persistent petitioning. The Heads of Houses deputed Jane and Aldrich to list the most heretical passages in the book. At a meeting on 18 August the Heads reached their decision and in full Convocation the next day the book was denounced as heretical and burnt publicly in the School quadrangle that same afternoon.[16]

The visitation and the condemnation of the book split the University into two camps. Many bitterly resented the way Trelawny had conducted the visitation. They were uneasy to learn of the peremptory power Canon Law allowed an ordinary at a visitation. Many did not like the way masters of arts had been allowed to force a judgement on the writing of a doctor of divinity. Others noted sourly the collusion of Christ Church men in both affairs. Bury did not lack for sympathy and support: he was ready to fight back on both fronts. About three days after his book had been burnt he was circulating in manuscript *An Apology for writing The Naked Gospel:* about two weeks before that he and some other Exeter Fellows had petitioned their majesties in Council.[17]

Trelawny received much encouragement and support from his friends at Christ Church, particularly the younger dons who had the time and energy. In James Harrington he had the services of a young barrister who was reckoned to be one of the greatest experts in the Common Law

86

and whose early death on 23 November, 1693 was considered a severe loss to his generation. Harrington went to London to brief senior counsel while, in Oxford, his fellow dons, Thomas Newey, George Smalridge and, above all, Francis Atterbury busied themselves in research. For them it was challenging, it was exciting and it was someone else's money they were spending. However, it would be wrong to think that Trelawny was a figurehead moved by the enthusiasms or policies of others. On 15 August the Queen in Council ordered the Bishop to reply to Bury's petition. From Trelawne the Bishop wrote a reply to the Lord President, the marquess of Carmarthen, which stands out among his surviving correspondence as the most dignified and magisterial letter he ever composed. He assured the Lord President of his deference for the Queen and his respect for the Lords of the Council, but expressed surprise that they should take notice of a petition in an affair in which the Council itself had already decided to do nothing. 'I cannot think that the same cause can reasonably be brought back to the same place where it was by general consent discharged as not falling under their lordships cognizance and determination.' He went on to point out that the College had already elected Mr. William Paynter as Rector and that he now enjoyed a freehold which, if contested, could be determined only in the Courts of Westminster Hall. Then he reminded Carmarthen of his privilege as a peer of parliament. No court of Westminster Hall would dare to try to control a legal proceeding in time of privilege of parliament and 'your Lordship must needs know how justly jealous the House of Lords is of having their privilege infring'd.' His power of visitation was a legal right and he had no intention of creating a precedent that would affect the honour and dignity of the House of Lords. He wondered out loud what aspect of the royal prerogative Bury and his co-petitioners were asking the Queen to invoke. Was it 'to issue out such an Ecclesiastical Commission as that which raised so much trouble in the last reign?', something he was sure her Majesty would never be brought to do. Finally, he stressed that in refusing to answer to the Council he was not trying to avoid a trial. On the contrary, he had chosen his course because he had been advised 'that this way only would bring the business to a speedy decision', and that if an action was brought against him even if it was in time of parliament, he himself would petition the Lords to be allowed to waive his privileges.[18] In the face of this reply the Council had nothing more to say.

While Trelawny busied himself with diocesan and family business, Oxford remained in a state of high excitement. Dr. Jane preached a sermon against *The Naked Gospel* in August[19] and the following month a pamphlet war broke out with the publication, on 23rd, of *An Account of the Proceedings of..... Jonathan Lord Bishop of Exeter,* written by James

87

Harrington. This soon went into a second edition to which was appended the censure of Convocation on *The Naked Gospel*. This was answered on 25 October by *The Account Examined or a Vindication of Dr. Arthur Bury,* written by James Harrington, an old republican pamphleteer (not to be confused with the young lawyer of the same name). More pamphlets followed in the winter and spring of 1691, two of them by James Harrington on the Bishop's side and one by Joseph Washington, a London lawyer and a favourite of Sir John Somers, the Solicitor General. The arguments in the later pamphlets tended to become increasingly technical and were intended for students of law. The early ones are the more entertaining. They contain carefully selected evidence, and, at different times, nearly all the logical fallacies of relevance. At one point the argument descends into farce with a string of affidavits designed to establish whether a large mole on Dr. Bury's foot was, or was not, public knowledge. In 1691 Thomas Long published his long awaited *An answer to Socinian Treatise called The Naked Gospel.* This book, dedicated to Trelawny, and concluding with a long history of Socinianism is a masterly attack on Bury. It takes and answers each of his arguments one by one. Archdeacon Francis Fulwood's book entitled *The Socinian Controversie touching the Song of God Reduced,* which he wrote in 1692 and dedicated, somewhat sycophantically, to Gilbert Burnet, is, in comparison with Long's book, a slight work and poorly argued. In addition to all this literature, Oxford was to be entertained for some years with the great Exeter College schism. King's Bench allowed Bury to manage the College pending a final judgement. William Paynter refused to accept this decision, and as both parties claimed to elect to vacant fellowships, several double elections took place. But the real focus of interest was no longer Oxford, but Westminster.

On 19 November, John Somers, the Solicitor-General, acting for Arthur Bury, moved the Court of King's Bench for a writ of prohibition. It is significant that Bury was able to engage the services of a law officer of the Crown. Trelawny's reply to the order of the Council could not have pleased the Whig lords and they sided with Bury. Moving for a writ of prohibition was a tried and tested way of interfering with an ecclesiastical judgement. The common law judges at this period were particularly hostile to the spiritual courts and Somers chose to move for a prohibition on the sentence of excommunication only, being grounds with which the judges were most sympathetic. The procedure was as follows. If the judges considered there was a *prima facie* case of the spiritual judge acting improperly or *ultra vires* then an order was sent to put a stop to proceedings or sentence. If the legal issue was unclear, the party applying for the prohibition would be instructed 'to declare in prohibition', that is, to assume by legal fiction that the spiritual judge could offer 'to declare'. Either way the merits of the prohibition could be argued before the judges by counsel representing both sides. If, after hearing the arguments, the judges decided that the case properly belonged to Common Law they would retain the case to be tried before them, and if not, then a consultation would be granted and the case remitted to the spiritual court.[20] Somers made the suggestion before the judges of King's Bench that a visitation was a temporal matter only, therefore the Bishop could not use canon law censure. The judges were strongly opposed to the Bishop's excommunication of Bury. Mr. Justice Dolben in particular objected to Trelawny's severity. They readily granted a prohibition on 28 November.[21]

Bury was not prepared to wait for a prohibition, so confident was he of success. Early in October he appeared in college chapel, looking upon the excommunication as null and void. Nor did he give up the Rector's lodgings, but, when leaving London in November, he instructed his wife to keep possession.[22] William Paynter, the new Rector, leased the lodgings to Robert Philipps. As he could not take possession Philipps, backed by Paynter and the Bishop, brought and action for ejectment. The prohibition had not affected the issue of whether or not the visitor had acted lawfully in expelling the Rector. The Bishop's lawyers continued to dispute the prohibition throughout 1691 and 1692, but the case got bogged down in legal niceties. By bringing an action for ejectment the whole question of the powers of a visitor could come to trial. Sergeant Pemberton, one of Trelawny's counsel, outlined the plan of campaign. The first issue to be decided in an action for ejectment was Paynter's right to bring such a case in the first place. Paynter's lawful election as Rector of Exeter College would, in turn, depend on the post being vacant, which raised the question of the validity of Bury's deprivation.[23]

The case of Philipps v. Bury came for trial before King's Bench in the Trinity Term of 1693 and was argued through its various stages until a final judgement was given on 16 June, 1694. By a verdict of three to one the judges delivered their judgement against the Bishop. Changes had taken place in the composition of the King's Bench during the course of the trial. Judge Dolben died suddenly early in 1964 which gave Lord Keeper Somers the opportunity to promote Sergeant Samuel Eyre to Dolben's post. The elder Justice Giles Eyre, who was on the bench already, had been violently against the Bishop throughout all the legal proceedings. On giving final judgement he could not forebear preaching a short sermon against the whole idea of a visitor having such absolute powers.[24]

The verdict did not dismay Trelawny's legal advisors. Lord Chief Justice Holt disagreed on all points with his three colleagues. Before the verdict was given, plans had already been laid to take the case on a writ of error to the House of Lords. At this period the Lords took their judicial function very seriously: all peers were entitled to take part and to vote. They were swayed at times more by family alliances and personal considerations than by legal argument. Nevertheless the arguments of a lawyer as distinguished as John Holt would have had their effect. The other side learnt of the writ of error with dismay and attempted, half-heartedly, to reach a compromise. The Bishop's advisors would accept only Bury's unconditional surrender.[25]

The Lords heard the case in December and proceeded rapidly to judgement. Perhaps it was fortunate for Trelawny that the Lord Keeper had an accident, for he had been opposed to Bury's deprivation from the outset. On 25 November Somers sat down heavily without realising that his servant had not placed a chair ready and he suffered mild concussion. He resumed his place on the woolsack on 3 December, but probably had little energy to steer the debate in the direction he would have wished to see it go.[26] Lawyers representing all parties were heard on 7 December, and the Lord Keeper reported the next day, summing up the arguments offered by counsel. Discussion began, but was adjourned until Monday, 10 December when, after a long debate, the judgement of King's Bench was reversed without a division.

One reason for the length of the debate was that Trelawny found an unexpected ally among his brother bishops. Edward Stillingfleet, bishop of Worcester, delivered a detailed argument in favour of the powers of a visitor which helped to determine the outcome of the debate.[27] Stillingfleet was the acknowledged legal expert among the bishops, and his speech helped to concentrate the minds of the peers on the central legal issue. This was not about the whole proceedings of the visitation of Exeter College, but whether or not the Bishop's decisions might be examined and reversed by the Court of King's Bench. Stillingfleet argued, with a wealth of legal precedent, that university jurisdiction is a branch of ecclesiastical law, so that the Court of King's Bench had no right to extend is jurisdiction as far as it pleased. He pointed out the consequences for all European universities if judges were allowed to interfere in their autonomy which had been their most treasured privilege since their foundation, and he argued that discipline and good order would be so undermined that they would be unable to function properly. The House was impressed by the force of Stillingfleet's arguments. Trelawny told Arthur Charlett that at the end of the debate only ten peers continued to favour Bury.

This judgement of the Lords was still not the end of the affair. Legal niceties delayed putting the judgement into effect until some words were added to it the following February. It was only a matter of time, however, and Trelawny could rest content. He was not a vindictive man and totally disarmed Bury's supporters among the Lords by the generosity with which he waived all claim to any money Bury had received as Rector pending the final outcome.[28]

This vindication of the rights of the visitor of Exeter College received little public comment; in fact it aroused more interest in Europe where Jurieu claimed that the Bishop of Exeter had done more to help combat Latitudinarianism in Holland than anyone else. Atterbury indicated mature reflection on the affair in England, when he wrote that the Exeter College case had,

> 'fix'd the Power of Visitors (not till then acknowled'd
> Final) upon the sure Foundation of a Judgement in
> Parliament; and by that means made so effectual a
> Provision for the future quiet of those Learned Bodies as
> may be reckoned equal to the greatest Benefaction'.[29]

At the time the judgement was given Trelawny had no doubt in his own mind as to what had been achieved. He disclaimed a personal victory. It was a victory of the Church of England in the University of Oxford. It preserved the University as an orthodox seminary for future clergy, and it inflicted a serious setback to the campaign of the anti-clerical common lawyers in Westminster Hall. The fact that the University of Oxford continued to be a conservative pillar of the Church of England owes much to Trelawny's memorable struggle.

One of the pieces of business to come before Trelawny in May, 1690 before he set out for Oxford to conduct his first visitation of Exeter College was a deed of presentation sent by Sampson Hele, patron of the rectory of South Pool, nominating Francis Hodder to that living following the death of the previous incumbent.[30] The Bishop ordered the necessary documents to be prepared and made an appointment for Hodder to attend him at the palace in Exeter to take his oaths and write in the subscription book his full assent to the Thirty-nine Articles. After Hodder had finished Trelawny looked at the page and spotted a grammatical error. Hodder had written *Triginta Novena articulis* instead of *Trigenta novem*. In the manner of a school master, the Bishop tested him on latin grammar. Hodder's replies revealed a poor grasp of latin. The Bishop went on to examine him in the Greek New Testament and some latin authors. Again Hodder displayed considerable ignorance. Finally, as a piece of irony, Hodder was asked to translate the twenty-fourth article into latin, which he proceeded to do in schoolboy fashion. Trelawny refused to grant him institution and wrote to Hele acquainting him of this and desiring him to send another priest better qualified. Hele insisted that Hodder was his candidate. Trelawny naturally wondered where and when Hodder had been ordained. Francis Cooke consulted his records. He found that Anthony Sparrow, when Bishop of

91

Exeter, had discovered, in 1670, that Hodder had counterfeited priest's orders. Nevertheless Hodder prevailed upon Sparrow to ordain him deacon in 1674, and priest in 1675. Trelawny continued to insist that Hodder was insufficiently educated and the moment six calendar months had elapsed from the date of the previous rector's death, he collated Gawen Hayman to the rectory of South Pool.

Hele sought a writ of *quare impedit* in the Court of Common Pleas in the spring of 1691. An advowson was a proprietary right and common lawyers were very jealous of safeguarding it. Hodder had been examined and admitted to holy orders; he had been licensed to a cure of souls. For a bishop suddenly to decide that Hodder was incompetent seemed to many to be an arbitary infringement of the rights of a patron. Thus Hele's lawyers argued and the judges of the Court of Common Pleas after some hesitation agreed. However, Trelawny did not question the right of the patron. He acted only as the ordinary and in that capacity he insisted that he could judge the qualification of a clergyman. That was a matter outside the competence of the judges of Westminster Hall. He appealed against the judgement but a similar verdict was given in the Court of King's Bench despite the marshalling of several precedents and ancient legal opinions by the Bishop's lawyers.

The case had already dragged on for three years when it was decided to take it on a writ of error to the House of Lords. The Lords heard the case on 15 March, 1694. On the same day the Dean of Arches wrote to Archbishop Tenison to point out that this case involved more than the Bishop of Exeter. It was a matter of concern for the whole Church and the Archbishops of Canterbury in particular, because, in the past, judges faced with similar cases had sent to the Archbishop to learn if the priest was or was not suitably qualified.[31] A case involving the rights of the whole episcopal order was sure to receive the sympathetic support of the bishops attending parliament and Tenison, who was one of King William's favourites, may have been able to neutralise the Whig Lords on this occasion. On 16 March the Lords ordered that the judgement of the two Courts be reversed and Hele was left without a remedy.

The Hodder case was an important one because it recovered some freedom for manoeuvre for the Church of England in an area where it had been on the defensive for centuries. It was recognised that a bishop could refuse to institute a felon, murderer or heretic, but if the crime belonged to ecclesiastical law he was required to explain to the patron 'specifically and directly', in Coke's words, why he was refusing to institute. The burden of proof lay with the bishop. The case against Hele established that as far as refusal for lack of ability was concerned, a bishop was not required to go into details nor have his judgement questioned in a court of Common Law.

It was a notable victory, and all the more remarkable that it should have been won in a decade so hostile to the legal rights of the Church of England.

The year 1694 was a legal *annus mirabilis* for Trelawny but success did not breed over confidence. He would dearly have liked to have proceeded against non-conformist education in his diocese. It was one of his personal hopes that the revival of Convocation in 1701 would enable the Church of England to proceed against Dissenting Academies. From 1687 until the middle of the eighteenth century, Exeter was one of the most important strongholds of Dissent outside London. Shortly after the re-founding of the Exeter Assembly of Presbyterian and Independent clergy, Joseph Hallett received its approval to set up an Academy in Exeter which lasted until 1719. Its four-year course was open both to layman and to candidates for the ordained ministry. It was a modest affair, seldom having more than six pupils studying at any one time. Peter King, the future Lord Chancellor, came under Hallett's influence, although it is not certain whether he attended the Academy. Its potential influence could always be over-estimated by suspicious Anglicans. However, Trelawny took note of the way the King had quashed proceedings against Richard Frankland who had been excommunicated by one of the courts of the Archbishop of York, and Joseph Hallett's Academy was left in peace.[32] Trelawny looked on this as a tactical withdrawal, not a retreat. When it came to the education of children in his diocese he was determined to maintain episcopal supervision as soon as he detected a change in the political climate.

It was the custom in the diocese of Exeter for the bishop to insert a clause in a schoolmaster's license forbidding any other to teach school within a given radius of the place where the licensed teacher was to keep his establishment.[33] This clause encouraged the active support of licensed teachers, so prosecutions of unlicensed schoolmasters were not unusual in the episcopal courts. Prosecutions were infrequent until 1699 when, possibly in collusion with the Church, the Mayor and seven Burgesses of Exeter petitioned the Bishop to act against several unlawful schoolmaster in the city. Trelawny took advantage of the triennial visitation of that year to enquire about the activities of schoolmasters elsewhere in the diocese. Two of these schoolmasters, who were unlicensed, took legal advice from Peter King, then a rising nonconformist Whig lawyer who offered suggestions for a prohibition which Lord Chancellor Somers readily accepted on 14 December. The Bishop's officers contested the Lord Chancellor's decision briefing the Attorney-General to appear on their behalf. By the time Somers put a stop to proceedings against unlicensed Devon schoolmasters it was clear that, politically, his days were numbered.[34] On 26 April, 1700 he was dismissed and Nathan Wright succeeded him as lord keeper on 21 May. Wright had a very different attitude. When the Bishop's counsel appeared before him on 21 November he discharged the prohibition leaving the way clear for the episcopal courts of Exeter to prosecute any unlicensed school teacher brought to their notice. The number of licences taken out for the period 1699 to 1708 indicates the degree of success which attended the policy of checking the growth of nonconformist education in the West Country.

The re-assertion of Church control over education must have been very heartening to all conservatives in the Church of England. It helps to explain why men like Atterbury and Bromley were convinced that an Anglican counter-revolution was possible. The means were to hand provided there was the will to use them. The episcopal right to license schoolmasters was not confined to the diocese of Exeter. In the use of rural deans, however, the Bishop of Exeter had an advantage enjoyed by no other Bishop.

The office of rural dean first appeared in England in the middle of the eleventh century as soon as the parochial system was fairly well developed.[35] From the earliest time the office had been elective, subject only to the bishop's confirmation. It was an office of which archdeacons were jealous, therefore a decree of Innocent III in 1214 making rural deans subject to archdeacons hastened their complete subordination and the decay in the effective working of the office. In the diocese of Exeter, however, no such subordination took place, and rural deans survied the Reformation as active officers with their power of visitation unabated. They continued to be elected by the clergy of the deanery with no suggestion at all that bishop or archdeacon attempted to interfere with their choice. During his term of office, the rural dean conducted a visitation of all churches, chapels and parsonage houses in his deanery. The court of the archdeacon of Cornwall had acquired something of the character of a commissary court so rural deans in that county returned their presentments to that court. All the other rural deans returned theirs to the Bishop's principal registry in Exeter. The rural dean's main concern was the fabric and furnishing of parish churches and the fabric of parsonage houses. In this annual visitation, the bishops of Exeter had, in theory, an effective weapon for strengthening episcopal surveillance of these particular matters in a large diocese. At the end of the seventeenth century it was a very different story in practice. A rural dean's visitation was often a formality. Parishioners in Devon and Cornwall took no great pride in their parish churchs and had no desire to spend money on repairs in renovating interiors. Churchwardens were reluctant to undertake repairs on their own initiative when they could not be assured of the

94

support of the parishioners in levying an increased church rate. In the face of lay opposition the clergy were not inclined to favour a vigorous policy. When submitting their presentments, rural deans either took refuge in a sweeping *omnia bene* or, alternatively, presented a number of minor defects and omissions in order to satisfy the court of Exeter, and to cover up more serious examples of neglect, decay or disrepair. The clergy had their own reasons for turning a blind eye. Rectors of small livings struggling to bring up large families and pay their taxes did not want to face large bills for repair of chancels and parsonage houses. The omission of known major defects from the presentments of rural deans suggests, in part, a conspiracy of silence among the clergy based on mutual sympathy and understanding.

However sympathetic Trelawny might be to these problems of his clergy, he could not ignore the situation indefinitely. The upkeep of churches and their furnishings had always been one of Trelawny's personal concerns. A poorly kept communion table and improperly used communion vessels he found personally distressing. As he learnt of the extent of the neglect in his diocese he decided that nothing less than an all-out campaign was needed if attitudes were to change. This began in earnest in November, 1706. The principal registry no longer accepted vague promises of repair. Informal request was superseded by formal admonition. All rectors and churchwardens presented by rural deans were summoned to appear before the court in Exeter and were ordered to verify, to the archdeacon at his visitation court, that repairs had been duly carried out. It is not possible to say for a certainty why the year 1706 was chosen. Probably Trelawny had intended such a course of action as soon as the accession of Anne created a more favourable political and legal climate. He delayed taking action in 1703 because the Archbishop of Canterbury seriously contemplated promoting legislation concerning the raising of money for the repair of churches and had gone as far as drafting a parliamentary bill. Trelawny would have wished to await the outcome of that proposal before proceeding. Then again, with so many parishes in the south west forced to replace the church roof in the months following the great storm of November, the year following was not an auspicious one in which to begin the campaign. Nor was the year 1705 any better when the Bishop faced an incipient revolt from the clergy of the archdeaconry of Exeter. A further reason for delay may have been the desire the win over Archdeacon Drewe. The cooperation of his court was essential if the campaign was to included Cornwall, because rural deans in that county returned their presentments to his court in his capacity as commissary and not to the principal registry. In fact Drewe never supported the campaign. It was extended to Cornwall only after his death, when Lancelot Blackburne succeeded him.

A number of small administrative changes were made in the procedure which followed a rural dean's presentment and this increased efficiency. Trelawny left Exeter shortly after the campaign began but he had the satisfaction of knowing that it continued with increasing intensity in the years that followed. The clergy's attitude changed: rural deans became zealous in presenting defects of all kinds. Churchwardens and others were compelled to undertake repairs and maintenance which ran the whole gamut from a tower about to collapse to a churchyard overgown with briars; from an unsafe gallery to a surplice of poor quality material. This campaign helped to preserve the ancient fabric of the many parish churches and chapels of Devon and Cornwall. When Prebendary Boggis in his *History of the Diocese of Exeter,* commented on the very small amount of church building in the eighteenth century it did not, as he thought, emphasize the 'lack of ecclesiastical enterprise'. Rather it was the case that very little major rebuilding was needed. The author of the *Thesaurus Ecclesiasticus Provincialis,* writing in 1782, summed up the situation as follows:

> The advantage resulting from this office (of rural dean) are examplified by constant experience: the Houses of the Clergy are, in general, kept in very good order, and Briefs, for the rebuilding or repair of Churches, so frequent in the other parts of the kingdom are here almost without an example.

In the course of the one hundred years before the publication of the *Thesaurus,* five hundred and two briefs were authorized for churches. Four were for churches in Devon and none were for churches in Cornwall.

When Dansey was collecting material for his book on the office of rural dean in the late eighteen-thirties, he learnt of an oral tradition in the diocese that Trelawny was repsonsible for breathing new life into the office. This owed much to the determination with which he championed the legal rights of the Church whenever he was in a position to do so, together with the vigorous way he exercised his authority through his own court. He so restored the morale of the officers of his courts that they felt confident enough to carry on his campaign even after he ceased to be their bishop. Given the spirit of the age it was a remarkable achievement, and to this day places all who love the churches of the West Country permanently in the debt of its Cornish Bishop.

1. W. Keatley Strode, *History of Exeter College* (1900), pp.72-9.

2. A. Bury, An Account of the unhappy Affair (Oxford, 1960); J. Harrington, *The Case of Exeter College* (Oxford, 1690).

3. Smith, Administration, p.287.

4. The Bishop's registers give indications of his movements.

5. A. Bury, *The Naked Gospel* (Oxford, 1690), p.14.

6. Bury, *op.cit.,* p.1.

7. Bury, *op.cit.,* pp.28-9.

8. T.J. Fawcett, *The Liturgy of Comprehension,* Alcuin Club Collections 54, (Southend, 1973), pp.26-46.

9. Anthony Wood, *Athenae Oxoniensis* (1721), ii.950.

10. Bodl. MS. Smith 47, ff.63-4, Bernard to Smith, 1 April, 1690; 9 April, 1690.

11. MS. Smith 47, f.65, same to same, 22 April, 1690.

12. Harrington, *op.cit.,* p.20; see also *Notes and Queries* (3rd series) i.264 a letter of John Harrington, 17 June, 1690.

13. T.C., Clarke Corresp. MS. 749, f.91, Edisbury to Clarke, 29 July, 1690.

14. Clarke Corresp. MS. 749, f.87, Rooke to Clarke, 27 July, 1690.

15. MS. Smith 47, f.69, Bernard to Smith, 14 August, 1690.

16. Wood, *op.cit.,* ii.950.

17. MS. Smith 47, ff.73, 74, Bernard to Smith, 27 September, 1690; same to same, 26 October, 1690; f.83, same to same, 4 April, 1691.

18. H.R.O., A/10/1, Trelawny MSS., T to Carmarthen, 31 August.

19. MS. Smith 47, f.71, Bernard to Smith, 24 August, 1690.

20. W. Blackstone, *Commentaries on the Laws of England,* 5th edn., (Oxford, 1773), iii. 112-4; Sir John Comyns, *A Digest of the Laws of England,* (1822), vii. 171-4.

21. *E.C.,* iv. 449 Newton to Charlett, 2 November, 1690.

22. MS. Smith 47, f.75, Bernard to Smith, 9 October, 1690; Clarke Corresp. 749 f.88, Rooke to Clarke, 11 November, 1690.

23. H.R.O., Trelawny MSS.

97

24. H.R.O., Trelawny MSS., Jones to T, 16 June, 1694; Luttrell, iii. 259, 265.

25. H.R.O., Trelawny MSS., Jones to T, 5 May, 1694; same to same, 5 July, 1694.

26. Luttrell, iii.404.

27. E. Stillingfleet, *Ecclesiastical Cases* (1704), ii. 411-36.

28. H.M.C., *MSS. of the House of Lords (NS), i.393-5; MS. Ballard 9, f.75, T to Charlett, 15 December* [1694].

29. Jurieu *La Religion du Latitudinaire*, p.416, quoted by Robert Burscough; *A Discourse of the Unity of the Church.....* (Exeter 1704). The Epistle Dedicatory; Francis Atterbury, *Sermons and Discourses on Several Occasions* (1708), dedicatory preface.

30. *The Case of Jonathan, Bishop of Exon, and Gawen Hayman, Clerk, Plaintiffs in the Writ of Error By them brought in the High Court of Parliament agains Sampson Hele, Esq., Defendant* (1694).

31. Lamb. Libr., Gibson MSS. 933, f.54, Oxenden to Tenison, 15 March, 1694.

32. A. Tindal Hart, *Life of John Sharp* (1949), p.136; Brockett, *op. cit.,* p.67.

33. Smith, Administration, pp.194-203.

34. W.L. Sachse, *Lord Somers: a political portrait* (1975), pp.154-8.

35. For a full discussion of what follows, see M.G. Smith, 'Bishop Trelawny and the Office of Rural Dean', *T.D.A.,* cxi (1979), pp.13-20.

CHAPTER SEVEN

The Convocation Controversy

The great body of the clergy, dismayed and resentful at the changes which had come upon them since 1687, seized on the call for a revival of Convocation as the one sure way of re-asserting the doctrine and discipline of the Church of England. Demand for synodical action came to a head in 1697. A Convocation which spoke with a united voice would, it was agreed, remind the country in general and the politicians in particular, of the status and divine authority of the clergy. Those who, like Francis Atterbury, argued for an active Convocation were confident that the clerical proctors elected to the Lower House would faithfully represent the wishes of the parochial clergy. However, only the sovereign could issue the licence empowering a Convocation to transact business. Many of the bishops were lukewarm to the idea of an active Convocation and the Archbishop of Canterbury was positively hostile. Therefore the clergy had to turn to the politicians to persuade some of them to bring pressure to bear on the King. To do this, it needed some sympathetic ecclesiastics of sufficient status to approach the politicians in order to persuade them to embrace the cause of an active Convocation. Who better to give a lead in this matter than the Canons of Christ Church, who had never abandoned their high church teaching, and those bishops of pre-revolutionary days who had already made known their conservative views.

The part played by Trelawny in the great convocation controversy is now very difficult to discern, despite the fact that one of the principal sources of evidence for the controversy is the long series of letters he received from Francis Atterbury which his descendant, Sir Harry Trelawny, generously handed over to John Nichols at the end of the eighteenth century. That Trelawny was an active supporter and advisor of some of the leaders of the clergy in the Lower House in the initial period is beyond doubt, but he worked behind the scenes. He was realist enough to know that he could achieve nothing in the Upper House where he and the Bishops of pre-revolutionary days were heavily out-numbered, but he did have high hopes that something positive would be accomplished. By the end of William's reign he had forged close links with Compton and Sprat. When these two Bishops formed a political alliance with the Earl of Rochester and Sir Edward Seymour to bring in a Tory ministry and revive Convocation, it was only to be expected that Trelawny should be included in the alliance. Many of the early discussions from 1696 onwards were centred largely upon Christ Church, and Trelawny would have known about them. It was probably old acquaintanceship with Subdean Blackburne which led Atterbury to glean from the archives of Exeter Cathedral so much about the *Praemunientes* clause in the writ summoning Convocation.[1] After the General Election of 1695 William selected his ministers from Whigs, some of whom were accounted the most outspoken enemies of the Church of England. Compton, Sprat and Trelawny took the threat seriously and, with others, watched the growing influence of Lord Somers with distaste and dismay. As Somers' latest biographer concedes, the belief that Somers looked upon the Church only as an adjunct to governmental power was 'not without some grains of truth'. Trelawny thought he saw in the changes made by Somers in the Commissioners of the Peace, a preliminary to an attack on the Church.[3] He could not forget how Somers had opposed his powers as visitor of Exeter College. He was alarmed and angered when Whig lawyers like Peter King of Exeter said 'that he thought all honest men should endeavour to advance the law above the power of the Church'.[4] Trelawny was prepared to work to overthrow Somers and the Whig Ministry. It was he who first introduced Atterbury to the Earl of Rochester and he joined Compton and Sprat in ordering that the clergy be summoned to elect proctors on the writ *praemunientes*. He gave Atterbury his seat in the Lower House by collating him to the archdeaconry of Totnes in January, 1701.

However, Trelawny's support of the alliance of high churchmen and old Tory politicians was cautious and conditional. He did not cooperate closely with the Earl of Rochester and never went out of his way to meet him.[5] He trusted neither Rochester nor Sir Edward Seymour. He had embarrassing memories of the deferential, even obsequious, way he had behaved toward the Earl of Rochester when, as a young clergyman, he was desperate for promotion. He knew something of the personal religious opinions of both men and, in Seymour's case, had positive evidence by 1699 of just how tender a regard he really had for the clergy of the Church of England. Seymour was prepared to sacrifice his local vicar, a stiff high churchman, rather than upset the Dissenters of Totnes.[6] These politicians would use the Church to serve their own ends. Probably Trelawny kept his opinions to himself and never imparted them to Compton, Sprat, or any one else in London. He did let his true feelings to be known to the discreet Francis Cooke in Exeter. He wrote from Cornwall in October, 1700:

'Your Idol, I hear, hath given you a glimpse and will be in
full shine upon you the 21st. If those that trust in him are
like unto him for reality they would make better courtiers
than patriots'.[7]

Only two men were so loved and fêted in Exeter at this period to deserve the
title 'idol'. One was Sir Edward Seymour, the other was the Earl of
Rochester who was in the habit of taking such journies in order to boost the
morale of the Tory gentry and their supporters.

Despite these reservations Trelawny, like so many churchmen, had
high hopes of what a sitting Convocation might achieve. All recognised
that the outcome might depend on the choice of prolocutor for the Lower
House. In mid-January, 1701 Trelawny ordered his archdeacons and
proctors to hasten to London to be there at the opening session in order to
defeat any candidate put forward by the Archbishop's friends.[8] He was
highly displeased when he learnt that, following a meeting at the Earl of
Rochester's London house, the elderly George Hooper had been chosen as
candidate and elected as prolocutor. Trelawny had wanted Dr. Jane to be
chosen as he had been in 1689. Jane was a strong character. Hooper was
well-meaning, but slow-witted and could be a more pliable tool in the
hands of a politician. Such turned out to be the case. In his letter explaining
the circumstances surrounding Hooper's selection, Atterbury put the best
construction possible on the choice. He was sure that all was not lost.[9]
Trelawny stayed in Cornwall, having been assured by Compton and Sprat
that there would be no further need for him to appear at Westminster until
later. At this stage they did not think that the Bishops would dare to resist
the clear mandate given to the majority in the Lower House. That Body
had appointed committees which were considering, among other things,
two matters dear to Trelawny's heart: the censure of atheist publications
and ways to suppress nonconformist centres of higher education. Dr. Jane
chaired the committee looking into Toland's *Christianity not Mysterious*
and the writings of Craig, a chaplain of Bishop Burnet. Trelawny hoped
that the committee would add Burnet's *Exposition of the Thirty-Nine
Articles* to the list.[10] Toward the end of March, however, he learnt from
Atterbury that the leaders in the Lower House were dragging their feet. By
the time he arrived in London early in April he heard from Compton and
Sprat of the Archbishop's determination to silence discussion. These three
bishops were the only ones to oppose the Archbishop in the Upper House
in April and May.[11] Recognising their isolation they encouraged Atterbury
to wrest the leadership of the Lower House out of Hooper's hands and lead
the clergy into constitutional deadlock with the Archbishop which stopped
all business. The King dissolved Parliament and Convocation in
November. No progress was made in the new Convocation although the

101

Lower House reactivated the committee dealing with heretical books, and produced a detailed indictment of Burnet's *Exposition*. When the King died the political situation changed and with it came renewed hopes that the Archbishop would be less intransigent. Trelawny, who had attended none of the sessions in the closing months of William's reign, was present for the opening sessions of the new Convocation in October 1702. Now the dispute between the two Houses revolved around the nature of episcopacy. This was a theological issue on which Trelawny set great store and lay at the root of his dislike of Gilbert Burnet.

Doubtless Trelawny disliked Burnet for several personal reasons as well. Apart from the loss of the nomination to be Bishop of Salisbury in 1689, Trelawny would hardly have approved of Burnet's background and upbringing. A Scotsman once destined for the presbyterian ministry who had supported those who sought to exclude James, duke of York, from the throne in 1680 and 1681, Burnet's past career would have stirred prejudices in one with Trelawny's background sufficient in themselves to cause dislike.

To one as conservative in his views at Trelawny Burnet's idiosyncratic approach to the government of his diocese of Salisbury occasioned further fear and dislike. Burnet's establishment of a nascent theological college at Salisbury not only looked like a copy of a dissenting academy, it was also an affront to the privileges of the Universities of Oxford and Cambridge.[12] Burnet contined Seth Ward's policy of collating to prebendal stalls the occupants of poorly endowed livings in the market towns of his diocese, but conservatives like Trelawny did not approve of compelling them to give a bond to resign the stall if ever they quitted the living.[13] There was no point in trying to persuade lay patrons to abandon the practice so long as they could cite episcopal precedent to justify them continuing it. The fact that Burnet stopped the theological college and abandoned the policy with regard to prebendal stalls would not have improved relations. Conservative English clergy would only wonder what this highly unorthodox Scotsman might get up to next. Trelawny commented sarcastically to his friend, Arthur Charlett, that Burnet's trouble was that he wanted to change everything to do with the episcopate unless it was liable to affect his power or his income.[14]

In addition to these causes for dislike two matters of far greater importance kept the two men in opposition. First, they differed fundamentally on the question of how to maintain pastoral discipline. Other Bishops appointed by William III may have expressed a preference for making use of the magistrates and Parliamentary legislation in the suppression of vice and profanity, and may have placed little faith in Canon Law and the church courts, but none of them was as openly contempuous of the whole system of canonical jurisdiction as was Burnet. A passage in his autobiography sums up his attitude:

'I tried next to regulate my Consistorial Court and for some years I went constantly to it but I found that that which is crooked cannot be made straight. All our proceedings are so dilatory and engage men in such an expense that I did not wonder to hear them so much cried out on as they were. They are a great grievance both to the Clergy and Laity'.[15]

To reject the ecclesiastical courts meant rejecting the Canon Law they administered and rejecting many of the concepts of canonical censures and the pastoral relationship between the parish clergy and the courts. It meant a rejection of what the older bishops believed in, and of one of the main reasons for reviving Convocation in the first place.

Secondly, the two men differed fundamentally on their understanding of episcopacy. In this respect, as has been shown already, Trelawny was a convinced Episcopalian in the mould of Cosin, Overall and Beveridge. Like them, he hesistated to place the divine origin of episcopacy on the same level as the doctrine of the Trinity. A protestant church which lacked bishops was a true, though errant, branch of the true Catholic Church. He agreed entirely with them that history demonstrated beyond question that the integrity of the Church had been sustained chiefly by Christians who recognized episcopal authority and the Apostolic Succession.[16] Furthermore, experience had taught the spiritual advantages of Sacraments administered by a validly ordained episcopal priesthood.[17] Even if episcopacy was not commanded by Revelation it was sanctioned by Divine Providence, and Trelawny always included the power to punish and correct as a part of God's design. 'The ordinary governing offices of the Apostles has descended down upon their successors', he wrote, 'and will continue through all ages as long as the Order [i.e. of Bishops] and Christianity'.[18] He was convinced that once the Apostolic Succession was subverted, England would see again the spiritual anarchy of the Commonwealth when 'each parochial church had its particular faith'.

Belief in the Apostolic Succession of bishops had obviously an integral connection with the maintenance of pastoral discipline. Once one denied that bishops were part of the divine plan and endowed with 'the governing office of the Apostles' then it really did not matter if the State took over the task of correcting the morals of society. Indeed, it could be argued further that the magistracy was the most competent branch of government to do so.

When Burnet published at long last his book on the Thirty-Nine Articles, he made public views which, in his usual tactless way, he had very

103

probably voiced frequently at meetings of the Bishops at Lambeth. These views were very different from those held by Trelawny and the older conservative Bishops. In his discussion of Article Thirty-three, 'On Excommunication', Burnet defended the practice but insisted that it should be rarely used, and hinted broadly that he had no time for pursuing an excommunicate with a writ *de excommunicato capiendo*. We should admonish brethren as sinners not use them as enemies 'whereas the other method looks like a power that designs *destruction,* rather than *edification,* especially when the secular arm is called in.' Burnet went on to show that he had in mind primarily the papal practice of calling on princes, under penalty of deposition from their thrones, to extirpate heresy in their territories. The phrase would not have been lost on his contemporaries who would also give it a local English context, especially as he chose to conclude his discussion with an attack on the church courts and Canon Law still operating in the Church of England.[19]

It was his commentary on the Twenty-third Article which aroused the greatest controversy and so outraged Trelawny that is the only known occasion when he seriously considered writing a pamphlet.[20] Burnet made it clear that he did not regard episcopacy to be God's choice for his Church. Lawful authority in the Church was not something God had ordained: rather it was a prudent provision the Apostles had made for the future. Burnet argued that the definition of lawful authority given in the Article 'is put in very general words, far from that magisterial stiffness in which some have taken upon themselves to dictate in this matter. The Article does not resolve this into any particular constitution, but leaves the matter open and at large for such accidents as had happened, and such as might still happen'.[21] Trelawny most emphatically did not consider that the Article 'left the matter open'. The phrase 'such as might still happen' had an ominous and chilling ring about it. Was this former Presbyterian, now official tutor to the young Duke of Gloucester, the heir presumptive, showing his hand as the spearhead of a calvinist fifth column, a Williamite mole, in the inner councils of the Church of England? When one considers that the publication of the book coincided with a time when Somers was thought to be tampering with the make-up of the commissions of the peace, Trelawny could be forgiven for thinking so. Burnet went further. In the manner of John Locke, he implies that lawful authority in the Church is derived from the laity. When a church is under persecution, then the natural state of affairs is for the pastors of that Church 'to satisfy the people in all that is done, to carry along their consent with it, and to consult much with them in it'. He goes on to say that in more settled times of history when the nation has a Christian ruler, then 'he comes to be in the stead of the whole people' and the outcome of this is that 'the Magistrate

104

has a power to make laws in sacred matters, he may order those to be prepared, by whom, and as he pleases'.[22] Again Burnet hedged his comments with qualifications and caveats but his words can be taken to imply that church synods have no inherent rights and that any authority possessed by the Bishops is only such as the King permits them to hold. If the King chooses to transfer all matters considered to be the cognizance of the church courts into the hands of secular magistrates he has a perfect right to do so.

If Convocation was going to deal with heresy then, in Trelawny's opinion, Burnet's book was as worthy of censure as any of Toland's writings. In the winter sessions of 1701 he pushed Atterbury unsuccessfully to persuade the Lower House to include Burnet's *Exposition* on the list of heretical publications to be examined by a committee. He took a close interst in the preparation of *A Vindication of the Twenty-third Article,* which appeared in 1702 under the name of Robert Burscough. Trelawny may even have had a hand it its writing.[23] It is reasonable to assume that Trelawny was concerned in the next dispute between the two Houses of Convocation. On 11 December, 1702 the Lower House agreed on a statement on the nature of episcopacy intended to compel the Bishops to disown Burnet and any other of their number who did not take the Apostolic Succession seriously. The Bishops and their supporters in the Lower House evaded the issue by arguing that the royal licence to transact business gave them no authority to enact any canon concerning doctrine or discipline.[24] Trelawny had to be content with the Queen's mark of disfavour with Burnet in January, when she turned him out of his grace and favour lodgings in St. James' Palace.

Trelawny did not give up all hope of having Burnet's book censured. Two years later he still hoped to get the Lower House to act on the *Exposition.* All he managed to achieve was a public restatement by the Upper House that episcopacy was of divine institution and with that he had to rest content. The attempt by the Lower House to get the Bishops formally to endorse a statement on the nature of episcopacy was not as pointless an exercise as some historians have thought. It was a re-assertion of the doctrine that the Church of England was part of the one Catholic and Apostolic Church and of divine origin, therefore its authority in matters of doctrine and discipline derived, in the last resort, not from the Crown, but from Christ. Trelawny's attack on Burnet was no personal vendetta. Later events were to prove that he was correct to fear that a denial of the divine authority of the episcopate would erode further the discipline of the Church. Three years after Burnet's death, Benjamin Hoadly preaching before George I took Burnet's speculations one stage further. Since the Kingdom of Christ was not of this world, 'He hath..... left behind Him, no visible Human *Authority;* no *Viceregents,* who can be so said properly to supply His Place; no *Interpreter,* upon whom his Subjects are absolutely to depend; no *Judges* over the Conscience or Religion of His People'.[25]

Trelawny continued to support the majority in the Lower House for the next three years but he had less interest in Convocation. Perhaps he considered that Convocation had achieved as much as it was likely to at that juncture without creating further tensions and enmities within the Church and the Nation. He always took Christian fellowship seriously and consciously tried to fulfil his ordination promise 'to set forward..... quietness, peace and love, among all Christian people'. For example, he made it absolutely clear to Atterbury that, no matter how he behaved toward Wake in Convocation, when he came to Exeter, he was to remember that Wake was his dean and his brother canon and that he was to behave charitably at all times.[26] Convocation had achieved something. It had restated publicly that episcopacy was of divine institution. Even the Archbishop's spokesman in the Lower House, Charles Trimnell, had conceded as much. Archbishop Tenison had started to draft some parliamentary bills on matters Trelawny felt very necessary, namely, the repair of churches, heretical books and censorship of the press. One of the weaknesses of Convocation at this period was that those who hoped for positive results did so for different reasons. Many of the lower clergy wanted to see the restoration of discipline over the laity. Some bishops wanted an increase of supervision over the clergy especially in the performance of weddings. Others wanted Convocation to impose some form of censorship. A failure to agree on priorities made it all too easy for politicians to manipulate the leadership, and, ultimately, to frustrate almost all its aspirations. Trelawny never seems to have expected revival of discipline over the laity in all respects. He accepted that the clock could not be turned back to 1685. What he did not accept was the attitude of mind which said that because some areas of discipline had ceased so all discipline over the laity might as well cease. He did not dream of claiming any powers which the Law did not allow him already. Having the courage and strength of will to maintain discipline in his own diocese he hoped that Convocation would stiffen the resolve of his brother bishops to do likewise. When Bishop Moore of Norwich began a prosecution of Dr. Coward in his consistory court for a book arguing against the immortality of the soul, it looked as if the Bishops were beginning to take heart.[27]

By the end of the summer of 1704, Trelawny had a further reason to lessen his interest in Convocation. Robert Harley had wooed and won Atterbury over to the side of the Ministry. In the autumn sessions Atterbury blunted the attack on the Bishops in the Lower House and had to explain to Trelawny why he could not bring himself to press on and censure the Bishops for neglecting to exercise the disciplinary powers they already possessed.[28] Trelawny was not pleased. It did not matter how hard Secretary Harley canvassed Atterbury's merits as a suitable successor to Wake as dean of Exeter in 1705. Trelawny did not consider him at all. The Queen accepted Trelawny's recommendation of Lancelot Blackburne. Blackburne was no Tory, but he did share his Bishop's conviction that all that was wanting to make the discipline of the church courts effective was the will to use them.[29] Convocation did nothing for the next few years. Atterbury tried to revive the Tory fortunes by publishing a collection of his sermons in September, 1707 with a dedication to Trelawny. In the preface he indicated that the Queen was prepared to support all those causes which the Lower House had hoped to have achieved in 1700. Having done so much to maintain the discipline of the church courts which Atterbury claimed still needed to be restored, Trelawny was justifiably angry at being associated with so transparent a political device.[30]

By 1707 Trelawny was out of sympathy with the extreme High Church party. He had to face an attempt to foment a rebellion among his Exeter clergy in 1705; he had to watch his careful scheme for re-invigorating the office of rural dean stand still in Cornwall because of Archdeacon Drewe's intransigence. He was vilified for accepting the bishopric of Winchester. In the spring of 1709, in defiance of the whole weight of the Christ Church interest, he licensed Henry Sacheverell to the readership of St. Saviour's, Southwark. In 1710 he collated the Archbishop's chaplain Edmund Gibson to the archdeaconry of Surrey. In the same year the High Church Tories watched him support moderate Whig candidates in the General Election with horrified fascination.[31]

However he might behave politically, Trelawny was still included among the handful of bishops and politicians who met at Sprat's house in 1710 to consider carefully the items of business to be laid before the new Convocation.[32] When the bulk of the bishops led by Wake objected firmly, but moderately, to the unprecedented and legally untenable form of royal licence, which was Atterbury's brain child, and which reduced the role of the Archbishop from president to the first on a list of bishops, any one of whom had to be present before business could be transacted, it was Trelawny who was asked to reply to Wake's arguments.[33] Whatever he said managed to remove the objections and the Upper House proceeded to business. Convocation appointed joint committees to deal with various topics and a number of proposals were drafted in the form of parliamentary bills. Atterbury intended to bring about a counter-revolution in alliance with the Tory majority in the House of Commons.[34] Trelawny was assigned to the committees dealing with the sanctions

107

employed by the church courts and the role of rural deans. He also seems to have been largely responsible for drawing up the form of service for consecrating new churches and churchyards.[35] However, when Convocation reassembled after the Easter recess, the life and heart had gone out of the High Church party. A more intriguing issue appeared in the shape of William Whiston, Lucasian Professor of Mathematics at Cambridge, and a holder of highly eccentric theological opinions. He published *An Historical Preface to Primitive Christianity Revived,* in which he cast doubt on the christology of the ante-Nicene Fathers and rated the authority of the Apostolic Constitution above that of the New Testament. He then had the temerity to dedicate his book to the members of Convocation. Both Houses embarked upon a heresy hunt, and foremost among the Bishops to do so was Trelawny. It is doubtful if he attended many of the joint committee meetings before Easter: he never had any taste for committee work, but Whiston's affair was another matter.[36] A move to suppress heresy was one of the practical results he had always hoped to see Convocation achieve. He pressed hard for Whiston to be given the severest sentence possible. Business proceeded slowly as more and more time was taken up with Whiston's book. In fact, it was only by the beginning of June the following year that Convocation had any items of business ready. On 18 June Trelawny headed a small joint delegation to wait on the Queen to ask her to publish the form of service for consecrating new churches and the condemnation of Whiston's opinions. The delegation was received coolly. The Queen complained of the failure of Convocation to complete any of the other business entrusted to it. A chastened Upper House promised the Queen on 20 June to hasten despatch of business, but nothing more was done before Trelawny produced the instrument of prorogation on 31 July.

　　　Disappointed by the failure of Convocation to produce any results in 1711, extreme high churchmen among the parish clergy enthusiastically supported the view of Roger Lawrence that any baptism not performed by an episcopally ordained priest or deacon was invalid. Some were sympathetic to the argument of Thomas Brett that a parish priest should admit to the Holy Communion only those who had made their confession. Such claims for priestly authority placed Trelawny and other High Churchmen in a dilemma. Having a high doctrine of episcopal authority he could hardly hold a low doctrine of sacerdotal powers. He had voiced his strong personal disapproval of the custom of licensing midwives so that they might baptise babies in an emergency, when he preached to the clergy of Exeter in 1699 and again to the clergy of Winchester in 1708.[37] On the other hand, he knew perfectly well that the temper of the English laity would never permit such views on priestly power to gain ground. He

108

always rested his case on the rights of the Church of England given to it by the Laws of the Land. Trelawny was busy with a triennial visitation in the month of May, 1712 when the issue of lay baptism was discussed in the Upper House, so he did not have to try to blunt the counter attack of the Archbishop and his supporters. He wrote letters to Atterbury in the new year, urging him to guide the Lower House in coming to no decision on the issue.

The next few years were a perplexing time both for the Church as well as for the Tory party. The Queen's health was known to be failing. Churchmen could not make up their minds whether the future lay with the old Harleian policy of moderation or Henry St. John's advocacy of a Tory High Church single party state. A restoration of the discipline of the Church was something all churchmen wanted to see. Even White Kennet had come round to realising, in the course of the Whiston affair, that a disciplinary line had to be drawn somewhere.[38] All churchmen recognised the need for some reforms, but did they really wish to see the discipline of the Church restored by a group of politicians whose personal opinions and private lives were the antithesis of all that was godly? Was parliamentary legislation the way forward? The Commonwealth had tried to produce a godly nation by legislation and that experiment had failed. Other churchmen questioned the wisdom of Atterbury's strategy. Only the judges of Westminster Hall had the right to interpret statutes. To embody a reform of the sanctions used by the church courts or of the system of issuing marriage licences in the form of a parliamentary statute was to play straight into the hand of the common lawyers. What Parliament allowed, Parliament could, at a later date, annul. One wonders if discussion on this issue between archdeacons and the proctors of their respective courts during the annual visitations after Easter 1711 may partly account for the reluctance of the Lower House to press on with business. There were other nagging questions connected with this Tory counter-revolution. Would it lead to civil war? Could it even end in an attempt to restore the Old Pretender? Trelawny was a bishop of such conservative opinions that he too must have doubted the wisdom of proceeding by way of parliamentary legislation. A new Licensing Act was one thing: a new sanction for the church courts based solely on parliamentary authority was quite another. Only on the issue of heretical and atheist publications did Trelawny still hope for some result. He urged Atterbury in February, 1713 to persuade the Lower House to concentrate on this. Following his débâcle at Christ Church the previous summer, Atterbury had no intention of allowing any business to be transacted in Convocation. He reminded Trelawny of the senility of the Tory prelates in the Upper House, and concluded that the clergy were 'sheep without a shepherd'.[39] Plagued with gout, Atterbury

109

was irritated with instructions from an elderly bishop who was doing very little himself to provide leadership in Convocation.

Trelawny could not always avoid attending. Archbishop Tenison was so crippled that he could not stir from Lambeth so he presided over the opening sessions of a new Convocation in February, 1714. He saw to it that the opening address to the Queen was safely drawn up and presented. After Bolingbroke had brought the royal licence to transact business, he ceased to attend. He appeared briefly at the end of April to learn the contents of a proposed parliamentary bill for a writ *de contumace capiendo* and then only appeared again to hear more about the fate of the form of service for consecrating new churches, and to join in discussion of another heretical publication. He was present at the opening session of the Convocation of the new reign and attended when the committees were drawn up, but he had little interest in Convocation affairs in April, 1715, or in the final sessions of the following year. There is nothing to indicate what Trelawny felt about Convocation's return to its slumbers. It is interesting to note, however, that throughout the controversy, he was consistently concerned not with administrative reforms, but with problems of theology. Nothing was more likely to encourage Erastianism and to destroy the mission of the Church of England than a failure to speak authoritatively on matters of doctrine. Trelawny would have derived some satisfaction from knowing that if Convocation was going to be prorogued indefinitely it should be the result of a desire to censure the theology of Benjamin Hoadley. It was an honourable battle to fight. It would have been no consolation to know that Hoadley was to follow him later as Bishop of Winchester, but he would have rejoiced to find in Samuel Johnson, who was prepared to stand before a battery of canon to restore the Convocation, a man after his own heart.

1. *E.C.*, iii. 11, Atterbury to T, 2 January, 1701.

2. Sachse, *op. cit.*, p.221.

3. Plymouth Libr., Kitley MSS. 190/3, T to Pollexfen, 25 March, 1702. Possibly Trelawny was over-reacting. See L.K.J. Glassey, *Politics and Appointments of Justices of the Peace 1675-1720*, (Oxford, 1979), pp.115-134.

4. D.R.O., Cooke Corresp., 30 November, 1700.

5. C.T., p.265, Fairfax (Tenison's secretary) to T, 19 November, 1698; p.254, Sprat to T, 1 July, 1703 (but Trelawny never stirred from Trelawne and never attended the rendezvous at Bath).

6. M.G. Smith, 'John Prince and the publication of 'The Worthies of Devon', *D.C.N. and Q.*, xxxiv, pt.viii (1981), pp.301-7. Seymour was Trelawny's maternal uncle, but there is never any acknowledgement of the relationship in the Bishop's letters.

7. D.R.O., Cooke Corresp., 5 October, 1700.

8. *Ibid.*, 18 January, 1701.

9. *E.C.*, iii. 28, Atterbury to T, 20 February, 1701.

10. Cooke Corresp., 15 March, 1701; *E.C.*, iii. 43-7, Atterbury to T, 18 March, 1701.

11. Lamb. Libr., Convocation Acts I/1/12, ff.33, 35.

12. Thomas Burnet, 'Life of the Author', appended to *Bishop Burnet's History of his own Time*, (1724), ii. 709.

13. *Ibid.*, 712.

14. MS. Ballard 9, f.73, T to Charlett, 20 August.

15. H.C. Foxcroft, *A Supplement to Burnet's History* (Oxford, 1902), p.503; see also Burnet's comment at the end of Article xxxiii, G. Burnet, *Exposition of the Thirty-Nine Articles of the Church of England*, (1826), p.376.

16. Trelawny, *Sermon..... and charge.....*, pp.12-13.

17. *Ibid.*, pp.9-10.

18. *Ibid.*, pp.29.

19. *Ibid.*, pp.372, 376.

20. *E.C.*, iii. 88*, T to Sprat, 20 July, 1702.

21. Burnet, *Exposition*, p.257.

111

22. *Ibid.,* p.258.

23. H.M.C., *First Report,* p.52, Newey to T, 9 March, 1702.

24. N. Sykes, *William Wake* (Cambridge, 1957), i. 119-20.

25. Benjamin Hoadley, *The Nature of the Kingdom, or Church of Christ* (1717), quoted by Bennett, *Tory Crisis.....,* p.214.

26. *E.C.,* iii. 119, Atterbury to T, 1 June, 1704; 124, same to same, 15 June, 1704.

27. Lamb. Libr., Convocation Acts I/1/12, Session 36, 15 December, 1703.

28. *E.C.,* iii. 253, Atterbury to T, 7 November, 1704.

29. Wake MSS. xxi, f.27, Blackburne to Wake, 23 August, 1718.

30. Bennett, *Tory Crisis.....,* pp.93-4.

31. MS. Ballard 9, ff.69-70, 71-2.

32. Sykes, *op. cit.,* i. 124.

33. Wake MSS. xvii, unfoliated, T to Wake, 24 February, 1711.

34. G.V. Bennett, 'The Convocation of 1710: an Anglican attempt at counter-revolution', *Studies in Church History* vii, pp.311-9.

35. Lamb. Libr., Codices MSS. 1114.

36. J.E. Hirst, ' 'Whiston's Affair': the trials of a Primitive Christian 1709-1714', *Journal of Ecclesiastical History,* xxvii (1976), pp.129-150.

37. Trelawny, *Sermon..... and charge.....,* pp.20-11; also MS. copy of a sermon in possession of Sir John Trelawny.

38. Hirst, *loc. cit.,* p.150.

39. *E.C.,* iii. 313, 10 February, 1713; 318, 24 February, 1713.

CHAPTER EIGHT

A Cornish Boroughmongerer

No politician of the period was unaware of the remarkable number of members of parliament returned for Cornwall. In addition to the two knights of the shire, twenty-one boroughs returned two members each. What is more remarkable is the distribution of the Cornish parliamentary boroughs. Two fifths were to be found within a small district centred on the town of Liskeard. In an area measuring twenty-eight miles east to west and twelve miles north to south lay the boroughs of Bodmin, Callington, Fowey, Liskeard, East Looe, West Looe, Lostwithiel, St. Germans and Saltash. The Trelawny family estates were concentrated in the same area, which helps to explain Trelawny control of two and, at times, of several more of the nine boroughs. By the beginning of Anne's reign English politicians became aware that Bishop Trelawny had come to wield an influence in general elections in Cornwall far greater than that held by his father and grandfather. By the year of his death that influence had dwindled to little more than that which he had inherited from them.

There were a number of personal factors which account for this remarkable achievement. Of a convivial sociable nature, Jonathan was prepared to enter into the sheer hard work of being a borough manager. He was prepared to enter upon the endless cultivation of people's goodwill so necessary for success in an election. When he could not reside at Trelawne he would make frequent trips to Cornwall to compliment the mayors on their election to office and to visit the gentry in their houses. His active involvement in local government before his consecration meant that many voters would have made his acquaintance. He was honest and open about what he believed and he was trusted. The Cornish gentry began to seek his advice when he was Bishop of Bristol.[1] A devout churchman himself, he did not hold aloof from the company of those less religiously inclined and in his own way he tried gently to convert them. This much is clear from a letter he wrote to George Clarke.[2] He must also have had a hand in helping Hugh Boscawen to declare himself so sincerely for the Church of England before the gentry at Liskeard in 1705. His position as bishop of Exeter

113

increased his influence and he put it to good use. Major-general Charles and Brigadier Henry also brought their influence to bear because borough-mongering was a family concern.[3] Success would not have attended these personal factors without two more important reasons. One was the decline and fall of the Earl of Bath, the other was the electoral alliance between the Godolphins and the Trelawnys. Unless national issues were strongly felt in Cornwall during an election campaign the returns were more likely to reflect the rivalries between leading families of Cornish gentry.

Cornwall was a royal duchy and up to the Civil War the Crown, through the Lord Warden of the Stannaries had had the predominant say in the borough elections. After the Restoration the Crown ceased to influence them directly, and let the initiative pass to the Lord Warden, who was John Granville. The Granville family had been important in west Cornwall ever since the eleventh century, but none had risen so far or so fast as the Granville involved in the negotiations which restored Charles II to the throne. Within three months of the King's return John Granville had been granted all the major offices in the duchy and the county. The following year he was created Earl of Bath, given three thousand pounds a year for life out of the duchy tin revenue and appointed governor of Plymouth. After his accession James II placed great reliance on Bath's direction of the General Election in Cornwall, where he blasted Sir Edward Seymour's hopes in that county and led John Evelyn to dub him 'the Prince Elector'.[4] When he declared for the Prince of Orange following the landing at Torbay, Bath's importance was acknowledged immediately with the commission of commander-in-chief of all forces in the West Country.[5] In 1689, the new monarchs confirmed him in all his offices, adding the lord lieutenancy of Devon in association with his eldest son, Lord Lansdown.

The rewards showered upon the Earl of Bath could not have pleased the other Cornish royalist families although they would not have said so openly. They had done much for the Stuart cause; they had suffered as much as the Granvilles but their rewards were meagre by comparison. Yet so long as Bath enjoyed royal trust and favour there was little that could be done against the Granvilles, so, for many years, there was little room in Cornwall for any parliamentary influence other than that of the Earl of Bath. Trelawny influence was confined to three boroughs, East Looe, West Looe and Liskeard. Only East Looe was a safe Trelawny seat. The franchise was vested in the mayor, corporation and a strictly limited and carefully vetted number of freemen. The Trelawnys nominated both members without any objection from the voters, who did not care if they ever saw their Members of Parliament because they always applied direct to Trelawne for any favours.[6] The franchise of West Looe consisted of approximately forty free burgesses whose loyalties were divided. The

Kendall family still contested the seat after 1660, and a Trelawny had to be elected mayor and returning officer in order to keep a Kendall out in 1678 and 1679. After 1685 the Kendalls relinquished all pretensions to independence and were content to be elected on Trelawny recommendation. The Bullers of Shillingham still had supporters in the town who were opposing the Trelawnys as late as 1690, but this opposition seems to have died with the passing of the Civil War generation.[7] Liskeard was not so much a family borough as the personal seat of Sir Jonathan, the second baronet, who held it only from 1679 until his death and had to share Liskeard with John Buller of Morval. In February, 1685 Trelawny made a clear distinction between those corporations 'where I have a helping influence' and those boroughs where 'my authority is absolute'.[8] One of the former was Lostwithiel but no one considered it to be a decisive influence.[9] It is difficult to determine whether the other Cornish landed families accepted this dominance of the Granvilles without demur, but what is clear is that by 1686 the Trelawnys were put on a collision course with the Granvilles. Family honour demanded that neither turned aside until the other had been defeated.

Wittingly or unwittingly, James II initiated the conflict by sending Sir Jonathan into Cornwall in June, 1685 with orders to mobilize the county militia against the landing of the Duke of Monmouth.[10] James, who had always taken an interest in maritime affairs, would have known Jonathan's efficient discharge of his duties as vice-admiral and had confidence in his ability to prepare the militia. However justified the decision may have been in terms of effective government, it could not hide a deliberate snub to the King's Lord Lieutenant, the Earl of Bath. Jonathan found his fellow deputy lieutenants were unwilling to cooperate. With typical Cornish procrastination they quibbled about the strict legality of mobilizing when the county was not directly threatened with an invasion. The only deputy lieutenant who supported Jonathan, and signed the orders with him to call out the regiments, was Jonathan Rashleigh. He felt the full weight of his Lord Lieutenant's displeasure and was dismissed in July.[11] Trelawny retaliated by intriguing against the Earl of Bath. Casting about him for allies he enlisted the aid of the Godolphins and other militia officers to frustrate Bath's aim of using the Cornish militia as a recruiting ground for the new regiment in the regular army the King had just authorised him to raise.[12] Control of the militia was then the first cause of friction between the Granvilles and the Trelawnys. A disputed election to the Stannary Parliament became another.

By 1684 tin production had risen sharply and the market price slumped. The Crown's right of pre-emption of all tin produced had been farmed out to a consortium of London pewterers and was due to expire in

1686. The farm was for a stated number of years and the price of tin was fixed for the duration of that lease. In practice, however, the purchase and export of tin was in the hands of a decreasing number of wealthy and powerful local merchants. 'They defrauded the London merchants who commissioned them to buy tin; they defrauded the king [of coinage revenue] by smuggling tin across the Channel when possible'.[13] These merchants combined to fix the price locally. It was felt by some, including Trelawny that the only way of helping the Tinners in a mining recession was to re-introduce direct Crown pre-emption. Only the Treasury had a pocket deep enough to defeat the price fixing of the local merchants. The Stannary Parliament of twenty-four stannators met seldom but only this Body would fix the official price of tin. The Earl of Bath, as Lord Warden, was ordered to summon a parliament to fix a new price and to agree that a new farm be negotiated with the London merchants. Secretly Bath wanted the farm to cease, so he proposed to urge the Parliament to accept a renewal of the farm but to raise the price to eighty shillings a hundredweight. The most merchants were prepared to offer was fifty-eight shillings, so there would be no takers for a new farm at so high a price. Bath expected no opposition in the Parliament; he might even gain some popularity for appearing to promote the welfare of the Tinners. Then he learnt that Trelawny, now Bishop of Bristol, happened to be in Truro on the day the precept for the elections arrived, and had promptly offered himself as a candidate. A tinner was broadly defined. It included anyone connected with mining from the tributors (the freelance prospectors) to the merchants or gentlemen who put up the capital to sink a new shaft. The stannators were always gentlemen of property in the districts of the four districts of the Stannaries, elected by the mayors and corporations of the principal towns. Here was a candidate for election whom Bath could not hope to overawe, and whose friendshp with the Godolphins made it very likely that, if elected, he would act as a Treasury agent. In a rage, Bath mustered his dependents at Stow, his family seat, and gave them one clear instruction: the election of the Bishop was to be stopped at all costs. Despite his efforts carried out 'with such a violence of passion as if the honour of his family and the preservation of his estates were now at stake'[14] Trelawny was elected a stannator for the Truro district by nine votes to six. The violent reaction to his candidature alerted Trelawny that something underhand was proposed. Once he learnt what it was, he wrote to Sir William Godolphin, explained the situation at length, and suggested that if the Lord Treasurer and Lord Godolphin would instruct him what price for tin the Treasury though reasonable, he, together with his friends, would try to insist on it when the Parliament met. Records of the Stannary Parliament have been lost, so the outcome of this affair is not certain.

Apparently the proposed high price was not adopted, nor was the farm renewed.[15] Trelawny was to raise the plight of the Tinners with William and Mary in the spring of 1690 and, in response, the Treasury was ordered to buy up as much tin as it could at that time. James II severely admonished his Lord Warden who was allowed to make his peace with the King. However, Bath arranged to have the nine gentleman tinners who voted for the Bishop, dismissed from the Commission of the Peace and would make no peace with the Bishop of Bristol. Lord Lansdown personally struck the Bishop's name from the Commission of the Peace for Devonshire in 1692.[16]

Faced with this Granville enmity the Trelawnys and the Godolphins drew closer together. Lord Godolphin consented to be godfather to the Bishop's eldest child, Charlotte (born 12 March, 1 688).[17] In later life, Sidney Godolphin's natural aversion to clergymen never extended to the Bishop. The two men had much in common. Godolphin, 'never in the way, never out of the way' was a hard-working administrator who eschewed self-publicity. He admired in others the same qualities and found them in the Bishop. They were both Cornishmen forced by their careers to spend much of their working lives outside Cornwall. They understood each others sensitivity to criticism; they shared similar views on major political issues. In an electoral alliance what Godolphin lacked, Trelawny could supply. Godolphin enjoyed the race meetings at Newmarket, but did not enjoy company otherwise. Trelawny on the other hand was a sociable man. he enjoyed the hearing and repeating of good stories.[18] He could do in Cornwall what Godolphin had neither the time or temperament to do. He could extend the parliamentary influence of the two families. A misunderstanding over the appointment of customs officers at Looe and Fowey toward the end of William's reign caused Trelawny to write a long letter of complaint to one of the commissioners of customs, Charles Godolphin. Written in a towering rage, the letter has the ring of honesty *in ira veritas;* and gives a rare insight into the Bishop's political motivation up to Lord Godolphin's death. 'I did not offer myself, my family, my interest everywhere to my Lord Godolphin', wrote Trelawny, 'as a person that really wanted or abmbitiously courted so sure a dependence..... I devoted myself to his Lordship because I found him to be a person of great wisdom and integrity and that as to the public, our principles suited though our fortunes and stations did not. I was as humbly his Lordship's servant when he was no minister as I can be now he is, and I hope will be for the Kingdom's sake these fifty years'.[19] In his political career, Bishop Trelawny has been described as 'pliant' and as a 'trimmer'. His conduct, in fact, was remarkably consistent bearing in mind that after his Church, his political loyalties were formed by Cornish affairs.

Immediately after the Revolution the Trelawny-Godolphin alliance made no mark. The Bishop campaigned unsuccessfully against old Hugh Boscawen in the county election in 1690, and his borough influence still did not extend beyond the two Looes. Both were filled with his own relatives and he refused to oblige either the Earl of Rochester, George, prince of Denmark or Sir William Trumbull.[20] Now he was bishop of Exeter he had some influence over the Cornish parish clergy and the borough of Penryn. Alexander Pendarves, who represented Penryn in Parliament from 1689 to 1705, had active Trelawny support. The Bishop's influence was with the mayor and corporation rather than with the scot and lot electorate. He failed to secure the return of a Godolphin in 1695 or to keep out the Whig, James Vernon. Nevertheless his influence with the corporation could not but increase with the passage of time. The Bishop of Exeter was lord of the manor, and Trelawny deliberately let the corporation lease on the town properties hang on one life throughout his episcopate, granting a fresh lease of three lives only after he knew he was to be translated to Winchester.[21] In 1689 this was for the future. Nothing looked like eroding the influence of the Earl of Bath.

The Granville ascendancy began to slip in the summer of 1690. The Tinners, who had been noted for their loyalty to the Crown a generation earlier, had been soured by the continued recession and government inaction. In June the militia was mobilized to prevent riots. For King William and his Dutch advisors, accustomed to guage the level of civilisation by the attention paid to civic discipline, the reputation of a Lord Warden who allowed such discontent to get out of hand at a time of national crisis was severely tarnished. The Granvilles had been leading supporters of James II. Could there be a more sinister motive behind the Tinners' disaffection? The Trelawnys also had close connections with James but now the Bishop was anxious to distance himself from his political past. When an Exeter clergyman baptised a baby with the name James the Just, Trelawny promptly sent for him and forced him to sign a recantation and forwarded it to Whitehall as proof of his loyalty to the new order. Several important Jacobite agents were at large in Exeter in 1690. Trelawny learnt of their presence, alerted the Council and was directed to have them arrested. The Earl of Nottingham conveyed the King's personal thanks for the services the Bishop was rendering.[22] When Trelawny learnt of other Jacobite agents in Exeter in 1692 he again wrote to the Council for authority to effect an arrest, pointing out that if Lansdown had not struck his name off the list of magistrates he could have issued the warrant himself. He did not fail to underline the fact that his letter would have been unnecessary if it were not for Lansdown's vindictiveness, and went on to regale Nottingham with an account of the irresolute and incompetent

118

leadership Lansdown was displaying as Lord Lieutenant at a time when a French fleet was in the Channel and a French invasion expected daily. Trelawny also pointed out that the officers appointed to muster the Devon militia were all known Jacobites. He implied that Granville loyalty lay overseas.[23] The King and his Ministers felt insecure and were ready to mistrust everyone. Bath's brother, the Dean of Durham, had chosen to share James' exile in France in March, 1689. Bath was a recipient of a letter from James requesting him to cross to France to witness his queen's lying-in in March, 1692. Trelawny's letter gave further confirmation of Granville Jacobitism.

The Granvilles were left alone until the following year. In March Lansdown offended the King by importuning for payment of arrears due to him for his recent journey to Spain as ambassador. Reprimanded by the King publicly he resigned his place as a gentleman of the Bedchamber.[24] In April he was dismissed from the lord-lieutenancies of Devon and Cornwall. Granville's decline from royal favour gained pace. Acting on a hint from the King in January, 1694, Bath resigned the governorship of Plymouth. In April, 1696 he was deprived of his two lord-lieutenancies. In May he was requested to sell the Lord Wardenship. Cornishmen noted the erosion of Granville influence and the Trelawnys speedily moved to fill the power vacuum in local parliamentary elections that this erosion created. In the General Election of 1695 men noted the contrast between the inertia of the Earl of Bath and the active campaigning of the Bishop of Exeter.[25] In addition to East and West Looe, the Trelawnys nominated one Member of Parliament for Bodmin and secured the return of one Member for Liskeard.[26]

Despite the King's gratitude for his services, the Bishop was never really *persona grata* at Court. His High Church sympathies saw to that. He had been included on the Commission of 1689 appointed to revise the liturgy but he never attended its meetings. He was not invited to join the Commission of English bishops and deans to consider the estates of the Church in Ireland.[27] Nor was it likely that William had forgotten that the Anne Trelawny he dismissed from his wife's service at the Hague in October, 1685 for her part in relaying domestic gossip from the Orange household to James II's ambassador was the Bishop's sister.[28] His efforts to make himself acceptable to the King were nearly wrecked by the behaviour of his brothers, who seemed, at times, to be trying to nullify any favourable impression the head of the family was trying to create. Major-general Charles Trelawny had grown increasingly restive with the behaviour of the military Higher Command in Ireland. He resented the criticisms of the English officers voiced by Dutch generals in the Irish campaign of 1689 to 1690; criticisms which he considered unjust. The poor equipment supplied and the neglect of his own regiment by the Treasury roused him to fury.[29] Although Bishop Sprat tried hard to dissuade him, he persisted in resigning his post of gentleman of the Bedchamber and the colonelship of his regiment. His brother, the Bishop, had to assure the Secretary of State that the resignations were entirely the General's own decision and in no way implied disloyalty to the King.[30] Charles was one of the most experienced and competent officers in the English army. He had commanded the brigade which turned the battle of the Boyne in William's favour and had been promoted major-general at the siege of Cork. His active concern for the comfort of his troops made him very popular with the Army. The public criticism of the Dutch Command which his resignation implied did nothing to diminish that popularity so the Government did not have much hesitation in appointing him to overall command of all regular troops stationed in the south west.[31] William agreed to the appointment, but he did not agree willingly. His subsequent appointment of Charles to be governor of Plymouth in July, 1695 was probably motivated by a desire to replace a Granville with an opponent and not a friend rather than any particular desire to show the General any favour. If anything, Henry Trelawny was more outspoken than Charles. In the spring of 1697 he acted as spokesman of a deputation of English colonels who waited on the King to protest at the lack of shoes and stockings for the men of their regiments about to embark for Flanders. Their demands were described as 'unreasonable' and the King dismissed them angrily. William considered it expedient to promote Henry to command the brigade,[32] nevertheless. William was unable to ignore Charles and Henry but he could afford to ignore their elder brother and did so throughout his reign.

The appointment of Charles Trelawny to be governor of Plymouth came as a surprise to the family. When he learnt of the King's intention in April, the Bishop wrote a letter couched in terms of guarded gratitude to the Earl of Portland, offering the interest of his family to the King in the most general terms, and praising extravagantly only those aspects of royal policy of which he approved. Portland's successful negotiation of the preliminaries to the Peace of Ryswick gave the Bishop a chance to write a second letter of thanks for favours to his brothers and for securing the Peace with France which he, like all Tories, wanted at that time. The laboured effusiveness of the letter suggests that Trelawny did not relish the task he had set himself. He was not anxious to receive promotion for himself or his family at the hands of Ministers of whom he strongly disapproved. Again Charles proved to be something of a thorn in the flesh because he was rumoured to be a candidate for the post of Lord Warden which went to Lord Radnor.[33]

The governorship of Plymouth was a significant boost to Trelawny prestige in parliamentary elections and a useful compliment to the growing influence Jonathan had as Bishop of Exeter. By 1696 he had all his major expensive legal battles behind him, and he was in full control of his diocese. The Major-general's control of the citadel of Plymouth strengthened the interest of the Tories on the corporation and of a cadet branch of the family in the Town. In the General Election of 1698 the Trelawnys wrested the second seat at Liskeard out of the hands of the Bullers and held on to their other gains of 1695. Charles and Henry Trelawny were returned for Plymouth, unseating John Granville, Bath's second son, in the process. The Bishop could now make skilful use of his episcopal patronage to enlist the support at election times of a spread of people with local influence. The deputy registrar of the consistory court was expected to canvass for the Bishop's candidate at Launceston. Canon Kendall did the same at Lostwithiel: Canon James influenced his local contacts at Liskeard. Francis Cooke was instructed to arrange a smooth institution and induction for Dr. George Hicks to the rectory of Whimple because Trelawny hoped to use Hicks to wrest Fowey wholly out of the Bedford interest. Many clergy could be relied upon to vote as their Bishop desired.[34]

When the Earl of Bath died on 22 August, 1701 the world learnt of the financial mess he left to his heirs. The long legal battle for the dukedom of Albermarle had been ruinously expensive. On 4 September, the second Earl was found dead in his bedchamber 'wounded in the head, with a brace of pistols by him, one discharged; 'tis said he had been melancholy for some time past'. The coroner's jury found a verdict of death by misadventure, but suspicion remained that the Earl had committed suicide.[35] He left a son five years of age. Temporarily the Granvilles were without a leader. John Buller of Morval died in January, 1698. His cousin, Francis Buller of Shillingham died of smallpox in March, 1701. With the death of Hugh Boscawen two months later there passed from the Cornish political scene the last representatives of the Civil War generation. The next generation of Bullers and Boscawens were Church of England men and although not necessarily Tories, would not feel compelled to oppose the Bishop on religious grounds. In the General Elections of 1700 and 1701 the Trelawnys consolidated and extended their influence. They captured both the seats at Bodmin and the Members for Launceston were returned with their support. They secured one Member for Fowey. From about this date the Trelawnys assumed responsibility for deciding which two Godolphins should be returned at Helston. Lostwithiel came definitely within Trelawny influence after 1702, by which date the Bishop could make his proud boast to the Earl of Nottingham

121

'I may without vanity say I have effectually served [the true interest of our English Monarchy] this session, having sent eleven members (whereof I shall answer for all but one which I need not because the Court must answer for him)'.[36]

The Bishop's influence extended well beyond the Cornish boroughs by this time. By 1700 the Knights for the Shire had his backing, and he was beginning to influence the choice for Devon. He was taking an interest in elections at Plympton, lending support to the Hearnes at Dartmouth, and even the voters of Seymour's own stronghold of Totnes acknowledged the weight of his opinion. Within Cornwall, the Robartes family had some working arrangement with the Trelawnys by 1698.[37] In the early years of Anne's reign no other family in Cornwall was in a position to challenge the Trelawny-Godolphin alliance and the Bishop had begun a methodical long term assault on the Seymour influence in Exeter itself, looking forward to the day when he could take control of the city, the greatest prize of all.

A combination of its location in the Exe Valley and of the social structure of the gentry in Devon gave Exeter a commanding position in the political life of the county. Living, for the most part, on modest incomes on their family estates, the Devonshire gentry could not afford to go regularly to Bath or London for 'the season'. The geographical accessibility of Exeter made it the substitute for 'the Town'. It was recognised that the way Exeter voted in a general election affected the voting pattern in the rest of Devon. To influence Exeter's electorate was a formidable task. The numbers voting in a general election could be as many as fifteen hundred.[38] Exeter was governed by a small, self-perpetuating, oligarchy of merchants who kept the ownership of all city property in their own hands. The surest way to influence the electorate was to win the favour and support of these city fathers who disposed of most local patronage. Bishop Trelawny courted the city merchants assiduously. He gave his services in Parliament to help forward any piece of legislation which affected their interests. In his acceptance speech at the Guildhall in 1698, Sir Bartholomew Shower waxed lyrical in his description of the Bishop's efforts on behalf of Exeter in connection with the Wool Bill. In 1700 Trelawny delayed his departure from Westminster until he was certain no bill would be brought forward to make the Exe navigable.[39] An enlargement of the franchise following a disputed election in 1689 had included all office holders, so the Bishop could reasonably expect to sway the votes of the officers of the ecclesiastical and admiralty courts. He looked to expand this narrow base by cultivating individuals. 'Is Mr. Carthew of Exeter a churchman and right in elections?' he enquired of Francis Cooke, 'because he has been recommended to me for a favour'.[40] A Bishop's party was in the making by the end of William's reign, but it had a long way to go before any challenge could be offered to the dominating influence of Sir Edward Seymour.

The accession of Anne brought fresh possibilities. The new Lord Treasurer lent his assistance in the matter of government appointments. At the end of William's reign Trelawny found the local customs officers at Exeter distinctly unaccommodating: by 1706 Lord Poulett complained that they were all the Bishop's creatures. The death of Edward Lake in 1704 gave the Bishop the opportunity to retain the archdeaconry of Exeter in his own hands in order to strengthen his surveillance of the clergy living in Exeter who might use the pulpits to canvass against any candidate who had their Bishop's backing. When some of Lord Godolphin's supporters wanted his son to stand for Exeter in 1705 Trelawny was well enough acquainted with the inclinations of the electorate to know that he would have lost by three hundred votes.[41] The year 1705 was a distinctly inauspicious one in which to enter a direct bid for control, because the relationship between the Bishop and the City Chamber was going through a delicate phase. The cathedral Close formed part of a baronial liberty in the heart of Exeter known as St. Stephen's Fee. The Bishop was lord of the manor and denizens of the Close believed that they lived in an enclave safe from both the jurisdiction of both city magistrate and city guild. In the summer of 1704 two officers of the mayor's court had entered a house in the Close in order to affect an arrest. This was a blatant infringement of the bishop's manorial rights which the Dean and Chapter urged Trelawny to challenge. This placed the Bishop in a dilemma. He did not wish to offend the City Fathers whose goodwill he had been cultivating for so long. On the other hand he could hardly withdraw support from the Dean and Chapter just as they were coming to grips with the problem of disturbances by the citizenry in and around the cathedral. He instructed the Dean to negotiate with the Mayor and members of the City Chamber. Wake held two meetings with some of them in September 1704 and reported to the Bishop that they acknowledged the existence of the Fee but were reluctant to make any public admission of guilt. After debating the arrest on 17 October the only resolution the Chamber passed was an order to the officers not to arrest anyone in St. Stephen's Fee in future.

Trelawny's legal advisor deemed this resolution an insufficient acknowledgement in Law. He drew up a strongly worded statement freely acknowledging the infringement of the Bishop's rights, and recommended that the City Chamber affix their common seal to it. In January Trelawny sent a copy of this statement to the Mayor with a covering letter in which he requested, in the politest possible way, that the Chamber endorse it. This was a remarkable lapse of judgement on his part. No self respecting city council was going to tolerate an outsider dictating a resolution for them to

123

pass. The Mayor sent the Bishop a polite refusal with the invitation to listen to his legal advisor when next the Bishop came to Exeter.[43]

Trelawny had his hands full of general election business throughout the summer so he was unable to meet with the City's legal advisor. He wrote to the new Mayor in October repeating his demand that the Chamber endorse the legal statement and, for the first time, threatening an action at the assizes if it did not. The City Fathers deeply resented this ultimatum, and showed it by resurrecting an old bone of contention between them and the Dean and Chapter. The Mayor's sword bearer ceased to drop his blade and doff his cap on entering the choir at the head of a civic procession. When the Dean and the Bishop protested, the Mayor and Councilmen boycotted cathedral services.[44]

Church and City remained deadlocked over the whole question of the Liberty of St. Stephen's Fee until Bishop Blackall succeeded Trelawny. Then the affair was resolved without loss of face for either party at a meeting in July, 1708 at the home of Nicholas Wood in Exmouth.[45] This wealth city cutler was the leader of the opposition in the Chamber to the Bishop. Trelawny revenged himself on Wood by having him dismissed from the receivership of the Land Tax in Devon. Wood feared further harassment at the hands of the customs officers and sought the protection of the Lord Lieutenant, Lord Poulett. Poulett wrote to Harley who consulted Godolphin. The Lord Treasurer pointed out that Trelawny was in such a good mood following the announcement of his translation to Winchester that he could easily be persuaded to forgive Nicholas Wood.[46]

The Bishop may indeed have ceased to persecute Wood but he had alienated the one man whose support was vital if he was to gain a controlling interest in parliamentary elections in Exeter. Wood was very popular in the City and could be assured of sufficient votes to be returned to Parliament himself. In the bye-election in April, 1708 following the death of Sir Edward Seymour, John Harris, a moderate Whig, was returned. Wood had declared his intention to stand for Parliament the previous year, so Harris may have been a compromise candidate put up in order to keep Wood out. If so, it was to no avail. At the General Election of 1708, Harris was returned with Nicholas Wood who unseated the Tory, John Snell.[47] Faced with the choice between seeking to gain control of Exeter and supporting the rights of the Church, Trelawny opted for the latter. It meant that full control of the city of Exeter was a prize which eluded him.

124

1. MS. Tanner xxviii, f.139, T to Sancroft, undated.

2. B.L., Egerton MSS. 2618, f.197, T to Clarke, 17 August, 1707.

3. Add. MSS. 28052, f.100, Charles Trelawny to Sidney Godolphin, 7 November, 1700; T.C., Clarke Corresp. 749, f.810, Charles Trelawny to Clarke, 2 July, 1691.

4. D.N.B., *sub nomine,* John Granville; *The Diary of John Evelyn,* ed. E.S. de Beer, (Oxford, 1955), iv.444.

5. U.N.L., Portland MSS., PwA 2263, Copy of Commissino, 20 November, 1688; 2264, f.31a, Prince of Orange to Earl of Bath, undated.

6. *J.R.I.C.,* ii (1866-7), pp.63-4; Add. MSS. 40772, ff.135, 137, 164; H.R.O., A/10/A, Bundle Two, T to Hedges, undated; same to same, 14 August, 1708.

7. Buller BO/23/73, Philip Hicks to Francis Buller, 15 October, 1690; same to same, 16 October, 1690.

8. *Cal. S.P. Dom.* Feb.-Dec. 1685, p.167, T to Sunderland, 22 February.

9. U.N.L., Philipps MSS. iii 8555 (PwV53), Blathwayt to Sir Robert Southwell, 13 March, 1686.

10. *Cal. S.P. Dom., loc. cit.,* p.185, Sunderland to T, 8 June, 1685.

11. 'Trelawny Papers', *Camden Miscellany,* ii (1853), pp.16-7, T to Sunderland, 14 June, 1686.

12. Add. MSS. 28052, f.96, T to Sidney Godolphin, 10 July, 1685.

13. Whetter, *Cornwall in the 17th Century,* p.77.

14. Exeter City Libr. 53/10/1, T to Sir William Godolphin, 12 October, 1686.

15. D.R.O., Cooke Corresp., Anstis to Cooke, 4 March, 1690; *Original Letters to John Ellis* (2nd series) iv, letter ccclxxiv, 24 November, 1688.

16. H.M.C., *Finch MSS.,* iv. 142, T to Nottingham, 11 May, 1692.

17. C.T., p.41.

18. *Memoirs of Thomas, earl of Ailesbury,* i. pp.227-8.

19. *J.R.I.C.,* iii (1869-70), p.18, T to Charles Godolphin, undated (but 8 February, 1701).

20. *Portland MSS.,* iii. 435, Edward Harley to Sir Edward Harley, 4 March, 1690; C.T., p.193, Prince George to T, 8 February, 1689; *Downshire MSS.,* i. 455, T to Sprat, undated (but June, 1694).

21. Add. MSS. 28052, f.94, T to Sidney Godolphin, 2 Novembr [1695]; D.C.O., Rental of Bishopric of Exeter taken 15 September, 1688; D.R.O., Chanter Box 4, 11034.

22. *Cal. S.P. Dom.* May 1690-Oct. 1691, p.16, Nottingham to T, 22 May; p.30, same to same, 11 June. *Finch MSS.*, iii. 379, Privy Council minute dated 11 June, 1690; 441, minute dated 1 August, 1690.

23. *Finch MSS.*, iv. 143, T to Nottingham, 11 May, 1692.

24. Luttrell, iii. 65.

25. B.L., Portland Loan 29/188, f.94, Francis Freke to Robert Harley, 22 October, 1695.

26. Buller BO/23/72/9.

27. T.J. Fawcett, *The Liturgy of Comprehension,* p.29; T.C., Clarke Corresp. 749, f.281, Edisbury to Clarke, 10 November [1690].

28. Henri and Barbara van der Zee, *William and Mary* (1973), pp.200-04.

29. T.C., Clarke Corresp. 749, ff.642, 810, 844a, 914, letters of Charles Trelawny to George Clarke, secretary of war in Ireland 1691.

30. C.T., p.271, Sprat to T, undated (but January, 1692); *Finch MSS.*, iv.134, T to Nottingham, 13 May, 1692.

31. *Finch MSS.*, iv. 161, Nottingham to Blathwayt, 16 May, 1692.

32. H.M.C. *Huntingdon MSS.*, ii. 290 [Eames] to Huntingdon, 25 March, 1697; Luttrell, iv. 231.

33. U.N.L., Portland MSS., PwA 1405, T to Portland, 22 April [1696]; 1406, same to same, 8 November, 1697; Luttrell, v.107.

34. D.R.O., Cooke Corresp., T to Cooke, 2 October, 1700, 2 December [1700]; Buller BC/25/8, John James to John Buller, 5 March, 1701; BO/23/72/35, memorandum dated 30 August, 1698; 23/65 Poll Book for Knights of the shire for Cornwall, 1705.

35. Luttrell, v.87; *Diary of John Evelyn, op.cit.,* v.476.

36. Cooke Coreesp., T to Cooke, 2 December, 1700; *E.C.,* iii. 15, Sprat to T, 14 January, 1701; Add. MSS. 28052, f.100, Charles Trelawny to Sidney Godolphin, 7 November, 1700; H.M.C., *Coke MSS.,* p.14, Bromley to Coke, 21 July, 1702; Add. MSS. 29584, f.95, T to Nottingham, 17 August, 1702.

37. Cooke Corresp., T to Cooke, 21 December, 1700, 11 January, 1701; Buller BO/23/72/25, John Buller to Earl of Radnor, 19 November, 1698; BO/23/72/29, P. Lyne to Buller, 31 December, 1698.

38. A.A. Brockett, 'The Political and Social Influence of Exeter Dissenters', *T.D.A.,* xciii (1961), pp.184-93.

126

39. *Cal. S.P. Dom.,* Jan.-Dec. 1698, p.379; Cooke Corresp., T to Cooke, 23 March [1700].

40. Cooke Corresp., T to Cooke, 2 November [1700].

41. Wake MSS. xvii, f.98, Blackburne to Wake, 6 June, 1705.

42. C.T., p.287, Wake to T, 17 September, 1704; Exeter City Libr., Chamber Minutes Act Book 13 (1684-1713), p.375.

43. D.R.O., P.R. 13, Box 517, T to Mayor and Chamber, 11 January, 1705; Mayor to T, 17 February, 1705.

44. Exeter Cathedral Libr., Dean and Chapter Records 4536/4/4, Webber to Edisbury, undated.

45. Exeter Chamber Minutes Act Book 13, pp.427, 429, 432; Exeter D. and C. 4536/4/6, Copy of Agreement.

46. *Portland MSS.,* iv.420, Poulett to Harley, 16 June, 1707; H.M.C., *Bath MSS.,* i. 175, Godolphin to Harley, 20 June, 1707.

47. J.J. Alexander, 'Exeter Members of Parliament', *T.D.A.* lxii (1930), p.186.

CHAPTER NINE

The Granville Revenge

Among the batch of dismissals and appointments at the beginning of Anne's reign, the Lord Wardenship of the Stannaries was taken away from the Earl of Radnor and given to John Granville, later Lord Granville of Potheridge. It was an act of generosity by the Queen to a family whose loyalty she appreciated. Lord Granville was willing to cooperate with Lord Godolphin. He steered through a proposal in the Stannary Parliament in 1703 to sell 16,000 tons of tin annually to the Crown at a price of seventy shillings a hundredweight. This massive government support for the industry was Godolphin's last great service to the Tinners. Granville made no attempt to challenge the Godolphin - Trelawny alliance. In 1704 Bishop and Lord Treasurer planned to sweep the board in the Cornish boroughs at the next election.[1] Godolphin was determined to revenge himself on all who had voted for the attempt to tack clauses against Occasional Conformity onto a supply bill. In April, 1705 he himself replaced Lord Granville as Lord Lieutenant of Cornwall and made his own son Lord Warden. Trelawny also took a further office in preparation for the General Election. When Edward Lake died Trelawny held the archdeaconry of Exeter *in commendam* so he could the better control the occupants of the pulpits of some Exeter city churches.[2] The task the two had set themselves was not an easy one. They wanted to see sufficient moderate Whigs returned in order to ensure the Ministry a working majority in the House of Commons. Marlborough and Godolphin moved toward the Whigs because they were convinced of the need to prosecute the land war against France. Trelawny was equally convinced of that policy. His sermon before the Queen in St. Paul's cathedral at the State Service of Thanksgiving for Allied victories in 1702 was imbued with the Old Testament prophetic consciousness of history. God had decreed the punishment of Louis XIV. The French King was a text book example of a ruler who disobeys and neglects the ordinances of God. Guided by divine Providence the Allies were destined to do to France what Assyria had done to Israel.[3]

In order to account for this attitude toward France, so

128

uncharacteristic of Tory high churchmen, one must recall again the family background. First, there was the long friendship between the Churchills and the Trelawnys; two families of professional soldiers at a time when that career was socially unfashionable, both of which had had first hand experience of the military power of France. Secondly, geographical isolation did not breed insularity among the Cornish. A sea-faring people having racial and linguistic links with Brittany never viewed events on the Continent with the indifference of the more parochially-minded English. They knew how British merchants and their families were treated by Louis XIV's officials.[4] The Revocation of the Edict of Nantes had a considerable effect on the south west of England. Many Huguenot refugees from Saintange, Auray and Poitou settled in Devon, bringing with them tales of dispossession and military brutality.[5] As a young bishop Trelawny had been concerned with raising money for the refugees. He continued to give financial support to refugee clergy throughout his life, and he and his wife offered a home to Claudia Sanxay, daughter of the first Huguenot minister of St. Olave's, Exeter, after her father died.[6] When he described the Old Pretender as one having 'as much cruelty toward protestants as the French tyrant hath given example of'[7] he was still evoking that lively fear of military despotism he had learnt from conversations with his brothers and with Huguenot refugees some twenty-five years earlier. Modern historians have tended to play down the importance of James II's Army as an instrument of government but, in recent years, Dr. Childs has demonstrated how wrong they are. He concludes that 'the ideal of government by the sword fits well with James's political character'.[8] Thirdly, on a more personal level, Trelawny was convinced that his opposition to James II would never be forgotten or forgiven. He still held the conviction years later, when he wrote to Lord Townshend, secretary of state, early in the reign of George I,

> 'believe me, my Lord, if they [the active Jacobites] keep
> their heads on their shoulders, you & all the King's
> friends must part with yours. I shall give mine for gone as
> the King's & your Lordship's'.[9]

Whenever men speculated on the qualifications to be looked for in the next bishop of Winchester, they tended to place political affiliation high on the list. Peter Mews, the aged and infirm bishop of Winchester, was a long time dying. Several churchmen had an eye on the rich rent rolls of that diocese. It was thought that the Whig Junto wanted the post for Gilbert Burnet, and Sir John Packington promoted a bill in the House of Commons in 1701 prohibiting translations of bishops very much with an eye to blocking Burnet's promotion.[10] The death of Bishop Mews came without warning. A clergyman mistook the old man's hand signal and administered medicine from the wrong bottle.[11] The death occurred on Saturday, 9 November, 1706. In London it was assumed that either Bishop Trelawny or Dr. Godolphin, the Lord Treasurer's brother, would succeed Mews. Writing to the Duke of Newcastle the following Tuesday, Harley thought that Trelawny would get the see. Queen Anne kept all major ecclesiastical appointments in her own hands and it was suspected that Trelawny was her choice. Trelawny, not Compton, had been chosen to give the sermon at the great Service of Thanksgiving in St. Paul's, held on 12 November, 1702, and the deliberate snub to Trelawny engineered in the Lords by the Whigs in deferring a vote of thanks until the sermon was printed suggests that the Junto feared that further perferment for him might be intended. In 1706, Godolphin only hoped to influence the Queen to delay her decision, and in a letter to the Duchess of Marlborough he hints that Trelawny had some kind of claim. Godolphin's instinct at that juncture was to keep the diocese vacant for as long as possible, but Anne's decision was known within a month.[12]

By the summer of 1705, Exeter clergy assumed Trelawny would get Winchester, but others had not given up all hope if Colonel Wyndham could tell Thomas Pitt early the following year that 'the expectations of the fat bishopric of Winchester..... is a great softener of obstinate dispositions'.[13] Contemporaries looked at the appointment through political eyes. If a survivor from pre-revolutionary days could be given so wealthy a prize at a time when the Ministry was pressing on with Whig appointments, and when knowledge of Trelawny's impending translation was known within days of the Earl of Sunderland's appointment as secretary of state (3 December, 1706), then this old High Church bishop must have betrayed his principles and done a deal with the Ministry. His rebellious clergy broadly hinted as much in 1705 and, by 1706, no vilification was adequate to convey the contempt felt for Trelawny by extreme High Church Tories.[14] In one sense, Trelawny's contemporaries were correct. A deal had been struck, but it was one made long before 1704. It was a pact arising out of the rivalries of Cornish landed families, and it had been consolidated by agreement on how the interests of the Nation and the Protestant Succession could best be served.

This translation to the diocese of Winchester gave Trelawny more money to spend on electioneering but it brought some loss in efficiency. He was forced to spend more time away from Cornwall and had fewer opportunities for cementing those personal contacts so essential to the borough manager's art. The city of Exeter is an example of this. Forced into making a choice between defending the privileges of the Church in Exeter and continuing to cultivate the goodwill of the City Chamber, Trelawny chose the former, as we have seen above. His translation took place in the middle of the dispute, removing him from Exeter and depriving him of an opportunity to influence the subsequent course of events. The return of John Harris at the bye-election and General Election of 1708 probably marked the highest point of electoral influence achieved by Trelawny in the South West.

If the years from 1705 to 1708 saw this electoral influence at its height, the next two general elections witnessed its collapse. The political climate was largely responsible. The Ministry's inept handling of the Sacheverell affair, and a growing weariness with a war which had largely achieved its aims, caused a revulsion of feeling among the electorate which no amount of threats or bribes could stem. Trelawny had hitched his fortunes to the political career of Lord Godolphin: when he fell from office Trelawny's reputation sank with him. However, Trelawny influence could not have collapsed as dramatically as it did if there had not been an alternative family in Cornwall ready and waiting to take over. The amenable Lord Granville of Potheridge died on 3 December, 1707. His death enabled George Granville, nephew of the first earl of Bath, to take up the reins of leadership of the Granville family and, in doing this, he was aided and abetted by Robert Harley.

At first George Granville had accepted the realities of power and had been willing to solicit the Lord Treasurer for employment. After two years of being fobbed off with vague promises, Granville's patience ran out and he offered his services to Robert Harley instead.[15] Devious by nature, a consummate politician, Harley could not resist the temptation to intrigue against a Lord Treasurer he hoped, one day, to replace. Despite the remarkable intelligence network at Harley's disposal he was ignorant of west country politics. The document he drew up in February, 1705, looking forward to the General Election to be held later that year, may show considerable understanding of the political make-up of other counties in England, but it displays an uncertain knowledge of Devon and no knowledge of Cornwall beyond the bare fact that it was the domain of the Lord Treasurer.[16]

Possessed with Granville's offer of service, Harley began to make enquiries. Defoe was despatched to the West Country in the summer of 1705. His visit, although hastened by a suspicious justice of the peace, proved most useful. Defoe supplied a clearer picture of Devon politics, including those of Plymouth, which was still a Trelawny borough. His report on Cornwall was brief and positively misleading. He penetrated no further west then Bodmin and stayed no more than four days. The Cornish were giving little away to inquisitive strangers, and all Defoe was told was that Lord Granville controlled somes seats and the Lord Treasurer many more.[17] The report was sufficient to satisfy Harley that he had been right to cultivate George Granville's friendship for use at some future time. Carefully, Harley played Granville along. In April the Lord Treasurer took the Lord Lieutenancy of Cornwall and made his son Lord Warden. In the summer Harley hinted to George Granville that the Lord Treasurer had something to offer him. Granville waited on the Lord Treasurer several times, but Godolphin said nothing. One suspects that Godolphin knew nothing of what Harley had hinted on his behalf. After the triumph of the Lord Treasurer's supporters at the polls, 'a certain undertaker in our county' (probably Boscawen) had announced his intention of having Granville dismissed from his governorship of Pendennis Castle. Harley ensured it did not happen, thus placing Granville under further obligation to him.[18] Harley continued discreetly to press Granville's case for promotion of some kind throughout the summer, but the Lord Treasurer was not enthusiastic. Unperturbed, Harley ceased to concern himself with Granville's present prospects, and began to consider in more detail the prospects of his future use. In October he asked Godolphin for a list of Cornish Members of Parliament. Godolphin furnished him with the list that Hugh Boscawen had given him, and unwittingly played Harley's game by telling him that Boscawen would be pleased to give him any further information required.[19] No evidence has survived to indicate whether or not Harley took up this offer, but it seems unlikely that he would have let slip the opportunity to learn more about the management of the recent Cornish elections, especially when the opportunity was so trustingly handed to him on a plate.

The cause of the sudden breach between Godolphin and Harley has never been explained to anyone's entire satisfaction. Harley's most recent biographer quotes the likeliest explanation, namely, that Harley and his friends intended to overthrow Godolphin, but he has reservations and points out that neither in his correspondence with Abigail Hill nor with his family does Harley hint of any plot.[20] Throughout 1707 Marlborough and Godolphin grew increasingly suspicious of Harley. They thought they detected his advice behind ever obstructive move by the Queen. When George Granville emerged as head of the Granville family on the death of Lord Granville of Potheridge at the end of that year, it is possible that his electoral alliance with Harley could be concealed no longer. Godolphin's last letter to Harley concludes 'I am very sorry for what has happened to lose the good opinion I had so much inclination to have of you, but I cannot help seeing and hearing nor believing my senses. I am very far from deserving it from you. God forgive you!' Some discovery caused Godolphin to write so blistering a sentence. Without denying the charge of contemporaries that Harley was plotting to overthrow the Lord Treasurer, Godolphin's discovery that Harley had been feeding a Granville

132

information of use in preparing for elections could account both for the bitterness of Godolpin's sense of betrayal and for Harley's protestations of injured innocence. Harley did not know, nor could he be expected to understand how keenly a Godolphin felt about his family honour. Cornish families confined their infighting to their own county, presenting a different front to the outside world. Four years later George Granville pointed out to Harley his ignorance in these matters:

> 'You may depend upon it nothing can be more prejudicial to you than the appointment of Lord Radnor as Lord Lieutenant of Cornwall, for however that family may be under your direction here [i.e. London] there is that general aversion to it there that they will give everything for lost if such a step is taken.'[21]

At the end of January, 1708, Godolphin made his sudden break with Harley and the Secretary went into the political wilderness on 11 February. Harley began at once to prepare for his return to power, slowly gathering together and coordination the efforts of his various supporters. At the General Election of 1708, George Granville worked hard. He recovered Camelford but confessed to a poor showing for his candidates elsewhere.[22] The death of Colonel Kendall in July meant a bye-election at Lostwithiel, and Harley's correspondence concerning this matter shows Granville and Atterbury trying to persuade Canon Kendall to nominate Henry St. John. The attempt failed but the tide of opinion among the Cornish gentry was moving in Granville's favour. Money was scarce; harvests were poor; prices were high and the war dragged on. Then, at the end of the year, Dr. Sacheverell preached his famous sermon. Granville busied himself cementing new alliances while Harley engineered a palace revolution in the summer of 1710. The Queen dismissed her Lord Treasurer.

With Godolphin's dismissal, the Trelawny-Godolphin influence began to crumble. Within days of the announcement, Francis Robartes placed his control of Tintagel and his interest in Lostwithiel at Harley's disposal with a promise to write again if he had any chance of influencing the elections at Bodmin and Tregony. At the General Election that autumn, Granville was chosen with John Trevanion for the county to the cry of

> 'Trevanion and Granville sound as a bell
> For the Queen and the Church and Sacheverell'.[23]

while the borough returns were equally satisfactory.

The Trelawnys were caught off-side. On many issues they were as Tory as they had always been. The Bishop was furious when he discovered that one of his nominees for Liskeard, John Dolben, was leading prosecutor of Sacheverell in the House of Commons and tried hard to get him to desist.[24] Trelawny's support of Lord Godolphin, however, had left him responsible for a number of Whig Members of Parliament. The Trelawnys knew they had a fight on their hands. John Trelawny, the Bishop's eldest son, admitted to Dr. Stratford that Liskeard intended to revolt. Both Bishop and son went into Cornwall in mid-August. John Dolben was dead so his replacement by Philip Rashleigh, a Cornish Tory acceptable to Liskeard, averted defeat in that place. The Major-general held his seat at Plymouth and the two Looes were safe, but in no other place was Trelawny influence sure. Lostwithiel, Bodmin and Launceston were lost. Helston gave some comfort by returning two Godolphins, but, overall, the elections had been a serious blow to Trelawny influence.

Robert Harley, now Lord Treasurer, and soon to be earl of Oxford, had no desire to deliver the Queen into the hands of the new high-flying Tory majority. His reluctance probably saved Trelawny interest from extinction. Stung by this Granville resurgence, the opposing families fought back fiercely in the mayoral elections of 1711 and 1712. Granville, elevated to the peerage as Lord Lansdown, pressed Harley in October 1711 to dismiss a number of Boscawen and Godolphin supporters from posts in the Stannaries and urged removal of the customs collector at Helston in July, 1712. He wanted government patronage to ensure a sweeping victory at the next election, and was pressing Oxford hard for answers and decisions within six weeks of the elections,[25] warning of the serious effects of any delay. In the eastern part of Cornwall another Harlyite had been busy. By August, John Friend, the Harley's steward, was confident he had secured a majority of twenty-three to seventeen of the voters of East Looe and that he could take both seats. He abandoned his plan reluctantly only when he learnt that Oxford wanted the Bishop to meet with no opposition. The Bishop had not been certain that West Looe would return his son, John, at the bye-election in April, 1713, so Oxford's intervention in August was crucial.[26]

Following an interview with the Queen in June, 1712, Trelawny reluctantly shifted his electoral support to Harley (now earl of Oxford) and in the General Election of 1713, placed one of the seats at East Looe at Oxford's disposal. Not that the Trelawnys had given up the struggle against the Granvilles. In the spring of 1711 Lord Carteret, although only twenty-two years of age, boldly applied for the post of lord lieutenant of Cornwall. He was the son of Grace Granville, daughter of the first earl of Bath, who was currently suing Lansdown over her father's estates. Carteret was a close friend of John Trelawny and of his father.[27] The application embarrassed and annoyed Lansdown. He was forced to propose a compromise candidate for the post he wanted to hold himself.

134

Even after the Whig triumph in the General Election of 1715, the Granvilles and the Trelawnys continued their electoral rivalry. In October 1717 the Bishop learnt to his rage, that Lansdown and John Anstis were trying to bribe the freemen of East Looe to elect one of their supporters at the next vacancy among their number.[28] When an opportunity arose to extend Trelawny influence in the borough of Saltash, the Bishop did not hesitate to sacrifice one of his daughters. It was the most shameful episode in his career.

John Francis Buller sought to marry Rebecca Trelawny, who was an attractive young woman of twenty. His face was hideously disfigured by smallpox which had very nearly claimed his life. Rebecca's father eagerly promoted the match, overriding her physical aversion to her suitor. The wedding took place on 22 July, 1716, in Trelawne chapel. The officiating clergyman was so unnerved by Rebecca's distress that he refused to proceed: whereupon the Bishop ordered him to continue or he himself would perform the ceremony. Rebecca could not answer 'I will' but kept bobbing up and down in her distress, an action which the minister took to signify an affirmative and so continued.[29] All that can be said in mitigation is that the Bishop was not alone in exploiting his women-folk in this fashion and for this motive. Lansdown did much the same in the autumn of 1717 when he insisted his seventeen year old niece marry Alexander Pendarves of Roscrow, who was well over sixty, in order to strengthen Granville electoral influence.[30] Rebecca accepted her fate and became a dutiful wife and mother. The Bishop used her to help win Buller's favour while he helped her husband to get the best price he could for outlying estates in Kent and Cornwall which he wanted to sell. John Francis Buller was returned for Saltash at a bye-election 1 December, 1718, with the active assistance of the Trelawnys.[31]

The continual manoeuvring and electoral intrigues of the Granvilles and Trelawnys after 1714 ignored the fundamental shift in the balance of power in Cornwall. In the General Election of 1715 the Crown reasserted its control over many borough elections in the Duchy. Hugh Boscawen became the recognised government electoral manager in Cornwall. The Vincents, who had given the Granvilles so much support, changed sides and joined Boscawen. Between them in 1715 they secured control of Camelford, Grampound, Mitchell, Penryn, Truro and a half interest in St. Mawes and Tregony. With Treasury money to back him, Boscawen's influence could not fail to expand in subsequent elections. The Granvilles were left with a secure hold on Launceston and the Godolphins on Helston. Liskeard a remained a Trelawny seat so long as the Bishop was alive. After 1721 the family was left with East Looe and West Looe and financial embarrassment forced the Trelawnys to become Treasury

135

electoral pensioners throughout the rest of the eighteenth century.

The passing of the Septennial Act meant that elections became increasingly venal as their frequency declined. The old electoral interest had rested partly on shared political principles, partly on an acknowledgement of the natural right of the gentry to govern, and partly on a network of carefully cultivated, carefully maintained personal relationships. It is not possible to say how much electioneering cost the Trelawnys in money. Granville confessed to Harley that the General Election of 1710 had cost him four thousand pounds, but he was a notorious free spender and had the harder task of challenging the families in power.[32] The cost in money to the Trelawnys, like the cost to the Duke of Newcastle later in the eighteenth century, was probably less than one might think. Only when Treasury money was available did the price of a vote suffer from run-away inflation. A comparison of the twenty pounds distributed among all the Saltash electors who voted for Sir Cholmody Dering in 1710 with the twenty pounds apiece paid to the electors of Lostwithiel in 1727 makes the point graphically.[33] Such growing expectations among the electorate made cash speak louder than ancient feudal ties. There is something rather touching at the sight of the Bishop assiduously cultivating the friendship of his son-in-law, or of the Major-general fussing over who could influence one voter at Saltash. It was an approach to electioneering out of tune with a new age in which every man was reckoned to have his price.

1. *Portland MSS.,* iv. 101, T to Harley, 15 July, 1704.

2. C.T., p.266, Hall to T, 24 January, 1704; Wake MSS. xx, unfoliated, T to Wake, 3 December, 1716.

3. Add. MSS. 43410, ff.83 *et seqq.*

4. G.H. Jones, ('The Problem of French Protectionism in the the Foreign Policy of England, 1680-8'), *B.H.I.R.,* xlii (1969), pp.145-157.

5. R.J.E. Boggis, *History of the diocese of Exeter* (Exeter, 1922), p.443.

6. MS. Tanner xxix, f.32; xxx, f.191; D.R.O., Cooke Corresp., John Cooke to Edward Cooke, undated (but September, 1717). See also, Theodore Sanxay, *The Sanxay Family* (New York, 1907).

7. Wake MSS. xvii, unfoliated, T to Wake, 28 February, 1713.

8. J. Childs *The Army, James II and the Glorious Revolution,* (Manchester, 1980), p.112. The whole chapter entitled 'Popularity and Politics', pp.83-113, gives a valuable corrective view.

9. P.R.O., S.P. Domestic, 35/3/35a.

10. *A letter from a clergyman in the Country to a Dignified clergyman in London Vindicating the Bill for Preventing the Translation of Bishops* (1702), p.6.

11. Luttrell, vi.110.

12. *Portland MSS.* iv. 198, Harley to Newcastle, 12 November, 1706; Henry L. Snyder, *The Marlborough - Godolphin Correspondence* (Oxford, 1975), ii. 773.

13. H.M.C. *Dropmore MSS.* i. 19, Wyndham to Pitt, 27, January 1706; 33, same to same, 18 December, 1707.

14. *Reasons in Particular Why the Clergy of the Archdeaconry of Exon cannot comply with His Lordship's present recommendation of Proctors,* p.2; Hearne, i. 315; *A Sermon and Charge,* p.37; *Portland MSS.,* iv. 295, Stratford to Harley, 22 April, 1706.

15. *Portland MSS.,* iv. 104, Granville to Harley, 25 July, 1704.

16. B.L., Portland Loan 29/9/12, List dated 7 February, 1705.

17. *Portland MSS.,* iv. 270, Defoe to Harley: Abstract of my journey, 1705, July 16 - November 6.

18. *Ibid.,* 216, Granville to [Harley], 4 August, 1705; 217, same to same, 8 August, 1705.

19. Longleat, Portland Papers, vii. f.113, Godolphin to Harley, 13 October, 1705.

20. Angus McInnes, *Robert Harley, Puritan Politician* (1970), pp.99-100.

21. *Portland MSS.,* iv. 693, Granville to Harley, 19 May, 1711.

22. *Ibid.,* v. 489, same to same, 20 May, 1708.

23. *Ibid.,* v.565, Robartes to Harley, 13 August, 1710; Roger Granville, *History of the Granville Family* (Exeter, 1895), p.414.

24. *Portland MSS.,* vii. 13, Stratford to Edward Harley, 19 August, 1710.

25. *Ibid.,* v. 97, Granville to Harley (Oxford), 6 October, 1711; 198, same to same, 4 July, 1712; 312, same to same, 28 July, 1713.

26. U.N.L., Portland Papers, Pw2 Hy932, Friend to Harley (Oxford), 27 August, 1713; Wake MSS. xvii, unfoliated, T to Wake, 28 February, 1713.

27. Basil Williams, *Cartaret and Newcastle* (1966), pp.10-12.

28. Downes MSS., T to John Francis Buller, 20 October, 1717; Buller to T, 20 November, 1717.

29. Nichols and Taylor, *op. cit.,* ii. 75. I am indebted to Mrs. Rosemary Parker for further details of this story handed down in her family.

30. Granville, *op. cit., p.448.*

31. Buller BC/25/11/3, T to Rebecca Buller, 10 April, 1717; 11/14, T to Buller, 25 August, 1720; 11/8, Charles Trelawny to Rebecca Buller, 24 November, 1718; 11/1, Major-General Charles Trelawny to Rebecca Buller, 18 May, 1720. See also letters in Downes MSS.

32. *Portland MSS.* v. 134, Granville to Harley, December, 1711; Granville, *op. cit.,* p.421.

33. Buller BO/23/76/1, Wills to Buller, 30 November, 1710; Sedgewick, Romney, ed., *The House of Commons, 1715-1754* (1970); i. *sub.* Lostwithiel.

CHAPTER TEN

Prelate of the Garter

On 14 June, 1707 Trelawny was finally translated to Winchester. As he informed his new clergy, it took place in spite of 'all the bitterest opposition which envenomed and consecrated lies could throw my way'.[1] Matthew Prior marvelled at the intensity of the opposition and remarked upon the sorrow the promotion caused at Lambeth.[2] Somers virtually ordered Tenison to remonstrate personally with the Queen. Anne cut the Archbishop short before he had a chance to say another word.[3] Trelawny entered upon his enjoyment of the rich rent rolls of Winchester vilified by both extremes of the political spectrum, but he could afford to be cheerful. He wrote in high good humour to his correspondents in August predicting that he would be bishop for the next twenty years.[4] Apart from the obvious financial gain, the translation conferred a certain status and some influence. A bishop of Winchester was *ex officio* Prelate of the Order of the Garter and Trelawny lost no time in procuring the accoutrements of that office. Winchester conferred a certain seniority among the bishops, but little more than that to which Trelawny was entitled after twenty-one years in office. As the visitor of five colleges, a bishop of Winchester had some influence in the University of Oxford, but it could be increased only by employing his other powers of patronage.[5] Only by use of the authority of the Chancellor of the University, and even then with much opposition, could Trelawny secure a senior degree for his business consultant, Charles Heron.[6]

Very few records of the diocese have survived for this period, so there is nothing to indicate how effective the ecclesiastical courts were, or how much authority a bishop of Winchester could command. Winchester was divided into two archdeaconries, Surrey and Winchester, with a commissary court for Surrey as well. London had an increasing influence on life south of the Thames. The population of Southwark and Bermondsey was growing fast. It must have been a far more daunting task to try to enforce a pastoral discipline in Surrey than in Hampshire. The bishop's patronage in Surrey was confined to the dignity of archdeacon.

139

Winchester was the larger of the two archdeaconries with twice as many churches and chapels. Forty-four parishes were peculiars, but jurisdiction appears to have been limited to matters of probate. In addition to the archdeaconry and cathedral canonries, the bishop could dispose of fifty livings and two hospitals, of which twelve were reputed to be worth three hundred pounds a year or more. He was patron of fourteen livings in other dioceses.[7] This considerable patronage gave the bishop some influence in itself.

Sir Peter Mews, son of Trelawny's predecessor, was chancellor of the diocese. Nothing survives to indicate the kind of relationship he enjoyed with his father's successor, but there are slight indications that it was not cordial. A passing comment on corrupt vicar-generals in Trelawny's visitation charge of 1708 was probably directed against Mews. The appointment of Dr. Robert Woods as judge of the commissary court of Surrey is significant. He had been Edisbury's deputy at Exeter and seems to have been a man Trelawny could rely on to keep him informed and to seek for his approval for all important decisions.[8] Ralph Bridoake, archdeacon of Winchester, was a supporter of Archbishop Tenison, so his relations with his new Bishop were probably cool to start with. They grew worse after his expulsion from Winchester College. When Thomas Sayer, archdeacon of Surrey died, Trelawny swallowed his pride and appointed Edmund Gibson on 6 June, 1710, a man he had singled out for public rebuke only two years earlier with the promise that he need never look to him for preferment.[9] Despite Gibson's obvious suitability for the post such a *volte-face* can only be explained by Trelawny's support for the Ministry of the day and his estrangement from the extreme High Church Tories. Judging by a comment he made to Wake, Gibson continued to dislike Trelawny despite this preferment.[10] Gibson's elevation to the episcopate in 1715 robbed Trelawny of the right to appoint his successor, and his right was lost a second time in November, 1719 when Dr. Boulter was promoted to Bristol. Much to his disgust Archbishop Wake prevailed upon the King to present Samuel Billingsby, a canon of Chichester, for whom Trelawny felt nothing but contempt.[11] Thomas Cranley, the registrar of the consistory court, seems to have performed his duties adequately enough. As a collector of tenths for the Southampton area he irritated the Governors of Queen Anne's Bounty by what they regarded as inefficiency, but Cranley exonerated himself.[12] Trelawny must have missed the industrious Francis Cooke. He took with him as many trusted subordinates as he could. Thomas Newey remained a domestic chaplain and was rewarded with a canonry at Winchester and the wealthy rectory of Wonston in Hampshire. John, the second son of Francis Cooke, was Newey's fellow chaplain: he too was made a canon and given the sinecure

140

of Oveton.[13] Edmund Drake continued as Trelawny's personal secretary. Charles Heron quit the service of the Duke of Somerset in order to work as the Bishop's business manager overseeing the stewards and manorial officers of the episcopal manors, negotiating fines on renewal of leases and on proposals for enclosures.[14]

The few records belonging to the diocese of Winchester for the eighteenth century which have survived give occasional glimpses of Trelawny at work. They show that he had lost none of his energy. Cranley was kept busy enforcing orders given to parishes in Winchester and Basingstoke deaneries after an episcopal visitation in May, 1712.[15] From the outset Trelawny's policy was to exercise as strict a supervision of his clergy as he had established in Exeter diocese. The sermon he preached at his primary visitation on the text 'This is a true saying, if a man desire the office of a bishop, he desireth a good work' (1 Timothy 3 v. i), was a detailed and uncompromising restatement of the High Church doctrine on the Apostolic Succession. In his visitation charge, the Bishop gave much sound pastoral advice coupled with stern warnings not to omit prayers or change the order of service in order to accomodate the objections of Dissenters. The clergy were ordered not to voice public criticism of the Government of the day, and not to solemnize clandestine marriages. They were encouraged to preach against simony. Incumbents were forbidden to engage and dismiss curates at will. Trelawny included comments on clerical political commentators which left no doubt in the minds of his hearers that Gibson of Lambeth and Stephens, rector of Sutton, were meant. Such a public rebuke of so influential a figure as Edmund Gibson must have impressed on the average clergyman that his new Bishop was not to be disobeyed with impunity. Dr. Bingham was deeply impressed and instanced recent 'Convincing Proofs' of Trelawny's discipline over the clergy in the dedication to the second volume of his *Origines Ecclesiasticae*.[16] Only in one part of his diocese, and that remote from the mainstream, do the records permit Trelawny's influence to be traced. The Church of England in the Channel Islands was still calvinist in practice and outlook. No bishop at this period could change this by personal intervention. Nevertheless, by making a wise choice of deans for Jersey and Guernsey, and backing them fully in everything they sought to do, Trelawny was able to begin the process of introducing Anglican practice into the Islands.[17]

In his correspondence with Archbishop Wake it is clear that Trelawny continued to exercise vigilance in the examination of candidates for ordination. From 1717, possibly earlier, he kept his own book in which all candidates wrote out and signed their subscription to the Thirty-nine Articles and their oaths. This book shows that he held ordinations

141

regularly four times a year up to a month before his death.[18]

As far as Church Societies were concerned, Trelawny showed an interest in the work overseas of the Society for the Propagation of the Gospel, but he was not actively involved and the large gift of money he intended for the Society was never given. The Bishop showed far greater interest in the Commission for the Fifty New London Churches. He attended meetings regularly throughout the summer of 1712, including the crucial meeting on 16 July, when the Commissioners drew up instructions for the architect and surveyor as to the style and furnishing of the new churches, instructions which reflected the High Church sacramental emphasis on an altar rasied up as well as railed off. He was one of those, when the Commission was reconstituted, who saw to it that Nicholas Hawksmoor was re-appointed architect.[19] Trelawny was never one to enjoy the minutia of committee work and he seldom appeared at meetings of the Commissioners after 1712, unless the case of St. Mary's, Bermondsey was on the agenda. Here he took a personal interest in negotiating with Lord Salisbury for the site of a new church, trying to beat the Earl down in price. He never got the new church for Bermondsey, but it was not for the want of trying.[20]

As Visitor of Winchester College Trelawny was faced with another legal battle which, although not of the same importance as those described earlier, involved him in considerable trouble and expense. The affairs of Winchester College came before Trelawny as Visitor several times between 1708 and 1715. The bulk of the Fellows of the College staged a rebellion against their Warden. The dispute was caused partly by dislike of 'a confident and capable adminstrator who enjoyed his office and had grown a little complacent in his long exercise of authority'.[21] In some respects Warden Nicholas was a man after Trelawny's own heart and he was inclined to support him. On the first occasion he heard an appeal, Archdeacon Bridoake, who was one of the leading mutineers among the Fellows, interrupted the Warden to say that what he asserted was entirely false. Trelawny reprimanded Bridoake very severely. The Archdeacon remained the most obstinate of all the Fellows. In 1710 the Warden and Fellows of New College issued a set of injunctions to the Fellows of Winchester College which greatly favoured Warden Nicholas. Upon the refusal of the Fellows to observe the injunctions, the Warden of New College appealed to Trelawny. The Fellows of Winchester, led by Bridoake, decided to contest the powers of the Bishop, claiming that he had authority over them as Ordinary but not as Visitor. If he was only their Ordinary then they had the right to appeal and could conduct a protracted law suit. The case was argued before Trelawny at a visitor's court at Chelsea in July, 1711 by a galaxy of legal luminaries from among both the

142

common lawyers and the Advocates of Doctors' Commons. Trelawny pronounced in favour of his own power as Visitor. Bridoake went to London seeking in vain for a superior judge to stop the proceedings. Gibson remarked to Wake that he supposed the affair would end up in a writ of error being taken to the House of Lords.[22] The Fellows even went so far as to engage Dr. Radcliffe, the famous physician, to persuade the Lord Treasurer to get an Order in Council to restrain the Bishop. Trelawny got wind of it and wrote to Radcliffe, with whom he was on good terms, to tell him not to support the Fellows. If he did speak to the Lord Treasurer he was to remind him of the reply Trelawny had given to the Privy Council in the affair of Arthur Bury. Radcliffe was told that the Bishop had expended a great deal of time and energy trying to get the Fellows to settle their differences with the Warden, even to employ the Dean and Chapter as mediators. He had, in his opinion, warned them clearly enough of the mischief they would bring on themselves if they forced him to conduct a visitation. He knew that one of the Fellows, (probably meaning Bridoake) was one of Radcliffe's patients so he concluded with the grimly humorous comment 'which I am sorry for, because if you knew him as well as I do, you could not think him fit to live'.[23] At a court held in Winchester College on 25 August, Trelawny forced the Fellows to acknowledge him as Visitor in a public ceremony, and two days later required them to signify their obedience to the injunctions of 1710. Only Bridoake held out, and Trelawny expelled him from his fellowship. This was not the end of the affair. Bridoake still appeared in the College, the other Fellows still obstructed the Warden and their proctor managed to delay an order against them for the costs of the legal proceedings until the end of October, 1715. Trelawny had upheld his own authority and the authority of the Warden, but at a cost. Not only must the legal fees of the eminent lawyers have been high, but the expulsion of Bridoake must have put paid to any willing cooperation with the Bishop in the administration of the diocese.

Trelawny's relations with the Dean and Chapter of Winchester appear to have been unexceptional, although John Wickhart, the dean and the senior canons could not have been entirely pleased with some of the Bishop's appointments. Newey was made a canon in 1712 and his other domestic Chaplain, John Cooke was collated the following year. Under the Winchester statutes the Vice-dean, Receiver and Treasurer were elected annually. It took seven years before the canons elected Cooke to the post of Treasurer, and Newey was never elected to any post. Making Anthony Alsop a canon in 1715 was another act of kindness to a member of Christ

Church. Two years later Mrs. Elizabeth Astrey of Oxford sued Alsop for breach of marriage and was awarded £2,000 damages. Trelawny presented Alsop to the rectory of Brightwell in Berkshire, and suggested that he place all his debt on that living, see it sequestered for debt, and live modestly off his canonry until the debt was paid. Alsop took this advice and lived abroad until his creditors agreed to a settlement. Trelawny protected him against charges for non-residence at the cathedral. Alsop only returned to England to take up residence in June, 1721. The senior canons may have been sympathetic to Alsop, but were probably not so pleased to learn that Trelawny had secured royal warrants for three of his appointees, dispensing them from all the obligations of the cathedral statutes except that of supplying preaching turns and the minimal residence of twenty-one days.[24]

Trelawny considered that the adminstration of the diocese of Winchester called for 'faithful diligence' in banishing and driving away 'all erroneous and strange doctrine'. Fear of Roman Catholicism as a potential recruiting ground for political despotism was deeply engrained in men and women of his generation. This accounts for his persistent intolerance of all Roman Catholic missionary or educational activity. Roman Catholic priests increased their level of activity in the early days of the eighteenth century. Other Anglican bishops did not approve of this activity either but the difference between their approach and Trelawny's is instructive. Nicholson of Carlisle complained bitterly of the inactivity of Cumberland magistrates, approved of the lord lieutenant's efforts to rouse them to enforce the laws against recusancy, but did nothing himself. Chandler of Lichfield and Coventry did not consider he or anyone else could move the magistrates of Derbyshire into action.[25] Trelawny, on the other hand, broke up one Roman Catholic school in 1708 and, when he learnt of two Roman Catholic priests openly ministering in Winchester in 1720, and of the establishment of a school for boys, promptly ordered all his clergy to be on their guard and wrote to the Mayor of Winchester, requiring him to tender the oath of allegiance to all suspected Roman Catholics. When the Mayor refused Trelawny travelled from Farnham to pay him a personal visit, with a list of actions he expected the Mayor to take. He threatened that if the Mayor failed to carry them out he would forward his name to the Privy Council and mention it in the House of Lords. The Bishop then turned his attention to other magistrates in the quarter sessions.[26] Other bishops complained, but did nothing: Trelawny asserted his authority, following it, if needful, with a personal confrontation with the offender, however unpleasant that experience might be. He had always understood his duty as a bishop in this fashion. He had hoped that the Lower House of Convocation would have shamed his brother bishops into asserting the

144

authority they still possessed. Had all the bishops on the bench been equally confident of their role and convinced of their duty, then the subsequent history of the Church of England might have been very different. The younger bishops had a certain sneaking admiration for the old war-horse. Trimnell of Norwich showed an affectionate concern for Trelawny's state of health in the winter of 1715 and Archbishop Wake told Echard that Trelawny was 'an honest and sincere Man; a Man of honour'. John Hough of Lichfield and Coventry paid tribute to his 'generous and public spirit'.[27] At the close of the Whiston affair church leaders who had opposed the Tory attempt at a counter-revolution, were becoming uneasily aware of the consequences. Even White Kennett was heard to complain that there had to be some kind of discipline, and Wake was dismayed to watch the Act against Occasional Conformity and the Schism Act repealed.

Apart from his strict supervision of his diocese, the last ten years of Trelawny's life were taken up with securing and maintaining the Protestant Succession. The demands of party so dominated all aspects of political and social life in Anne's reign that any person in a public position who was not firmly on one side or the other was bound to earn someone's dislike. Despite the pressure to conform, however, there were always those prepared to take a line of their own. Cornishmen in particular tend to be individualists, and Trelawny's churchmanship did not predetermine his stand on foreign affairs. He continued to give his support to Godolphin and Marlborough up to and beyond Godolphin's dismissal from office in 1710. He had a strong personal dislike of the Pretender and had no doubt in his own mind that were James III to be king, a despotism would be imposed on Britain with a ruthless proscription of all opponents, and Roman Catholicism advanced at the expense of the Church of England. He was convinced that, unless checked, French military might be used to restore the Pretender and suppress all English liberties. Defeat of the French in Europe and the Union in Scotland were two effective ways of frustrating the Pretender. He did not share the fears of his fellow High Churchmen that the Union with Scotland might lead to an attack on the position of the Church of England. He supported actively the extension of the Malt Tax to Scotland as one additional strand in the cord binding the two countries together.[28]

After Godolphin's dismissal, the Harley Ministry started preliminary negotiations for Peace with France. The Queen herself made it clear that she, too, was for the Peace and told Burnet, at one point, that she hoped none of the Bishops would oppose her.[29] The vote in favour of Nottingham's amendment in the Lords on 7 December that no peace should be made if Spain or the West Indies went to a Bourbon King

145

shocked the Queen and she began to assert her authority in order to discipline the recalcitrant. Marlborough was dismissed, followed by Somerset. If Trelawny were as pliant and as time-serving as some historians have thought, he would have toed the line before the summer of 1712. In fact he voted with the Whig leaders on the motion to allow the Duke of Hamilton to sit as an English peer, and sought a reluctant reconciliation with Harley only after a personal interview with the Queen.

Being the senior bishop available and the one most closely involved in the form of service for consecrating new churches, Trelawny headed a small delegation of bishops who waited on the Queen on 18 June. She may have taken him aside and reminded him bluntly of the loyalty he owed her because he forgot to ask for the return of the documents presented to her, (thus forcing the Upper House to send two more bishops to see the Queen to ask for them back), and the very next day he used Atterbury to sound out Harley with a view to a reconciliation. This was followed by two meetings over dinner with Bromley, the speaker of the Commons, after which it was thought in ministerial circles, that Trelawny's objections had been satisfied and that he would now support the Ministry.[30]

Trelawny was not fully satisfied. He accepted that the Ministry would negotiate a peace which placed effective checks on the power of France and that it would not negotiate away all that Marlborough had fought for. On the other hand he was not satisfied that the present Ministry would do enough to serve the Hanoverian Succession. By the end of 1712, if not before, he was numbered with that handful of 'whimsical' or Hanoverian Tories who were a thorn in the side of the Ministry and who were to play a crucial role in Parliament over the next two years. He probably influenced the young Lord Cartaret. In the Commons the whimsical Tories included his son, John, and Sir Henry Bateman who later sat for West Looe in the Parliament of 1715.

In the winter of 1713 Trelawny tried to form a party among the Bishops to press for more active measures to be taken against Jacobites. His canvassing did not produce the hoped for address to the Queen, but Wake assured him that even the knowledge that an address had been thought of had had a good effect. His letters to Wake give the fullest indication of his motives. He was in favour of peace with proper safeguards, yet it would not be right for the Bishops to comment on a matter which belonged to the royal prerogative, unless they wished 'to die as Whigs & not as guardians of our religion.' He did not wish to embarrass the Ministry by calling for further measures to protect the Queen's personal safety but he was convinced that a Jacobite plot was in preparation and that, if not prevented, a coupe d'état would be mounted. He concluded that the Pretender had 'as much cruelty towards the protestants as the French tyrant had given him the example of & the Jesuit will furnish him with arguments for with a sweeping vengeance for his suppos'd Father's & his own disgrace and injuries.'[31]

Both Lansdown and Harcourt tried to win Trelawny over to the side of the Ministry during the spring but all he would say was that he had 'a great respect' for the Lord Treasurer.[32] This was enough for Oxford to mark him down as a government supporter in his estimate of how the peers would vote on the commercial articles of the Treaty with France.[33] Oxford may well have mis-read the Bishop's signals: the Lords never had to vote on the issue because the Commons threw out the commercial clauses by nine votes. In the General Election of August and September, the Bishop, for tactical reasons, placed one of the seats at East Looe at Oxford's disposal but he did not trust a man who consorted with such known Jacobites as the Granvilles. When Parliament assembled in February, fear for the Succession outweighed all other considerations in the minds of the 'whimsicals'. During the months of in-fighting between Bollingbroke and Oxford, Trelawny may have come round to thinking that Oxford did indeed support the Hanoverian Succession. When Nottingham estimated how the peers would vote on the Schism Bill, he listed Trelawny as doubtful. For Trelawny to be doubtful about a matter on which he had hoped to see Convocation act fourteen years earlier he must have suspected the motives of the Bill's proposers and that it was designed simply to embarrass the Lord Treasurer.[34] Oxford's conciliatory speech in favour of the Bill made it possible for Trelawny to put loyalty to the Church before his fears for the Protestant Succession and he voted for the Bill. Nevertheless his friends among the Bishops had changed. Sprat died in May, 1713 and Compton two months later. Atterbury, the new bishop of Rochester, still corresponded, but the letters were noticeably fewer and the strain in their relationship was difficult to hide.[35] They continued to correspond about third parties until Trelawny's death but their political beliefs pulled them steadily apart. Atterbury made no secret of his Jacobite sympathies. It is just as well for their relationship that Atterbury took elaborate precautions to preserve his anonymity as the author of the crudely anti-Whig, anti-Hanoverian election broadsheet *English advice to the Freeholders of England* which came out in January, 1715. Among the copies directed to key political figures in the south

147

west and intercepted in Exeter, was one addressed to the mayor of West Looe.[36] One can only hope that Lord Lansdowne made the decisions to whom to send copies of the pamphlet and that Atterbury himself did not try to stir up trouble in a borough where the voters had been restive under Trelawny's control since 1713. On the other hand, Atterbury had no scruples in intriguing with Lansdown against Trelawny in the Lostwithiel bye-election of 1708. Despite his conscious gratitude to Trelawny, in Atterbury's mind politics joined love and war in having an ethic of their own. By the end of Anne's reign Trelawny consorted with Trimnell of Norwich, Wake of Lincoln and Evans of Bangor.

By the beginning of April, 1714 all the Bishops, led by Dawes, the new archbishop of York, had consolidated in opposition to the Ministry. Trelawny could then have the satisfaction of knowing that a policy position he had first advocated before Christmas 1712 had now been accepted. He had not intended to embarrass the Ministry whereas Dawes told the Queen bluntly that the Ministry must be changed, but then much had happened during the intervening months. So when on 1 August Anne died, Trelawny had no reason to be apprehensive of the new King. He seems to have established an alliance of sorts with Lord Townshend almost immediately. By the end of the year Townshend was helping him to fend off an attack on his influence when he was forced to spend freely among the voters of Liskeard and Looe.[37]

Trelawny continued to support the Hanoverian Succession during the reset of his life. Enthusiastically he supported the Declaration drawn up by the Archbishop and Bishops in and near London pledging their support for King George at the opening of the Jacobite Rebellion of 1715. He considered it to be 'admirably well drawn' and signed it with both his long names - Jonathan Winchester - 'to show I did it heartily'.[38] The reasoning in the Declaration, of which he approved so strongly, was a mixture of commonsense and fear of popery. It was naive of members of the Church of England to contemplate putting the clock back thirty years. So much had been done to ensure the Protestant Succession that it would be ridiculous to support a bloody reversal of that policy. The lesson of the history of Europe over the last one hundred and fifty years taught, unmistakably, that a succession of Roman Catholic rulers led to the ruination of Protestantism. So long as Roman Catholic canonists taught that heresy was a greater crime than murder, then a proscription of Protestants inevitably followed on a return to power of a Roman Catholic ruler. Over fifty thousand had been put to death in Flanders recently. What

148

the clergy of the Church of England had done to James II 'will certainly be remembered and resented'.[39] In reading through this Declaration Trelawny could see nothing that he himself could not have written. He wished it had been drawn up sooner and wanted to know why it had not been published immediately.

Trelawny supported not only the new King: he also gave his backing to Lord Townshend and Sir Robert Walpole. When they disagreed with the King over foreign policy, resigned from the Ministry and formed an alliance with the Prince of Wales in opposition, Trelawny made his support of them public by returning Horatio Walpole, the Prince's secretary, as a member for East Looe in a bye-election in December, 1718, despite the displeasure of General Stanhope who was now the King's leading Minister. Trelawny was the last man to be deflected by Stanhope's bullying. It was inevitable that by the summer of 1717 Trelawny should find himself in the not unfamiliar role of political opponent. No doubt Stanhope's threats in the House of Commons in April, for which he was compelled to apologize, offended Trelawny's prejudices as a country gentleman. A more important reason was George I's decision to try to implement the promise he had made to the Privy Council and to a large deputation of Dissenting ministers in the autumn of 1714 to repeal the Acts of Occasional Conformity and Schism. In April the Prince of Wales let it be known that he would support those bishops opposed to repeal. Wake, Nicholson, and Trelawny were frequent visitors at St. James before the King expelled the Prince and Princess in December. In his visitation charge that summer he enjoined obedience to the House of Hanover warning his clergy 'to let no knavish whisper of a mistaken lost part [the Jacobites] discourage, fool or frighten you'. He devoted much of the charge to describing the virtues of the Prince and Princess of Wales.[40] Wake, Nicholson and Trelawny opposed the Ministry's attempt to impeach Oxford and they continued in opposition together.[41]

The outlook for the privileged position of the Church of England looked very bleak in the winter of 1718. Gibson was moving away from supporting that privileged position and most other bishops were not prepared to defend it. Trelawny gave his proxy to Wake for the winter session announcing that he had no wish to leave Wolversey Palace before his gardens and buildings were finished.[42] The habits of a country gentleman died hard. However, once he learnt that the Dissenters were switching their tactics away from demanding repeal of the Acts of Occasional Conformity and Schism and into making a breach in the Test and Corporation Acts, Trelawny rode up to Westminster by the middle of December. 'The corporations must remain as they are,' he told Wake, 'or the fanatics [his invariable term for Dissenters] by their own money and

149

the Government's will have a Parliament which will do our business at once.' He was convinced that a Parliament with Dissenters in the majority would abolish the Church of England.[43] He strongly opposed the Bill exempting the officials of the Bristol workhouse from the Test and Corporation Acts, and when it passed the Lords in March, he was one of four bishops who signed the protest in the Lord's Journal.

After repeal of the Acts of Occasional Conformity and Schism Trelawny seldom appeared at Westminster. A theological issue of great importance brought him back. Thirty years earlier his expulsion of Arthur Bury from Exeter College had helped to put a stop to the teaching of Socinianism but it had not brought an end to speculation on the nature of the Trinity and of the person of Christ. Trelawny had been foremost in securing a condemnation of Whiston's Arian tendences. In his book, *Scripture Doctrine of the Trinity,* published in 1712, Samuel Clarke, another Anglican clergyman, postulated the subordination of Christ to God the Father. He did this not so much on the grounds of natural reason as of the insufficient evidence to be found in the Bible for the doctrine of the Trinity. Clarke's opinions met with rapid success among Dissenters, especially among the respected and influential dissenting ministers of Devon.[44] Their Trinitarian disputes were seized on by those in Parliament opposed to the repeal of the Occasional Conformity and Schism Acts in December 1718. It could be alleged that those dissenting from the Church of England were not simply opposed to Anglican church order; they were inimicable to orthodox Christianity.

John Shute Barrington, one of the Members of the House of Commons who had led the campaign for repeal of the legislation protecting the Church of England, wanted this Trinitarian dispute resolved at national level. The Committee for the Three Denominations in London was a loose association of Presbyterians, Independents and Baptists which looked after matters of common interest among Dissenters. Barrington requested the Committee to discuss the proposal that Scripture should provide the only rule of faith and the Committee resolved to have the proposal debated at a general assembly of London ministers. This assembly held three sessions in February and early March 1719 in Salter's Hall and divided into two opposing parties. What had begun as an unorthodox speculation among a few Anglican divines had developed into a major split, at national level, in Nonconformity.

Within the Church of England some of the bishops took this spread of Arianism seriously, none more so than Wake and Trelawny. The latter visited the Archbishop at the end of March to urge that some step be taken to challenge Arianism, and was overjoyed to learn that the King was to include a mention on the doctrine of the Trinity in his message to

150

Parliament at the end of the session, and to authorize the Archbishop to instruct his suffragans to commend careful instruction in orthodox belief.[45] Some saw in the Trinitarian dispute an opportunity to embarrass a Jacobite bishop. It was rumoured that George Smalridge of Bristol held Arian beliefs. The idea that a Christ Church man, and a regius professor should be guilty of such beliefs filled Trelawny with alarm. He asked Smalridge point blank if it was true, and when Smalridge fully vindicated himself, Trelawny had copies of his reply circulated in order to scotch the report.[46] He encouraged the Bill for the more effectual suppressing of Blasphemy and Profaneness which Wake introduced in the winter of 1720 and this brought him to Parliament again in May to vote with the minority in favour of the Bill. Wake, Trelawny and three other bishops voted for the Bill: eight other bishops voted against.[47] It demonstrates once again the consistency of Trelawny's position. He had argued for legislative control of the dissemination of anti-religious literature for over twenty-five years. Despite the Ministry's anti-clerical policy, he remained a firm supporter of the House of Hanover. He went into Cornwall in September 1720 partly to congratulate the mayors of the boroughs on their election, partly to visit known or suspected Jacobites. If his visits should make the Ministry suspect his loyalty or accuse him of treason,

> 'I would do them all the spite and mischief I could though
> I resolved to cut the pretender's throat the first moment I
> could come at him.....
> Gentlemen may be won but can't be frightened'.[48]

This kind of distinctly unclerical language shocked contemporaries: it would cause raised eyebrows even today. Colourful language had ever been a Trelawny family trait.

1. *Sermon..... and charge,* p.67.

2. Longleat, Prior Papers xiii, f.133, Prior to Weymouth, 28 June, 1707.

3. Gregg, *op. cit.,* pp.146, 238.

4. H.M.C., *Bath MSS.,* iii. 436, T to Prior, 2 August, 1707; B.L. Egerton MSS. 2618, f.197, T to Clarke, 17 August, 1707.

5. Wake MSS. xx, unfoliated, T to Wake, 7 December, 1716.

6. Hearne, i. 165.

7. *Special and General Reports made to his Majesty by the Commissioners appointed to inquire into the Practice of the Ecclesiastical Courts in England and Wales,* xxiv (1831-32), Appendix D, No. 6; H.R.O., Book of First Fruits and Tenths.

8. L.C.C., AH-3, Archdeaconry of Surrey Office Papers, 1700-1727.
9. *Sermon..... and charge,* p.62.

10. Wake MSS. xx, unfoliated, Gibson to Wake, 14 September.

11. Add. MSS. 28275, f.103, T to Echard, undated.

12. C.C., 379, QAB Minute Book ii (September 1716-October 1725), f.105, 2 March, 1719; 197, Letter Book (1718-22), f.53, 7 March, 1719.

13. S.H. Cassan, *Lives of the Bishops of Winchester* (1827), p.196-203.

14. H.R.O., Bishopric of Winchester: Estate Administration, Eccles. 415809, E/B9-E/B13.

15. H.R.O., Trelawny Papers A/10/A Bundle One, miscellaneous No. 12, Cranley to T, 12 May, 1712.

16. Joseph Bingham, *Origines Ecclesiasticae: or the Antiquities of the Christian Church* (1710), ii. the dedicatory preface.

17. M.G. Smith, 'Bishop Trelawny and the Church in the Channel Islands' 1680-1730, *Annual Bulletin Societe Jersiaise* (1983), xxiii (3), pp.320-330.

18. Wake MSS. vii [Cant ii], unfoliated, T to Wake, 28 October, 1716; H.R.O., F/10/viii, Subscription Book 1717-1721. For Trelawny's ordinations in Exeter see Smith, Administration, pp.180-98.

19. Lamb. Libr., Lambeth MSS. 2690, Minute Book (1711-17), ff.42-4; C.T., pp.218-9, Duchess of Marlborough to T, 23 December, 1715, 31 December, 1715.

20. Lambeth MSS. 2690 and 2691, Minute Books *passim;* Wake MSS. vii [Cant ii], unfoliated, Case of the Inhabitants of St. Mary's, Bermondsey.

40. Wake MSS. vii [Cant. ii], unfoliated, T to Wake, 2 October, 1717.

41. C. Jones, 'The impeachment of the earl of Oxford and the Whig Schism 1717', *B.I.H.R.* lv (May 1982), pp.66-7.

42. Wake MSS. xx, unfoliated, T to Wake, 25 November, 1717.

43. *Ibid.,* same to same, 1 December, 1717.
44. Brocket, *op. cit.,* pp.74-95.

45. Wake MSS. xxi, f.118, T to Wake, 1 April, 1719.

46. *Ibid.,* f.161, Smalridge to T, 23 September, 1719 (còpy); see also, MS. Ballard 9, f.79.

47. *Portland MSS.,* v.621, Edward Harley junior to Abigail Harley, 4 May, 1720.

48. Wake MSS. xxi, f.272, T to Wake, 9 September, 1720.

CHAPTER ELEVEN

A Family Man

There does not appear to be any early portrait of Jonathan Trelawny. The best picture hangs at Downes in Devon. It depicts a proud man with a touch of arrogance, resplendent in his robes as a prelate of the Garter. A long straight nose and a strong jaw suggests one who could be physically intimidating if he were in a temper, the more so as his garter cloak indicates that he was tall. The full generous mouth, however, does not belong to a cruel man. The hard drinking of his early days at university took toll of his health shortly after be became a bishop. Thenceforth he suffered the agony of periodic bouts of the stone. In his late fifties he had to hide his corpulence inside corset stays.

He was an intelligent man, but intellectually lazy. The polished latinity which was the hallmark of an old Westminster stayed with him throughout his life. He was quick to spot the smallest grammatical error as Hodder learnt to his cost, and, when he chose, he could produce an apt latin tag. Only two published sermons appear to have survived together with one visitation sermon and two visitation charges. Their style is plain and their construction easy to follow. The visitation charges are full of sound pastoral common sense. The sermons reveal a mind thoroughly familiar with the Scriptures, with a fondness for the historical books of the Old Testament. Their appeal is directed to the mind rather than to the heart. It is a restrained, disciplined and, above all, reasonable Christianity that they commend. In this respect Trelawny did not differ from the bulk of contemporary preachers of the Church of England. Any deeper currents of Cornish mysticism were curbed by an education received in an age which firmly separated fact from feeling. For example, he could not forbear telling readers of the new edition of Camden's *Britannica* about recent reports of miracles performed after drinking at Saint Madron's Well; but, as one of the people cured was a sceptical clergyman who only drank the water but did not himself pay a visit to that holy place, Trelawny concluded, in the spirit of the men of the Royal Society, that 'the virtue of the water claims the whole remedy'.[1]

154

Although Jonathan Trelawny's overall contribution to Edmund Gibson's new edition of Camden's *Britannica* was small he does deserve to be remembered for the new sections on Devon and Cornwall which he wrote. It was an important contribution which helped to stimulate interest in local history. Jonathan also took a keen interest in numismatics, especially in the coinage of the Civil War.[2] He did nothing toward preserving the Cornish language but he was anxious to preserve Cornish literature for his non-Cornish speaking Countrymen. It was at his request John Keigwin translated into English William Jourdan's *Gureans an bys* (Creation of the World).

The Trelawnys were east Cornish folk and quite prepared to consider marriage alliances outside Cornwall. Jonathan's mother was a Seymour and he married Rebecca, the daughter of Thomas Hele of Babcombe in Devon, and a co-heiress of Matthew Hals of Efford. This marriage was arranged partly with an eye to family fortune, a scheme consolidated later when Jonathan's brother, Henry took as his second wife the other co-heiress, Rebecca Hals, who was Rebecca Hele's aunt. Nevertheless, Bishop Lamplugh and others heartily approved of the marriage which took place at Egg Buckland on 31 March, 1684.[3] Jonathan was thirty-four years old, Rebecca was barely fourteen. Yet the marriage turned out to be a very happy one. The muniment room at Trelawne once contained many letters written by Jonathan to 'my dearest Becky'. Rebecca's portrait shows a woman of soft, almost languid beauty. She was not dominated by her husband. She had her own income and kept her own accounts. He confided to Francis Cooke on one occasion 'I hope you mind my wife, or we shall have a melancholy Christmas for she will not be Patience'.[4] One suspects that the painted frieze in the drawing room at Trelawne House and the appallingly bad cherub memorial on the wall of the Trelawny Chapel in Pelynt Church reflect the taste of Rebecca and that they were a part of her domain in which Jonathan did not interfere, even though his association with the University of Oxford must have imbued him with somewhat higher canons of artistic taste.

Jonathan and Rebecca went against the trend of the aristocracy in the late seventeenth century and had a large family, thirteen children, of whom eleven survived. One gets an occasional glimpse of the harrassed parent worrying over childhood illnesses and coping with a coach load of fretting, bored, offspring cooped up on a long journey. It was natural that the Cornish love of family and close fellowship meant that the parents would not dream of leaving their children behind in Cornwall when duty required the Bishop to be in London. Jonathan was a stern parent but he enjoyed his children and was proud of them. When Matthew Prior recounted how he had met two of the boys coming from Westminster

School, Charles with his nose in a book and his younger brother, Edward, scruffy and dirty 'having just before boxed with a beggar boy bigger than himself' Jonathan replied fondly that 'each was in his way'.[5] He never bothered to conceal his preference for sons, but he had all the natural delight of knowing that one of his daughters was to present him with a grandchild.[6] It was a pleasure that he could not share with his wife. She died on 11 February, 1710. Their eldest child, Charlotte, was born deformed. She was of a gentle and affectionate disposition but very conscious of her humped back. She always sat on a chair in the corner of the room and left instructions that she should be buried in a sitting position.[7] Laetitia, the second child, was of a lively, equally affectionate nature, but with the strong family will. She fell deeply in love with her first cousin, Harry. For many years her father refused to permit the marriage. No doubt he had the madness of his brother, Chichester, in mind and did not wish to see the family inter-breed still further. Laetitia's maternal grandmother, Elizabeth Hals, was also Harry's aunt. As well as being first cousins, the young couple were also first cousins once removed. Harry and Laetitia maintained a correspondence over several years, even managing occasionally to meet secretly in defiance of her father's orders. Laetitia spiritedly refused to marry anyone else so, finally, her uncle Charles persuaded her father to let the cousins marry. Harry succeeded Laetitia's brother and the baronetcy descended in his line.[8] John, the first son, the apple of his father's eye, was born in 1691. He inherited the estates and title. Henry was born a year later and was a midshpman serving under Sir Cloudisley Shovell on H.M.S. Association when she went down off the Scillies in 1707. His body was recovered and he lies buried in the parish church of St. Mary.[9] Charles, the next son, was a studious youth. He did well at Westminster School,[10] went to Christ Church and was ordained at the highly uncanonical age of eighteen. His health was never good and he died five weeks after his father. It may well have been his father's anxiety for his future which left him so well provided for. Jonathan collated him first to the Rectory of West Meon, worth betwen £300 and £340 a year, to which he added in July, 1720, the Rectory of Cheriton, worth a further £400. A month earlier he was given a vacant canonry and his father would dearly have liked to have given him the archdeaconry of Surrey. After Charles, the next two children were daughters. Rebecca grew up to be a local beauty greatly resembling her mother. She was the daughter forced to marry John Francis Buller. Of the next daughter, Elizabeth, nothing is known. Edward, the young boxer, was the next in line. He followed an army career, was appointed governor of Jamaica and rendered important services to his country in the West Indies. Two more sons, Hele and Jonathan, and a fourth daughter, Anne, complete the list. Hele also

156

became a clergyman and was studying at Oxford when his father died.

All bishops at this period expected to use their powers of patronage to provide for their dependents. Trelawny leased South Farm, East Meon, to his brother Charles in 1709 and give him the office of Keeper of the Wild Beasts in 1711 at an annual wage of twenty pounds. His son, John, was made Steward of Winchester at one hundred pounds a year, and his son Charles was given the reversion. Edward was given the reversion of the office of registrar of the consistory court. Had he every taken it up, he could always have appointed a deputy. When John was given the post of Keeper following his uncle's death, Hele was confirmed in the reversion of the office of Constable of Taunton Castle, at twenty pounds a year. In all this, Jonathan's old secretary, Edmund Drake, was not forgotten. He was given a reversion of the post of surveyor of episcopal lands at twenty pounds a year, and shared the office of steward to the bishop at forty pounds a year.[11]

Among the few intimate family letters which have survived, the correspondence conducted by the Bishop with his son-in-law, John Francis Buller, from 1716 to 1718 gives a fascinating glimpse of Jonathan when he relaxed. Once he came to know and like his son-in-law, he reveals a measure of caring and a keen sense of humour which his portrait could never show. He fusses over John Francis's health; he is shocked to learn that no baby clothes were ready shortly before Rebecca's first child was due. He is anxious about her health after the birth of his grandson. He pokes fun gently at Buller's purchase of an officer's commission for the boy as soon as he was born.[12] Granger related a story of Jonathan being visited by an old friend from Christ Church days and described 'the usual good humour in his countenance'.[13] It is hazardous to claim insight into another's character. We all live our lives in the presence of invisible beings. It is an even greater presumption to comment on a man's spiritual development. Yet something must be said, even if only to combat the modern tendency to assume that such a development is non-existent. Jonathan was not forced to choose a clerical career; indeed the wording of his father's will suggests that his doing so was not entirely in accordance with parental wishes. There was a vein of deep piety in the Trelawny family. Jonathan's deaf aunt, Elizabeth, was one of George Fox's earlier converts in Cornwall, an embarrassing defection to Nonconformity which may account, in part, for her nephew's strong detestation of 'fanatics' though the social exclusiveness of Dissenters offended him much more. A spiritual book which had a deep and abiding influence on Jonathan was George Bright's *Treatise on Prayer*. He possessed a copy of the 1678 edition and was still using it in later life, because at a book sale in the nineteenth century it was noted that on the fly leaf was written 'August the 8th a night

157

never to be forgot. Jonat. Winton'. One cannot say to what incident or experience this note refers but it may well record a spiritual experience of some kind. Bright taught the importance of composing one's own prayers and one knows that Jonathan did this. The two prayers he wrote for his use before and after preaching were preverved by one of his descendants. In an anecdote it was recalled that he invariably said prayers with his family before they retired for the night. His daughter, Laetitia and his nephew, Harry both wrote prayers at a time of deep personal grief.[14] One cannot be sure that the note on the fly leaf of the book records a profound spiritual experience but the use of Bright's method of developing the life of prayer makes that a probable interpretation. He did deliberately curb in himself that Cornish enjoyment of revenge. Some clergy disliked his discipline and resented the haughtiness with which he behaved. Yet he was always fair in his dealings with them and never pursued a personal vendetta against one of them. For one who used his parliamentary privileges to the full he never brought or even threatened an action of *scandalum magnatum* against anyone, unlike Burnet and Compton, who did. Jonathan was able to gain and retain the friendship of people as diverse as Thomas Sprat, Launcelot Blackburne, Sarah Churchill, Charles Trimnell and William Wake. Thomas Newey and Edmund Drake were content to remain in his service until his death. In an age of bitter partisan politics Jonathan never confined his friendship to the Tories.

Like other members of the Trelawny family, Jonathan had a violent temper which comes out in some of his letters. His language was distinctly unclerical on those occasions. Yet his fits of temper quickly passed and he was seldom vindictive. Possibly the most attractive trait in Jonathan's character is his openness. He had all the Cornish reticence with strangers but in his letters to those he knows and trusts, he seldom pretends to be someone other than he is.

A Cornish gentleman gew up expecting to command his inferiors and Jonathan quickly assumed that to be his right. He would ply Francis Cooke with instructions concerning the administration of the diocese, as one would expect from a bishop to his registrar, but Cooke was also expected to run domestic errands in Exeter like buying red lozenges for heartburn, or guitar strings for his wife, and taking parcels to the carrier. Cooke was thanked for a Christmas present with the words 'Your brawn was good though small' and was told, roughly but kindly, that his bishop hoped that his gout was 'the sign of a long life'. Jonathan would peremptorily dismiss a servant for inefficiency, but take his cook's advice on the best method of conveying books to Trelawne. He was generous, but when short of ready money, grumbled over small expenses. Having spend hundreds of pounds building a private chapel at Trelawne House he complained about Cooke spending seven pounds on repairs to the palace stables at Exeter and grumbled for weeks about a printer's bill for five pounds twelve shillings for printed letters sent to each parish. Cooke was told 'the prints stick in my stomach, I'll be caught no more' and a few days later was ordered to reimburse his bishop whenever some commutation money was available. When dealing withh the clergy he readily acknowledged a mistake. 'If I have injured Mr. Collins by doing (as I thought) a justice to Mr. Chilcot, I beg his pardon.' But if simony or some other irregularity was suspected it was a different matter. If a certain clergyman came to the commissioners for institution with a deed of presentation, Cooke was told, ominously, 'let them turn him over to me!'[15]

The main reason why Trelawny's character is so difficult to understand stems from the marked contrast between his formal correspondence and his private letters. When writing to men in public office his style is flamboyant and effusive and he displays an exaggerated courtesy and deference to men of higher rank. On the other hand his writing style when writing to people he knows and trusts is blunt and humourous. One must seek for an explanation partly in his background, for among the Cornish it is not thought strange to appear to be one person to a stranger and another person to a friend, and partly in his own highly developed sense of hierarchy and the behaviour fitting between men of different social rank. He believed strongly that a proper deference strengthened and upheld the hierarchial structure of society. He was as keenly aware of the deference due from him as he was of that due to him and expected others to behave accordingly. Thus he could write to the Duke of Marlborough using phrases like,

> 'permit me to give myself the great honour of this opportunity to throw myself with my son at your feet'

or

> 'to see the best army under the greatest general in the world'

which, if taken out of context by those ignorant of the fact that the Duke and the Bishop were very good friends, could easily be mistaken for odious flattery.[16] It was not flattery but his way of showing a form of deference to his social superior. On the other hand, Trelawny expressed his distaste to Cooke on receiving from the patron of a living what he considered to be 'a paper fitter for his proctor'. He rebuked Archdeacon Bridoake for rudely interrupting Warden Nicholas because, in his opinion, Bridoake had displayed sheer bad manners. Trelawny was shocked to learn that the same archdeacon could thrust himself 'with rudeness and impudence' on the new Lord Keeper, Lord Harcourt:

> 'some men of late days give themselves strange opinions

of their having made the late change in the Ministry [i.e. Godolphin's dismissal and Harley's promotion] and, on that account, think they may use them with familiarity, perhaps command'.[17]

When Wake who was once his dean became his archbishop, Trelawny had no difficulty in changing the tone of his letters from one of polite direct order to one of verbose deference. To read the one without the other always gives a distorted picture. The real man underneath the effusive deferential language was a shrewd judge of character, honest and humourous. Even when writing to friends he could be at times disconcertingly blunt. Those who knew him appreciated these qualities. On one occasion Francis Cooke told him of the death of a certain Colonel Hulford. Trelawny was not surprised. What would have surprised him was 'to learn of a single man or woman who was sorry for it!' Jonathan may be criticised for his lack of charity: he cannot be faulted for his honesty.

1. E. Gibson, ed., *Camden's Britannica* (1695), p.22.

2. Bodl. Dep. C. 225, Gibson MSS., f.167, T to Bennett, undated.

3. C.T., p.261, Lamplugh to T, 25 February, 1684.

4. D.R.O., Cooke Corresp., 22 May [1700], 21 December [1700].

5. *Gentleman's Magazine,* xxv, pt.ii (1805), p.915; *Bath MSS.* iii. 436, T to Prior, 2 August, 1707.

6. C.T., p.275, Trimnell to T, 28 December, 1714; Buller BC/25/11/4, T to Rebecca Buller, 26 April, 1717; 11/7, Major General Charles Trelawny to Rebecca Buller, 10 July, 1718.

7. (Stothard) Bray, *op. cit.,* p.69.

8. *Trelawny Correspondence: Letters between Myrtilla and Philander* (1884). This small volume, privately printed, containes the love letters.

9. *J.R.I.C.* ii (1866-7), pp.18-20.

10. C.T., p.291, Sprat to T, 30 August.

11. Winchester Cathedral Libr., xx Ledger Book (1708-18), ff.30, 40, 42-45, 63, 72, 73, 76; xxiv Ledger Book (1718-25), ff.10, 21.

12. Downes MSS., *passim.*

13. Granger, *op. cit.,* ii. 521.

14. *Trelawny Correspondence,* pp.77-8, 123-4.

15. D.R.O., Cooke Corresp., 1 August, 31 August, 17 September.

16. Blenheim MSS., B2-20, T to Marlborough, 15 March, 1711. It may not be without significence, in this context, that Leonard Welstead dedicated his book on literary style to Trelawny, see *The Works of Dionysius Longinus* (Bristol, 1712).

17. 'Trelawny Papers', *Camden Miscellany* (1853), p.22, T to Radcliffe, 29 July, 1711.

161

CHAPTER TWELVE

The Road to Bankruptcy

Few topics attract as much cant and misrepresentation as the reputed income of the clergy of the Church of England. It would seem that the reluctance of the average Englishman of the twentieth century to believe that the Church of England is not subsidsed by the State can be parallelled by the obstinacy with which Englishmen in the seventeenth century insisted that all bishops were well off. It was conceded that the same could not be said for the holder of a Welsh diocese, but no one could understand what any English bishop had to complain of. Misinformation was rife: the values of richer livings were frequently quoted with no regard for accuracy. Luttrell, for example, reported in 1708 that the income of the rectory of Witney was £700 a year. Two and a half years later he quoted £500 as the figure, but then he was prepared to believe that a bishop of Winchester was worth £7,000 a year, a figure double the actual income.[1] A book of valuations published in 1680 still gave the income of the bishop of Exeter as £1,566 14s.6d., a figure taken, uncritically, from the *Valor Ecclesiasticus* of Henry VIII and ludicrously unrealistic by the reign of Charles II.[2]

In some respects the English bishops were much better off than their parish clergy. Their income was derived from fixed rents and fees unaffected by fluctuating harvests which made tithe so unreliable. On the other hand their outgoings were much higher. All livings over ten pounds a year were charged with payment of first fruits and tenths, but by the late seventeenth century assessments bore no relation to actual income. Episcopal first fruits and tenths kept in line with actual revenue. For example, a dean of St. Buryan, Cornwall, paid. £58 8s.1½d. for first fruits and £5 16s.9¾d. for tenths, out of an annual income of approximately £150. When Trelawny went to Winchester he paid £3,124 12s.8d. for first fruits and £250 14s.7d. for tenths out of an income for the year of £3,502 15s.11¾d.[3] What little income a bishop might receive in his first year after payment of tax could easily be swallowed up in the legal fees payable at the various stages of his confirmation, consecration or translation, enthronement and introduction into the House of Lords. A list of these fees is preserved among Archbishop Sharp's papers and it shows that they were far from trifling.[4]

A diocese provided three sources of income: rents and fines from episcopal estates; fees from various legal and sacramental acts, and the grant of reversions. The size and extent of episcopal estates varied greatly. The more scattered or remote from the diocese, the more difficult it was to collect the rents and the more officers needed to oversee manorial courts and collect their lord's dues. The alacrity with which the Somerset tenants of the bishop of Winchester ceased to pay rent on the death of Peter Mews in noteworthy, and problems connected with the illegal felling of timber and poaching of deer during the years of Mew's dotage remained to plague Trelawny for some time after his translation. Income from fines and reversions was a lottery enlivened by horse trading. Small properties, like town houses, were leased for a number of years but large properties, especially in the south west, were leased for a term of three lives. These leases could be renewed or a new life added upon payment of a large and uncertain fine. Annual rents were kept low. Tenants approved of the security of this form of tenure and preferred 'a sharp pain to a perpetual ache' as one old Cornish writer put it. Reversions were part of a limited market. Officers of the bishops' courts, both ecclesiastical and manorial, held office by virtue of a patent of appointment. A bishop might sell the promise to appoint during the lifetime of the existing holder. No bishop could rely on a lease falling in or an office holder dying. If he was fortunate in this respect then everything depended on how hard a bargain he was willing to drive, and how skilfully negotiations were conducted. It was always embarrassing to be seen trying to secure a just proportion of treasure on earth while advocating a search for treasure in heaven at the same time. A politically active bishop had to balance the further consideration that too hard a bargain might offend an influential landowner and political supporter. The political disincentive to re-negotiate the lease for Penryn Town had been mentioned already.[5]

A bishop received a fee for every institution, licensing and ordination. In a large diocese this source of income amounted to a significant sum. Income from this source can be calculated fairly accurately for the diocese of Exeter. Trelawny added an average of sixty five pounds a year, twelve per cent above the annual rent roll,[6] and this was a welcome source of money because it involved little expenditure. It was a different matter when it came to procurations. These fees were paid to the bishop at his triennial visitation, but his expenses far exceeded them. Parishes in the diocese of Exeter paid procurations of two shillings and sixpence. Assuming that all paid, for thirty parishes were still in arrears eighteen months after the primary visitation of 1689, then the 474 parishes subject to a triennial visitation produced a sum amounting to £59 5s.0d. The bishop employed five servants, namely a porter, a footman, a groom, a coachman and a postilion all at one shilling a day. It took between 25 and 29 days to complete the circuit. Horses could be hired for one shilling a day and the presence of a postilion implies that four horses were needed to pull the coach. Servants expected board and lodging, which could not have been less than one and sixpence a day each. Fodder and oats for a horse came to sixpence a day, so assuming the hire of only four horses and the use of the bishop's own coach, expenses came to twenty-five pounds at least. The bishop divided the cost of a sumpterman and his horses equally with his registrar. This came to a further two pounds ten shillings. Nor was that all. The leading clergy and local gentry who attended the court expected to be entertained to dinner that evening. Even if the expense was shared between the bishop and his registrar, at an average price of one and sixpence a head excluding drink and tobacco, it is difficult to picture any bishop of Exeter pocketing any procuration money at the end of the month.

After 1689, the burden of taxation, both the Land Tax and poor relief, bore heavily on the parish clergy. The bishops were better off because they could often pass these taxes on to their tenants without having them deducted from the rents. This arrangments was in force for fourteen out of the twenty-two estates of the Exeter bishopric by 1717 and it spread slowly through the manors of Winchester.[7] The cost of maintaining a palace was proportionately higher than a parsonage and, beyond that, a bishop's expenses mounted steadily. The demands of hospitality were considerable. Trelawny reckoned that his two years at Bristol had cost him £1,500 of which hospitality accounted for the largest part. Fuel for heating bedrooms for friends or relatives wanting to stay a night or two, six dozen bottles of claret for the assize judge, a meal for the officers of the local garrison, bills of this sort soon mounted up. Attendance at Parliament was another burden. Some bishops had the advantages of a house near or in London. Others had to rent accommodation from Londoners eager to fleece the unwary provincial. Cost of travel was not light. Nicholson of Carlisle reckoned a journey south to Westminster cost him one hundred pounds: it could not have been much less to travel from Trelawne.[8] If one adds to all these expenses the legal costs of defending his rights and the rights of his consistory court in the courts of Westminster Hall or at the local assizes, then one can appreciate that the financial burden of a bishop might be crippling.

How individual bishops reacted to their financial situation has been a neglected area of study. When Stratford of Chester died, his son wrote that many of his father's episcopal colleagues would not approve his

164

example of leaving less than he started with after enjoying one or more dignities of the Church for forty years.[9] Disappointment may have soured his son's judgement, but some of his contemporaries also felt that bishops could be less than faithful stewards. The anonymous letter writer of a pamphlet in support of Sir John Packington's abortive Bill to prohibit the translation of prelates made a bid for popular support for this parliamentary manoeuvre, designed principally to block Burnet's appointment to Winchester, by airing the grievance that short tenure of a see tempted the less scrupulous to exploit estates at the expense of his successor. It was alleged that Patrick felled and sold all the available timber on the episcopal estates of Chichester during the brief time he was there, passing off the depredation with the joke that it mattered little seeing he was to be succeeded by a Grove.[10] Offspring Blackall's greed for money so incensed Launcelot Blackburne that when he succeeded Blackall at Exeter he ordered an enquiry and unearthed the fact that in eight years an active campaign to persuade tenants to renew leases had brought Blackall £2,600 in fines. This policy of active realisation of potential revenue was probably not followed by all bishops: it could not be concealed from public disapproval for long. It was easier to cut back on expenditure by incurring as little administrative or legal expense as possible while gaining a reputation for modesty and humility in the process. As a matter of family pride, temperament and conviction Trelawny could not behave in this fashion. Family pride demanded that social rank incurred responsibilities. Trelawny was impulsively generous as well as combative by nature. He was also convinced of the divine rights and obligations of the episcopal order. In the difficult years following 1689 such a combination was fatal for achieving financial solvency.

Financially Trelawny's career began badly. It was acknowledged that a royal chaplain needed the income of a good living to support the expense of attendance at Court. St. Ive brought Trelawny £109 a year out of which he had to allow £30 for a curate. South Hill was reckoned to be worth £140 a year. Trelawny was faced with a bill of £700 in repairs to two parsonages. He inherited his father's debts when he succeeded to the baronetcy and was forced to take out his first mortgage of £2,000 in 1681.[11] It is not possible to discover how frequently or by how much the family rent roll of £300 a year was supplemented by heriots and fines, but the expenses of a vice-admiral of the coast, a deputy lieutenant, and travel as chaplain to the household of Lord Conway would have eaten up much of the income from this source. A gentleman in Trelawny's social position was in a cleft stick. If he resided quietly and lived modestly on his estates he had little or no hope of freeing himself from debt. If he plunged into the world of affairs he might win the rewards of lucrative office but he would

165

have to incur further debts in the hope of doing so. Trelawny was painfully aware of this dilemma when he pleaded for a wealthier bishopric than Bristol. He was allowed to supplement his £350 a year with the income of his two Cornish livings, but his request to be excused first-fruits although looked upon favourably, does not appear to have been granted.[12] By the time he had paid first-fruits, all the fees for a newly consecrated bishop, his share of the trial of the Seven Bishops, journey to and from London to attend either at Court or upon the Archbishop, Trelawny could have had little left. He paid no tenths at all. He was motivated neither by greed nor by bravado when he solicited William and Mary for the diocese of Salisbury. That bishopric had an income large enough to need no *commendam*.[13] Burnet secured Salisbury, however, and Trelawny had to be content with Exeter and a new *commendam* in which St. Ive and South Hill were given up in exchange for Shobrooke in Devon, and the Royal Deanery of St. Buryan at Land's End, with permission to retain any two dignities in his gift as bishop.[14]

This new *commendam* was not generous. The Exeter rent roll was £558 3s.5¾d. a year. Shobrooke was assessed at £260 3s.0d. for the Land Tax, and paid £3 12s.0d. annually in tenths. Trelawny paid his curate thirty pounds a year, which left him with approximately £175 a year. He reckoned St. Buryan to be worth £140 a year clear of all charges.[15] Charges and tenths on the bishopric amounted to £61 9s.8d. An average of £65 a year came in by way of fees. Therefore, Trelawny's annual income as bishop of Exeter amounted to about £875 (excluding fines, heriots and profits from fairs). Assuming that the mortgage of 1681 was carried at the maximum interest rate of five per cent, then a third of the income from the family estates was servicing that debt. Had Trelawny chosen the line of least resistance when carrying out his episcopal duties, he could have contrived on around £1,000 a year to live within his means and reduce his debts. He did nothing of the sort.

Within a year of his primary visitation, Trelawny became embroiled in the Exeter College Case, followed closely by the case of Hele v Hodder. One cannot discover how much those two cases cost; they must have been expensive for both were carried on a writ of error to the House of Lords. In later years Bishop Hough alleged that he had been told that Hele v Hodder had cost Trelawny £1,000.[16] This figure looks suspiciously high, but the cost must have run into hundreds of pounds. In 1696 Trelawny had to face a rebuilding of part of the palace of Exeter.[17] It is not surprising to learn that he conducted no personal visitation of his diocese between 1692 and 1699 and seldom appeared at Westminster during the same period. When he admitted to the Duke of Portland in 1696 that he could not afford to attend Parliament, he wrote the simple truth.[18]

Throughout these years his family increased. Eight of his twelve children were born between 1688 and 1700.[19] Rebecca, his wife, brought some welcome financial relief in 1698 when she received her portion of the Efford estate of her maternal grandfather, Matthew Hals. This amounted to land worth over £6,500 with a rent roll of £206 3s.1½d.[20] Not that the Bishop personally spent any of this money while his wife was alive. He was an affectionate husband and Rebecca was a woman who knew her own mind. Judging by the few bills that have survived, Rebecca was determined to make Trelawne House a less spartan home to live in.[21] Her husband, in response, decided to make Trelawne a grander house by adding a large chapel in 1701. It was an extravagance he half regretted, costing as it did several hundred pounds. He confessed to Francis Cooke that he would have 'to pinch for it' and wondered if any one was in the mood to take up a reversion.[22] Yet, by the end of the year, Trelawny was offering to foot the bill for fitting out the interior of the meeting place of the Lower House of Convocation! It was just as well for him that this offer was declined,[23] but such impulsive generosity was typical of the man. Gifts of church plate to Pelynt and Shobrooke churches; support for his old college, including a statue of Cardinal Wolsey commissioned by him from Grinling Gibbons for one hundred guineas; small but frequent sums to help poverty stricken French ministers in England are just some examples. He bore the cost of repair and refurbishing the chapel at East Looe. This was as much a shrewd political investment as it was an act of charity, being designed to check the growth of nonconformist worship in the town, but payment of forty pounds a year to the curate was remarkably generous when the Church at large only hoped to raise curates' stipends to thirty pounds.

In a letter to the Earl of Nottingham, Trelawny hinted that the inclusion of two dignities in his *commendam* was a compensation for the loss of Salisbury.[24] In his seventeen years at Exeter, Trelawny invoked this clause sparingly. He held the archdeaconry of Totnes from 27 August 1693 to 1 May 1694 before giving it to George Snell. In so short a time Trelawny could have done little more than recover the charge of assuming it. It was the archdeaconry with the least income. However, in 1704 Trelawny took the prebendal stall vacated by George Hooper and the archdeaconry of Exeter. A prebend was worth little more than twenty pounds a year; the archdeaconry about sixty pounds. Judging by one of Atterbury's letters Trelawny was apprehensive of public criticism at having done so.[25] His motive may well have been political rather than financial. He held the archdeaconry until his translation to Winchester. One story circulating in Pelynt in the late eighteenth century was to the effect that, shortly before he left Exeter, he refused £7,000 for the reversion of Cuddenback,[26] the wealthiest of the episcopal manors in Cornwall, on the grounds that he

167

would not prejudice his successor. If the story is true, it shows that his honour as a gentleman meant more to him than financial redemption. It may well hint the extent of his financial embarrassment that someone should have thought he could be tempted in this way.

By 1706 Trelawny's insolvency was no secret. When the Governors of Queen Anne's Bounty refused to consider a proposal of the Committee for Rules and Order that all arrears of first fruits and tenths should be answered *before* a promotion passed the Great Seal, a proposal strongly advocated by the Bishop of Salisbury ahead of the Committee's final report, it may well be they saw through a Whig manoeuvre to make it impossible for Trelawny to be translated to Winchester.[27] In 1710 it was understood that Trelawny's support for Henry Seymour's election to Parliament was a foregone conclusion because of the sum of money the Bishop owed him.[28] Early in 1713, the Bishop re-mortgaged all his family estates for a further £9,000.[29]

Why Trelawny should have taken this step is still something of a mystery. Presumably his credit was so bad that he had to satisfy a number of creditors. Yet by that time he had enjoyed the rent rolls of the diocese of Winchester for six years. The only surviving rental book shows that his income from 1707 to 1711 totalled £17,611 18s.4¾d.[30] So large a sum should have been sufficient to discharge all debts from the past. However, this is the period when the Governors of Queen Anne's Bounty were busy pursuing arrears of tenths and first fruits from all the 'chiefest dignitaries'. In the reports submitted to the Governors by the First Fruits Officers on the order of the Lord Treasurer the casual and haphazard methods of collecting tenths in the diocese of Exeter became obvious to anyone who perused the figures. It was a distasteful task for any bishop and an anathema to one with Trelawny's generous and understanding nature. Not only do the figures reveal that he passed no accounts for tenths while he was bishop of Bristol; they show also that up to Christmas 1705, £6,630 4s.½d. of the tenths of the diocese of Exeter were still unpaid. Out of this sum a negligible £163 was owed by Bishop Lamplugh's executors. The rest was made up of £2,824 7s.10½d. due from the clergy and £3,785 12s.3¾d. due from the bishop. Apparently Trelawny had paid no tenths for over seven years. The Governors considered Trelawny's case in 1710: he agreed to pay £500 down and the balance by the end of 1711.[31] Assuming that Trelawny was liable for all the tenths for Bristol for 1686 and 1687 and for his own tenths for Exeter, the deductions from his income would be as follows:-

	£	s	d
For Bristol	650	0	0
For Exeter	3785	12	3¾
For Winchester first fruits	3,124	12	8
For Winchester tenths for five years	1,560	10	10
Total	9,120	15	9¾

Of the first five years rent there remained £8,491 2s.7d. When the charges of translation to the see of Winchester and installation as Prelate of the Order of the Garter are added to the costs of rebuilding part of Farnham Castle, and laying out the gardens at Wolversey, Trelawny had a much smaller disposable income than the total rent roll. The remainder could easily have been swallowed up in the costs of the General Election of 1710. Unfortunately, without evidence, any estimate of cost on that score is pure speculation.

There is no doubt that Trelawny sought to improve his episcopal income the moment he was translated to Winchester. He employed Charles Heron for a number of years as his business agent with orders to tighten up the administration of the episcopal manors where it had grown slack, and to increase income by exacting worthwhile heriots and pressing fines for the renewal of leases upwards. In doing this he anticipated by a number of years a policy pursued by several bishops and capitular bodies from about 1720 onwards. Christopher Clay has pointed out that few institutional owners of land had any experience in estate management. It took some time for them to realise that an increase in the fining rate had become long overdue. As a country gentleman, Trelawny was in a position to know what changes were taking place both in the price of freehold land and in the bargains being struck between landowners and their tenants. In this matter he appears to have blazed a trail other ecclesiastical landlords might follow.[32]

In pursuit of this policy, Bishop and Business Agent were prepared to use fair means or foul. Action was taken in manorial courts to break old tenures. Tenants were prosecuted for having committed waste of timber, for which they forfeited their copyholds. The Bishop and Heron pressed ahead with sale of timber, even going to the extent of concealing tree felling from the bishop's Woodward who had the right to licence all wood cutting and take up to a third of the value of the timber as his fee. Between 1709 and 1710 Trelawny piloted through the Lords a Bill to enclose Ropley Common and quietly tacked on a clause which enabled him to 'improve'

Farnham Old Park. After years of lax administration under Bishop Mews, his successor had some justfication for being firm with his tenants and manorial officers, but there is little doubt that Heron's methods aroused deep fear and resentment among the tenants of the bishopric. The Hampshire tenants, in particular, hated his authority and this largely explains why deer poaching from the bishop's parks increased greatly toward the end of Trelawny's life. The policy carried out by Heron and his successor, Forbes, in the Bishop's name, a policy for which Trelawny must carry responsibility, contributed directly to formation of the notorious 'Blacks', the masked and armed raiders with black gloves who committed depredations in the deer parks and meted out their own rough justice in local disputes.[33]

It was not the practice of the aristocracy and gentry at this period to pay back the principal of a mortgage, but Trelawny even ceased to pay interest after the first two years. The mortgages of 1681 and 1713 were outstanding three years after his death with interest accumulating on both. Sir Charles Wager, a family friend, acquired the mortgages. The need to pay him led to the Private Act of Parliament which permitted sale of as many Trelawny estates as were needed to raise £15,939 10s.0d. The Bishop's sudden death, on 19th July, 1721, upset the family's financial strategy. He died intestate which shipwrecked his charitable intentions too. He had intended to give £1,000 to endow a school in East Looe, and £1,000 to the Society for the Propagation of the Gospel for work particularly in the West Indies, but his son, John only learnt of this some years after his father's death. Between 1713 and 1721 Trelawny received a full eight years' income, at least £25,000, yet he was spending money so fast that some of his servants' wages were perpetually in arrears and one litigant, awarded costs by the Court of Exchequer in July, 1719, had to wait until 1736 before he got his money, because he had refused to accept, in the Bishop's life-time, a cash payment at the insultingly low figure of twelve pence in the pound.[34]

Lacking any definite documentary evidence, only tentative answers can be given for this outflow of cash. John, his eldest son must have cost him dear. The purchase of an army commission of colonel must have been expensive. The expenses of the General Election of 1713 must also have been high. Trelawny family estates lay in east Cornwall, but wealth was shifting to west Cornwall where more tin was to be found, so the Bishop was still investing in land further to the west. He bought all the land holdings of Peter Jenkins and took a lease on the episcopal manor of Tregair and Burmeir. He was also purchasing leases of tenements in the manor of Port Looe whenever opportunity occurred.[35] His son, John, to whom his father committed the management of the Cornish lands in 1713, seems to have invested in Wheal Vorr, which produced a great quantity of tin in 1717 but the seam had run out completely by the following year.[36] Hard evidence of the involvement of many landed families in the speculative fever which led to the South Sea Bubble of 1720 is difficult to come by. Certainly bishops were not immune. Offspring Blackall's will revealed that he left £2,300 in South Sea Stock, and Benjamin Hoadley had purchased £2,000 in the Third Subscription of 1720 and 1721.[37] The Trelawnys were concerned with the fate of the whole venture. A manuscript copy of the report of the House of Commons secret committee on the South Sea Company was preserved among the family papers. The Bishop's last appearance in the Lords was six weeks before his death when the affairs of the Company were being discussed.[38] John Trelawny's name appears on the Third Subscription List of Sir Theodore Jannson himself for £1,000. Living with a mortage was part of a way of life for so many gentry in the south west but the Bishop always regretted the fact. He told his son-in-law 'I have smarted too much by mortgages to bring any person I have a kindness for under that plague which seldom is cured and whenever it is it leaves great scars behind'.[39] In 1719 he had begun pulling down part of Trelawne House as a preliminary to an extensive rebuilding,[40] so, presumably, cash for the builders was a higher priority than wages for his servants.

In December, 1714 Charles Trimnell was commiserating with Trelawny's heavy expenses in the General Election[41] but there was no General Election for him to fight after 1715. It would be tempting to conclude that Trelawny's bankruptcy, leading to the sale of many family estates as well as the Bishop's personal library can be explained by unwise investments and large sums squandered in bribing the Cornish electorate. Such a view would do less than justice to the complexity of the Bishop's financial situation. Had he less love for the Church of England, had he cared less about the responsibilities of the office of a bishop, he might have spent far less money in defending the doctrine and discipline of the Church. One hundred years after his death the large incomes enjoyed by many bishops and dignitaries of the Church of England were thought to be a national scandal. No episcopal duty, as it was understood in the early nineteenth century could justify remuneration on the scale then available to some diocesans. But, by then, the whole concept of a bishop's responsibilities had changed and a bishop like Philpotts of Exeter, who tended to revert to an earlier understanding was looked upon as somewhat eccentric. Trelawny would have welcomed in Philpotts a kindred spirit. By 1721, in the eyes of the younger generation, Trelawny's understanding of a bishop's income as a trust not to be enjoyed but to be employed in protecting the Church had made him something of an eccentric too.

171

1. Luttrell, vi. 106, 372, 690.

2. *Book of Valuations of all the Ecclesiastical Preferments in England and Wales,* (1680), quoted by A. Browning, *English Historical Documens 1660-1714* (1953), p.418.

3. See J. Ecton, *Thesaurus Rerum Ecclesiasticarum* (1742); H.R.O., Trelawny Papers, Rental of the bishopric 1702-1711.

4. G.R.O., Lloyd-Baker-Sharp MSS. D. 3549, Box 4, Bundle 0.

5. See above, p.118.

6. D.R.O., Chanter 725, gives a list of all fees.

7. D.R.O., Chanter 1104, Rental of the bishopric 1717; H.R.O., Rental 1702-1711.

8. F.G. James, *North Country Bishop* (Yale, 1956), p.117.

9. *Portland MSS.* iv. 390-91 Stratford to Harley, 24 February, 1707.

10. *A Letter from a Clergyman in the Country......* p.14.

11. 11 George II, *cap.* 34 (1725).

12. *Cal. S.P. Dom.,* Feb.-Dec. 1685, p.419, December 19.

13. Add. MSS. 29584, f.109, T to Nottingham, 7 February, 1704.

14. *Cal. S.P. Dom.,* Feb. 1689-April 1690, p.58.

15. Wake MSS. xx, unfoliated, T to Wake [December 1716].

6. W.D. Macray, 'Table-talk and papers of Bishop Hough, 1703-1743', *Oxford Historical Society* (1890), p.396.

17. Lamb. Libr., Tenison's Register i, 23 March, 1698.

18. U.N.L., Portland Papers PwA 1405, T to Portland, 22 April, 1696.

19. The children cost £36 in taxes because three were born while that curious statute 6 & 7 *Gul. & Mar. cap.* 6 was in force. In 1707 corsets for the females of the family, and for the Bishop, cost over £22, *Tre Pol and Pen* (Truro, 1928), p.50.

20. D.R.O., C.R. 636.

21. D.R.O., C.R. 647.

22. D.R.O., Cooke Corresp., T to COoke, 6 February, 1701; same to same, 20 February, 1701; same to same, 20 March, 1701.

23. E.C., iii. 56, Atterbury to T, 17 November, 1701.

172

24. *Loc. cit.*

25. *E.C.,* iii. 189, Atterbury to T, 30 May, 1704.

26. C.T., p.213.

27. C.C., 378, Q.A.B. Minute Book (1704-1716), f.37, 22 January, 1707.

28. Margaret Maria, Lady Verney, ed., *Verney Letters of the Eighteenth Century from the MSS. at Claydon House* (1930), i.304.

29. 11 George II, *cap.* 34 (1725).

30. *Loc. cit.*
31. Alan Savidge, *The Foundation and early years of Queen Anne's Bounty* (1955), p.44.

32. Christopher Clay, ' "The Greed of Whig Bishops"? Church landlords and their lesses 1660-1760', *Past and Present,* lxxxvii, (May 1980), pp.128-157.

33. E.P. Thompson, *Whigs and Hunters: the origin of the Black Act* (1977), pp.119-41, gives a detailed account. It is written from a marxist standpoint and includes a caricature of Trelawny worthy of the pages of the soviet satirical magazine *Krokodil.*

34. D.R.O., C.R. 636.

35. C.R.O., Buller BS/14/22, Rental, 1711, of manor of Port Looe.

36. *Portland MSS.* v.196, Atterbury to Harley, 25 June, 1712; *Cal. Treasury Papers* v (1719-1721), 379, Roger Corker to John Anstis, 25 May, 1718.

37. Boggis, *op. cit.,* p.440; H.L., Box 158, Sir Harcourt Master's List.

38. *Lords' Journal,* 10 June, 1721.

39. Downes MSS., T to John Francis Buller, 19 November, 1717.

40. D.R.O., Cooke Corresp., John Cooke to Edward Cooke, 9 August, 1719.

41. C.T., p.275, Trimnell to T, 28 December, 1714.

Conclusion

Jonathan suffered no lingering illness. His death on 19 July, 1721 came quickly.[1] It took the family a fortnight to prepare for the removal of the corpse from Chelsea but there was never any question where it should be interred. Jonathan must rest with his ancestors in the family vault at Pelynt parish church. On Thursday, 3 August the coffin was carried with 'great Funeral Pomp and State' through the streets of Chelsea and Kensington, then on to Salisbury and Honiton, Exeter and Plymouth, across the Tamar and down the steep treacherous roads to Liskeard and Trelawne. Crown and cushion, mitre and crozier, great banner and bannerets preceded the hearse. No doubt but that the final stage of the journey was well attended for the Cornish dearly love a funeral.[2]

He had been a bishop for nearly thirty-five years and, on any showing, had enjoyed a remarkably successful ecclesiastical career. No one thought to perpetuate his memory by writing a biography or by erecting a monument. Indeed, the massive episcopal throne he ordered to be built in Winchester Cathedral was dismantled in the next century. Annually (on or near 30 June), many dinner guests helped him to celebrate his release from the Tower of London, and, to that extent, helped to perpetuate a piece of popular history. Apart from that Jonathan was not anxious to record any particular view of himself for posterity. Years earlier Atterbury had recorded in the dedicatory preface to his sermons the Trelawny preferred to work unobtrusively, and, in contrast to Atterbury himself, who left instructions that only his sermon notes and incriminating papers should be destroyed after his death, Trelawny left a simple note that all papers should be destroyed. Only his young son Hele's disbelief that his father really meant 'all papers' led to the bulk of them being transported to Trelawne, there to lie for a further two hundred years before disappearing for good. If they remembered him at all, men remembered him fondly. He was, wrote Granger, 'friendly, open, generous and charitable, a good companion and a good man.' George Clarke recalled being entertained at Bristol in 1686 'in that kind and generous manner with which his Lordship always uses his friends'.[3] It is ironic that he should owe a measure of posthumous fame to the great Lord Macaulay, aided and abetted by the Reverend R.S. Hawker of Morwenstow. He would have been distinctly uncomfortable in the role of a hero in a Whig interpretation of history. Hawker palmed off a ballad of his own on to an unsuspecting Macaulay. The Song of the Western Men

174

probably has nothing to do with Bishop Trelawny or with any of his ancestors.[4]

In the late nineteenth century the publication of some of Trelawny's letters led historians to pass a harsh judgement. In 1882 Nichols and Taylor in their history of Bristol reversed the judgement of the past.

'How far Trelawny was in earnest in his resistance to the Declaration of Indulgence is a question; that he was a disappointed man, a truckler and a time server is, we fear, beyond dispute'.[5]

Twemlow wrote a fairly balanced article for the *Dictionary of National Biography* in 1899 but modern historians have tended to repeat this type of snap judgement. They have passed opprobrious comments on Bishop Trelawny on the basis of occasional letters read in the course of their research into something else. Certainly Trelawny's language was vigorous and colourful at times. Only when it is taken out of the context of the writing of his contemporaries does it appear unduly 'obsequious', 'pliant' or 'odious'. It is conceivable that an 'essentially timid' man could govern his diocese 'with vigour' but vigorous administration must, sooner or later, lead to personal confrontations which the naturally timid find impossible to sustain. If his fear of the consequences of Jacobite success are thought to betray a cowardly nature then one can only point out that the author or authors of the Bishops' Declaration of 1715 were equally cowardly, and so were all the Bishops who associated themselves with it. The Declaration repeated Trelawny's own opinions. He endorsed it heartily but he did not compose it. What seems with hindsight to have been timid over-reaction was judged realistic at the time. Englishmen were uneasy at the speed with which France recovered after the wars. If the Pretender's return were to be accomplished with French military aid the consequences may well have been bloody for some.

If the occasional letter of Trelawny has twisted the judgement of historians, the reliance on Burnet's *History of Mine Own Time* has confirmed the distortion. Trelawny has been labelled a lightweight bishop whose success in the shady world of boroughmongering earned him an unjustified promotion. Popularly he is remembered only by the phrase from the refrain of an old song:

'And shall Trelawny die?
Here's twenty thousand Cornishmen
shall know the reason why.'

Why has Trelawny been remembered best as the subject of a doubtful ballad? The answer is that he espoused a cause that failed. In the age of Walpole and Newcastle the ecclesiastical issues, so important to men in the reign of Queen Anne, seemed to be but echoes from a distant past.

175

Trelawny was convinced of the rightness of the doctrine and discipline of the Church of England as he had learnt it as a young man. His idea of a Church in alliance with 'the landed interest' exercising pastoral and supervisory oversight, guiding and correcting the moral development of the Nation had been rejected by the time of his death. His sermons reflect the rational appeal of the age but included a belief in divine Providence which was largely discredited by the beginning of the eighteenth century. Grey does not record the name of the peer speaking in the debate after the collapse of the South Sea Company who said that he truly believed that the collapse was God's punishment on a nation that permitted blasphemy to flourish unchecked. Such an assertion cut little ice in the House of Lords in 1721, and evoked the riposte that 'the noble lord must be a great sinner since it was said that he had lost heavily when the value of the stock plummeted'.[6] It was either the Bishop of Winchester or Lord Bathurst who spoke but, whoever it was, this belief in divine intervention was something with which Trelawny wholeheartedly concurred. Other parts of his theology were also out of date. The high doctrine of episcopacy he held had but a small following in the eighteenth century and had to await the Oxford Movement before it was revived. Restricting the right to educate the young to one particular Church became hard to justify in the Age of the Enlightenment. Censorship of the religious press was just no longer acceptable. By his death, in his theological opinions at least, Trelawny was not unlike that bird his contemporaries had allowed to be harried into extinction on the island of Mauritius. Like the dodo his theology was uncomplicated, unadaptable and very vulnerable.

To be an effective conservative in a period of change is the most difficult task of all. Bishop Trelawny lived through one of the most formative periods in the history of the Church of England. Behind all the debate, party intrigue, political error and lost opportunities a change was taking place in the relationship between the clergy and the laity, a change that was to have a far reaching effect on how the clergy saw themselves and their role in society. Parish clergy ordained in the early eighteenth century did not have the same confidence in the authority of their office. The older clergy were more assertive because they had been accustomed to the backing given by bishops, archdeacons and the church courts. For the new generation this support was given haphazardly, if it was given at all. The slowly growing secular outlook in society was gradually edging the clergy into an enclave labelled 'religious practice' and leaving them there, unattended. When he had conducted his primary visitation of Dorset in 1686 Trelawny had found the clergy negligent in saying the Litany in church on weekdays, but the neglect had far more to do with concealed Dissent than with lay indifference. In his primary visitation charge in 1716

176

Atterbury remarked on the number of Rochester clergy who had abandoned the practice of saying the litany in church on Wednesdays and Fridays, discouraged by the lack of congregation. Atterbury did not approve but he did sympathize.[7] The Honourable Henry Brydges, archdeacon of Rochester, was brother to the duke of Chandos and so not a typical archdeacon of his time, but he was so far from understanding the obligation of public worship that he not infrequently celebrated the Holy Communion at Christmas and Easter for his family in the drawing room.[8] The respect and authority expected and assumed by the clergy of the late seventeenth century had given way by the reign of George I to the exact opposite. As Thomas Burnet told George Duckett in 1719 once upon a time ' a word against the clergy passed for rank atheism and now to speak tolerably of them passes for superstition'.[9]

When one considers Trelawny's career against this background it is remarkable that he achieved as much as he did and maintained to the last a reduced but effective discipline in the Church. In the diocese of Exeter he made possible a continuing policy of preserving the fabric and interior of parish churches which involved an exercise of discipline over the laity which few dioceses could match. The results can be seen and enjoyed today. In the Channel Islands he made possible a discipline in church affairs which finally saw the end of schismatic practices in the Islands. He prevented socinian teaching from getting a foothold in the University of Oxford, thus contributing to the preservation of orthodox trinitarian belief in the Church of England when unitarian teaching tore apart the world of Nonconformity after 1715. He contributed to keeping Oxford largely a clerical institution and, in that sense, preserved those conditions which gave rise to the Oxford Movement. In the great political crises of 1688 and 1714 others played a more important role than he. At the same time there are indications that he made the running on issues which others took up later. His opposition to the religious policy of James II had begun before that stormy interview which led to the imprisonment of the Bishops in the Tower. He was urging a 'Hanoverian' Tory position by the end of 1712 and may well have led others to adopt that stance. Both in Church and State he showed that courage in a crisis and coolness in the face of danger which had been a family trait.

His political attitude was determined by his religion.

'Forasmuch as the mercies received from Almighty God do call for suitable returns of gratitude on our part, and yet all our goods are nothing unto Him who is all-sufficient; and therefore the best way of expressing our thankfulness to Him for the good things we have received of Him is by doing good to others.....'[10]

177

This preamble to the proposed but unfulfilled gift of one thousand pounds to endow a school at East Looe and a further thousand pounds to the Society for the Propagation of the Gospel is a simple statement of Christian stewardship instantly appreciated by fellow Christians in any age. Is it right then to describe him as a 'trimmer' or as 'pliable', one who adjusted his opinions to the political climate? A distinction needs to be made between his outward behaviour and his inner convictions and actual deeds. The latter changed little. Devoted to 'our true Reformed Episcopal Religion', as he described it, he was convinced that the safety of that Church was best lodged in the hands of the gentry who should occupy the bulk of the seats in the House of Commons and support any ministry that was anti-Jacobite and an enemy to the pretensions of France. Trelawny's outward behaviour was another matter. Here that Cornish preference for ambiguity came uppermost. In old age he quoted approvingly a story concerning Lord Godolphin's father:

'a gentleman having with some surprise observed him to
be very ceremonious with an ill man, but in power, asked
him with a kind of resentment how he could be so? His
answer was, "I always put off my hat to my occasions'.[11]

It was as a Churchman and as a Cornishman Trelawny would wish to be remembered. It is as a Churchman and as a Cornishman he should be judged.

1. *Biographia Britannia* (1766), vii. 240.

2. Hearne, vii. 267.

3. Granger, *op. cit.,* iv. 263; H.M.C. *Leybourne-Popham MSS.,* p.265, autobiography of Dr. George Clarke.

4. R. Morton Nance, 'The Reason Why', *Old Cornwall* (Oct. 1927), pp.38-40.

5. Nichols and Taylor, *op. cit.,* iii. 118.

6. Grey, *Parliamentary Debate* (1740), viii. 118.

7. *E.C.,* ii. 256, Charge to the Clergy of Rochester, May, 1716.

8. Add. MSS. 61999, Diary of Henry Brydges D.D. (Jan. 1718-Mar. 1729), *passim.*

9. *Letters of Thomas Burnet to George Duckett,* p.161.

10. Buller BO/22/48.

11. *Ibid.,* BC/25/11, T to John Francis Buller, 25 May, 1718.

I MANUSCRIPT SOURCES

Belvoir Castle	Rutland MSS in possession of his Grace, the duke of Rutland.
Buller Papers at Antony	In possession of Col. Sir John G. Carew-Pole, Bart., D.S.O., T.D., Antony House, Torpoint, Cornwall.
Bodleian Library, Oxford	Department of Western Manuscripts Ballard MSS Gibson MSS Tanner MSS Smith MSS
Bristol Record Office British Library	Diocesan Papers Blenheim MSS Egerton MSS Portland Loan 29 Additional Manuscripts

Additional Manuscripts:

15892	32095
28052	38507
28275	40772
28875	43410
28927	46942
29584	61999

Christ Church Library, Oxford	Wake MSS
Church Commissioners Records	1 Millbank London Queen Anne's Bounty Commissioners Books
Collectanea Trelawniana	A manuscript book in the possession of Mrs. Francis Williams (a copy is now in Cornwall Record Office).
Cornwall Record Office	Archdeaconry papers Buller records Parish registers Wills
Devon Record Office	Cooke Correspondence Diocesan Papers Exeter City Chamber Minutes Grigson Collection (formerly in Exeter City Library)
Downes MSS	In possession of Mrs. Rosemary Parker of Downes, near Crediton, Devon

180

Duchy of Cornwall Office	Buckingham Palace Gate Rental of Exeter Bishopric
Exeter Cathedral Library	Dean and Chapter Act Books and Papers
Gloucester Record Office	Diocesan Papers Lloyd-Baker-Sharp MSS
Hampshire Record Office	Diocesan Papers Trelawny Papers Wolversey Papers
House of Lords Record Office	South Sea Company Papers Private Act 11 George II cap. 34
Lambeth Palace Libarary	Convocation Act Books Commissioners for New Churches Minute Books Court of Arches papers Gibson MSS Tenison MSS S.P.G. Papers
London County Council Record Office	Archdeaonry of Surrey Office Papers
Longleat House	Portland Papers and Prior Papers in the possession of The Marquess of Bath
Magdalene College, Cambridge	Pepys MSS
Plymouth City Library	Kitley MSS
Public Record Office	High Court of Admiralty Papers Lord Chamberlain's Papers State Papers Domestic 35
Trinity College, Dublin	Clarke Correspondence Lyons Collection
University of Nottingham Library	Portland Papers Phillips MSS
Winchester Cathedral Library	Dean and Chapter Ledger Books

II PRIMARY SOURCES IN PRINT

(Published in London unless otherwise stated)

ATTERBURY, Francis,	*Sermons and Discourses upon Several Occasions* (1708)
AILESBURY, Thomas,	*Memoirs of Thomas, earl of Ailesbury, printed for the Roxburghe Club* (Westminster, 1890)
BEER, E.S., ed.,	*Diary of John Evelyn,* 6 vols. (Oxford, 1955)
BINGHAM, Joseph,	*Origines Ecclesiasticae: or the Antiquities of the Christian Church,* 2 vols. (1710)
BURNET, Gilbert,	*Exposition of the Thirty-nine Articles of the Church of England* (1826)
BURNET, Thomas, ed.,	*Bishop Burnet's History of His Own Time* (1724)
BURSCOUGH, Robert,	*A Vindication of the Twenty-third Article from the Bishop's Exposition* (1702) *A Discourse of the Unity of the Church..... being an Answer to a Book, Entitled, Dissenters no Schismatisks ec.* (Exeter, 1704)
BURY, Arthur,	*An Account of the Unhappy Affair* etc. (Oxford, 1690) *The Naked Gospel* (Oxford, 1690)
CALENDAR OF STATE PAPERS DOMESTIC,	1677-8, 1678, 1679-80, 1685, 1686-87, June 1687 - Feb. 1689, 1689-90, 1690-91, 1693, 1698
CALENDAR OF TREASURY BOOKS	1685-89, 1704-5, 1719-21
CARDWELL, E., ed.,	*Documentary Annals of the Reformed Church of England,* 2 vols. (Oxford, 1839)
COOPER, W.D., ed.,	'Trelawny Papers', *Camden Miscellany* ii. (1853)
COUCH, Jonathon,	'Correspondence (Anno 1700) between the Bishop of Exeter and Mrs. Charles Godolphin', *Journal of the Royal Institution of Cornwall,* iii. (1868-70)
DOVER, Lord, ed.,	*The Ellis Correspondence,* 2 vols. (1831)
ECCLESIASTICAL COMMISSION,	*An Order directed against Clandestine Marriages,* (1686) 4 November.

182

ECTON, John,	*Thesaurus Rerum Ecclesiasticarum* (1742)
FOXCROFT, H.C., ed.,	*A Supplement to Burnet's History* (Oxford, 1902)
FULWOOD, Francis,	*The Socinian Controversie touching The Son of God Reduced.....* (1693)
GRIGSON, Geoffrey,	*Tre Pol and Pen* (Truro, 1928)
GUTCH, J,	*Collectanea Curiosa* 2 vols. (Oxford, 1781)
HARRINGTON, James,	*An Account of the Right Reverend Father in God, Jonathan, Lord Bishop of Exon, in his late visitation of Exeter College in Oxon* (1690) *A Defence of the Proceedings of the Right Reverend The Visitor and Fellows of Exeter College in Oxford* (1691)
HARRINGTON, James,	*The Account Examin'd: Or, a Vindication of Dr. Arthur Bury, Rector of Exeter College, from the columnies of a late pamphlet* (1690)
HARRISON, T,	*The History of King James' Ecclesiastical Commission* (1711)
HEARNE, T,	'Remarks and Collections of Thoams Hearne' *Oxford Historical Society* (1885)
HISTORICAL MANUSCRIPTS COMMISSION,	*First Report* (1874) *Seventh Report* (1879) *Ninth Report* (1884) *Bath MSS.* i, iii *Coke MSS.* *Downshire MSS.* i *Dropmore MSS.* i *Finch MSS.* iii, iv *House of Lords* (New Series) i, v *Huntingdon MSS.,* *Leybourne-Popham MSS.* *Portland MSS.* ii-v, vii *Townshend MSS.*
HOADLEY, Benjamin,	*The Nature of the Kingdom, or Church of Christ* (1717)
HUNTER, J,	*The Diary of Thomas Cartwright,* Camden Society first series xxii (1843)
JOURNALS OF THE HOUSE OF LORDS,	1685-1721

A Letter from a Clergyman in the Country to Dignified Clergyman in London Vindicating the

	Bill for promoting the Translations of Bishops (1702)
LONG, Thomas,	*An Answer to a Socinian Treatise call'd The Naked Gospel which was Decreed by the University of Oxford in Convocation, August 19, A.D. 1690 to be Publickally Burnt* (1691)
LUTTRELL, Narcissus,	*A Brief Historical Relation of State Affairs,* 6 vols. (Oxford, 1859).
MACRAY, W.D.,	'Table-Talk and the Papers of Bishop Hough, 1703-1743' *Oxford Historical Society* (1890)
NICHOLS, J., ed.,	*The Epistolary Correspondence of the Right* Reverend Francis Atterbury D.D., Lord *Bishop of Rochester,* 4 vols. second edn. (1789-90) *Reasons in Particular Why the Clergy of the Archdeaconry of Exon cannot comply with His Lordship's present recommendation of Proctors* (Exeter, 1705). Notes and Queries (third series) i.
SCOTT, Walter, ed.,	*A Collection of Scarce and Valuable TRACTS..... particularly that of the Late Lord Somers* (1813)
SMITH, D.N., ed.,	*Letters of Thomas Burnett to George Duckett, 1712-1722* (Roxburghe Club, 1914)
STILLINGFLEET, Edward,	*Ecclesiastical Cases relating to the Exercise Ecclesiastical Jurisdiction as far as it is allowed by law,* 2 vols. (1704)
STILLINGFLEET, James, ed.,	*Miscellaneous Discourses on Several Occasions, by the Right Reverend Edward Stillingfleet, D.D., Late Lord Bishop of Worcester* (1735)
TENISON, Thomas,	*Circular Letter to the..... Bishops of his Province on the growth of vice and prophaneness in the Nation* (1699)
TERRILL, E.,	*Records of the Church of Christ, meeting at Broadmead, Bristol 1640-1687,* ed. E.B. Underhill (Hanserd Knollys Society, 1847)
THOMPSON, E.M., ed.,	*Letters of Humphrey Prideaux, sometime dean of Norwich to John Ellis, sometime Under Secretary of State 1674-1722* (Camden Society, Oxford, 1875)

184

TRELAWNY, Bishop J.,

Letter of the Bishop of Exon to the Archdeacon of Exon (1699)
The Case of Jonathan, Bishop of Exon and Gawan Hayman, Clerk, Plaintiffs in a Writ of Error By them brought in the High Court of Parliament against Sampson Hele, Esq., Defendant (1694)
Letters between Myrtilla and Philander (1884)

TRELAWNY, Bishop
Sir Jonathan

A Sermon on [1 Tim. iii, 1] by the Right Reverend Sir Jonathan Trelawny, Bishop of Winchester: and charge to the Clergy of that diocese, 1708 ed. Sir John Salusbury Trelawny (1876)

VERNEY, Lady Margaret
Maria, ed.,

Verney Letters of the Eighteenth Century from the MSS. at Claydon House, 2 vols. (1930)

WASHINGTON, Joseph,

The Case of Exeter College in the University of Oxford Related and Vindicated (1691)

WOOD, Anthony,

History and Antiquities of the University of Oxford (Oxford, 1786)
Athenae Oxoniensis (1721)

III SECONDARY SOURCES

(Published in London unless otherwise stated)

ALEXANDER, J.J.,

'Exeter Members of Parliament'
Transactions of the Devonshire Association
lxii (1930)

BAKER,
Sir George Sherston,

The Office of Vice-admiral of the Coast
(1884)

BEDDARD, R,

'The Commission for Ecclesiastical
Promotions, 1681-1684', *The Historical
Journal* x (1967)

BENNET, G.V.,

'King William III and the Episcopate',
*Essays in Modern Church History in Memory
of Norman Sykes,* eds. G.V. Bennett and
J.D. Walsh (1966)

BENNETT, G.V.,

'The Convocation of 1710: an Anglican
attempt at Counter-Revolution'
'*Studies in Church History,* vii, eds.
G.J. Cuming and Dereck Baker (Cambridge
1971)

BENNETT, G.V.,

'The Seven Bishops: a reconsideration',
Studies in Church History, xv (Cambridge
1979)

BENNETT, G.V.,

The Tory Crisis in Church and State 1688-1730
(Oxford, 1975)

BIDDLE, Sheila,

Bolingbroke and Harley (1974)

BLACKSTONE, W,

Commentaries on the Laws of England
(Oxford, 1773)

BOGGIS, R.J.E.,

History of the Diocese of Exeter
(Exeter, 1922)

BRAY (Stothard), A.E.,

Trelawny of Trelawne (1837)

BROCKETT, Alan A.,

'The Political and Social Influence of
Exeter Dissenters', *Transactions of the
Devonshire Association* xciii (1961)
Nonconformity in Exeter 1650-1875
(Manchester, 1962)
Biographia Britannia vol. vii (1766)

BROWNING, Andrew,

Thomas Osborne, earl of Danby
(Glasgow, 1951)

BROWNING, Andrew, ed.,	*English Historical Documents 1660-1714* (1953)
CARPENTER, E.,	*The Protestant Bishop* (1956)
CASSAN, S.H.,	*Lives of the Bishops of Winchester* (1827)
CHILDS, John,	*The Army of Charles II* (1976) *The Army, James II and the Glorious Revolution* (Manchester, 1980)
COMYNS, Sir John,	*A Digest of the Laws of England* (1822)
CRUICKSHANKS, Eveline,	'Divisions in the House of Lords..... Ten new Lists' *Bulletin of the Institute of Historical Research* liii (1980)
ENGLISH LAW REPORTS	Vol. clxi (Edinburgh, 1917)
DAVIES-FREARE, E.T.,	*A Guide to Pelynt Parish Church* (Liskeard, 1960)
FAWCETT, T.J.,	*The Liturgy of Comprehension 1689* (Alcuin Club Collection liv, 1973)
FINBERG, H.P.R.,	*West-Country Historical Studies* (Newtown Abbot, 1969)
GIBSON, Edmund,	*Codex Juris Ecclesiastici Anglicani* second edn., (1761)
GLASSEY, L.K.J.,	*Politics and Appointments of Justices of the Peace 1675-1720* (Oxford, 1979)
GRANGER, J,	*Biographical History* vol. ii
GRANVILLE, Roger,	*History of the Granville Family* (Exeter, 1895)
GREGG, Edward,	*Queen Anne* (1980)
GRIGSON, Geoffrey,	*Freedom of the Parish* (1954)
HAMILTON JENKIN, A.K.,	*Cornwall and the Cornish* (1933)
HARRIS, F.L.,	'Education by Charity in Eighteenth Century Cornwall' *Journal of the Royal Institution of Cornwall* new series ix pt. i (1982)
HART A. Tindal,	*Life of John Sharp* (1949)
HIRST, J.E.,	'Whiston's Affair': the trials of a primitive Christian 1709-14' *Journal of Ecclesiastical History* xxvii (1976)

HOLMES, G.,   *British Politics in the Age of Anne* (1967)

HORWITZ, H.,   'Parliament and the Glorious Revolution'
Bulletin of the Institute of Historical Record
xlvii (1974)

IAGO, W.,   Bishop Trelawny *Journal of the Royal
Institution of Cornwall* vii, (1881-83)

JESSOP, A., ed.,   *Lives of the Norths* (1890)

JONES, C.,   'The impeachment of the earl of Oxford and
the Whig Schism 1717' *Bulletin of the
Institute for Historical Record* lv (1982)

JONES, F.G.,   *North Country Bishop* (Yale, 1956)

LACEY, D.R.,   *Dissent and Parliamentary Politics in England
1661-1689* (Rutgers, 1969)

LATHAM, R.C.,   *Bristol Charters 1509-1899* (Bristol Record
Society, 1947)

McINNES, Angus,   *Robert Harley, Puritan Politician* (1970)

NANCE, R. Morton,   'The Reason Why', *Old Cornwall* (1927)

NICHOLS, G. and   *Bristol Past and Present* 3 vols.
TAYLOR, John,   (Bristol, 1882)

OGG, David,   *England in the Reigns of James II and William
III* (Oxford, 1957)

PARLIAMENTARY   xxiv (1831-32) *Special and General Reports
PAPERS,   made to his Majesty by the Commissioners
appointed to inquire into the Ecclesiastical
Courts in England and Wales*
(1883) Report of the Commissioners appointed
*to inquire into the Constitution and Working of
the Ecclesiastical Courts*

POOL, P.A.S.,   *The History of the Town and Borough of
Penzance* (Penzance, 1974)

POUNDS, N.J.G.,   'Barton farming in Eighteenth Century
Cornwall', *Journal of the Royal Institution of
Cornwall,* new series, viii, pt.1 (1973)

SACHSE, W.C.,   *Lord Somers: a political portrait* (1975)

SANXY, Theodore,   *The Sanxay Family* (New York, 1907)

SAVIDGE, Alan,   *The Foundation and Early Years of Queen
Anne's Bounty* (1955)

188

SCHWOERER, L.G.,	'A Journal of the Convocation at Westminster', *Bulletin of the Insititute of Historical Research* xlix (1976)
SEDGEWICK, Romney, ed.,	*The House of Commons, 1715-1754* 2 vols. (1970)
SINGER, S.W., ed.,	*Correspondence of Clarendon and Rochester* (1828)
SYMPSON, Alan,	'Notes of a Noble Lord' *English Historical Review* lii (1937)
SMITH, M.G.,	'The administration of the diocese of Exeter during the episcopate of Sir Jonathon Trelawny, 1689-1707' (Oxford University unpublished B.D. thesis, 1964)
SMITH, M.G.,	'Bishop Trelawny and the office of rural dean' *Transactions of the Devonshire Assocation* cxi (1979)
SMITH, M.G.,	'John Prince and the publication of The Worthies of Devon' *Devon and Cornwall Notes and Queries* xxxiv pt.viii (1981)
SMITH, M.G.,	*Pastoral Discipline and the Church Courts: the Hexham Court 1680-1730* (York, 1982)
SMITH, M.G.,	'Bishop Trelawny and the Church in the Channel Islands 1680-1730' *Annual Bulletin Société Jersiaise* xxiii (3) (1983)
SMITH, M.G.,	'The Cathedral Chapter of Exeter and the Election of 1705: a reconsideration' *Transactions of the Devonshire Association* cxvi (1984)
STRICKLAND, Agnes,	*Lives of the Seven Bishops* (1866)
STRODE, W. Keatley,	*History of Exeter College* (1900)
SYKES, N.,	*William Wake, Archbishop of Canterbury* 2 vols. (Cambridge, 1957)
THOMPSON, E.P.,	*Whigs and Hunters: the origin of the Black Act* (1977)
TURNER, F.C.,	*James II* (1948)
WHETTER, James,	*Cornwall in the 17th Century: an economic survey of Kernow* (Padstow, 1974)
WILLIAMS, Basil,	*Cataret and Newcastle* (1966)
WYNNE, William,	*Life of Sir Leoline Jenkins* (1724)

Trelawne House

INDEX

Address of thanks, 43, 70.
Admiral's Regiment, 9.
Admiralty, High Court of, 10-11.
Advowson, right of, 92.
Agincourt, battle of, 5.
Ailesbury, Thomas, Earl of, 44, 49, 59.
Aldrich, Henry, 15, 86.
Almondsbury, Gloucestershire, Parish of, 28.
Alsop, Anthony, 143-4.
Anne, Princess, later Queen of England, 57, 74, 107-8, 128, 130, 134, 139, 145-6, 148.
Astis, John, junior, 10, 135.
Apostolic Succession, 24, 103, 106, 141.
Apostolic vicar, activity of, 49.
Archdeacons' courts, 67, 95-6.
Archdeaconry of Exeter, clerical opposition in, 95, 107.
Argyle, Earl of, 19.
Arianism, 150-1.
Army, Commissions in, 9, 158.
Army of Charles II, 9.
Army of James II, 39, 129.
Arundell, John, 6.
Astrey, Elizabeth, 143.
Atheist publications, 66, 101.
Atterbury, Francis, Archdeacon of Totnes and Bishop of Rochester: 70, 73, 100, 107;
helps in Exeter College Case, 87;
promoted by Trelawny, 73;
in alliance with Trelawny in Convocation, 101-7;
intrigues against Trelawny in bye-election, 133;
strained relationship with Trelawny in later years, 147-8.

Baptism, administration of, 108-9.
Barlow, Thomas, Bishop of Lincoln, 40.
Barrington, John Shute, 150.
Basset family, 12.
Bath, City of, 32, 111 note.
Bath, John Granville, 1st Earl of, 50, 114-21.
Bath, Charles Granville, Lord Lansdown and 2nd Earl of, 114, 117-9, 121.
Bateman, Sir Henry, M.P. for West Looe, 146.
Bathhurst, Ralph, 20.

Bathhurst, Earl of, 177.
Bedford, Duke of, 68.
Beaufort, Duke of, 27.
Bedminster, Gloucestershire, Parish of, 28.
Bermondsey, Surrey, Parish of, 140.
Bernard, Edward, 84.
Bill of Rights, 41.
Bill for supressing blasphemy, 151.
Bill to prohibit translation of bishops, 129, 166.
Bill to repair churches, 95, 106.
Billingsby, Samuel, 140.
Bingham, Joseph, 141.
Bishoprics, revenue of, 163-4. Method of appointment to, 51.
Bishops, role of in seventeenth century, 24-5.
'Blacks', The, 171.
Blackall, Offspring, Bishop of Exeter, 124, 166.
Blackburne, Launcelot, Canon, later Dean, of Exter, 15, 95, 107, 159, 166.
Blandford Forum, Dorset, 29.
Blathwayt, William, 49.
Bodmin, 113, 119, 121, 131, 133-4.
Boggis, R.J.E., 96.
Bonrepas, 49.
Borlase, William, 7.
Boscawen, Hugh Senior, 4, 18, 121.
Boscawen, Hugh Junior, 113, 132, 135.
Bouchier, Dr., 79, 85.
Boulter, Hugh, 140.
Boyne, Battle of, 120.
Braunton, Devon, peculiar of, 71.
Brett, Thomas, 108.
Bridoake, Ralph, Archdeacon of Winchester, 140, 142-3.
Briefs for repair of churches, 96.
Bright, George, 158-9.
Brightwell, Berkshire, Parish of, 143.
Bristol Cathedral, 27.
Bristol, City of, 26-8; hostility towards Roman Catholics, 31;
rists in, 29, 31;
episcopal residence in, 32;
mayor and corporation of, 31;
celebrated acquittal of Seven Bishops, 49;
parish in: St. John's, 33;
St. Mary Redcliffe, 28;
St. Peters, 33, 54 note;
St. Thomas', 28.

194

195

Pitt, Thomas, 130.
Place Bill (1692), 57.
Playford's version of metrical psalms, 68.
Plymouth, 16, 67, 114, 120-2, 131, 134.
Plympton, 122.
Poaching of deer, 171.
Polperro, 69.
Poole, Dorset, Peculiar of, 29.
Port Looe, Manor of, 171.
Portland, William Bentinck, Duke of, 120, 167.
Portsmouth, 32.
Portugal, 9.
Poulett, Lord, 124-5.
Praemunientes writ, 100.
Praemunire, penalty of, 47.
Preaching, style of, 155.
Preston, Lord, 51.
Prideaux, Humphrey, 17.
Prior, Matthew, 139, 156.
Privy Council, decisions of, 19, 85, 87.
Procurations, 164.
Prohibitions, 63, 88-9.
Prolocutor of Lower House, The, 101.
Protestant Religion, The, 58, 179.
Public morals, regulation of, 60, 63, 104.

Quare impedit, 46, 101.
Queen Anne's Bounty, Governors of, 70, 140, 169.
Queen Consort's Regiment, 31, 32.
Queen Dowager's Regiment, 'Kirke's Lambs', 9, 32.
Quo warranto proceedings, 28.

Radcliffe, Dr., 143.
Radnor, John Robartes, Earl of, 18, 120, 122, 133.
Rashleigh family, 4.
Rashleigh, Jonathon, 115.
Rashleigh, Philip, M.P. for Liskeard, 134.
Rebellion of 1715, 148.
Reforming Societies (see under name of society).
Restoration of 1660, 8.
Revelation and Natural Religion, 82, 150.
Reversions, 164, 168.
Revocation of Edict of Nantes, 38, 129.
Reynell, John, 68-9, 70.
Rich, Samuel, 35.
Riots in Bristol, 27, 29, 31.
Robartes, Francis, 133.

Robartes, John, 48.
Rochester, diocese of, 178.
Rochester, Lawrence Hyde, Earl of, 18-9, 20, 42, 100-1, 118.
Roman Catholicism, 31, 32, 43-4, 144.
Romsey, John, 32.
Rowe, Thomas, 69.
Royal Chaplains, 16.
Royal Household, office in, 8-9.
Rural Deans, 94-7, 141.
Ryder, land agent, 68-9.
Ryswick, Peace of, 120.
Sacheverell, Henry, 107, 133-4.
St. Augustine, Abbey of, 27.
St. Buryan, Royal Deanery of, 52, 71, 163, 167.
St. Germans, 113.
St. Giles-in-the-fields, 40.
St. John, Henry, Lord Bolingbroke, 109-10, 133, 147.
St. Ives, Parish of, 8, 16-7, 51, 166-7.
St. Madron's Well, 155.
St. Mary, Bermondsey, Parish of, 142.
St. Martins iuxta Looe, Parish of, 49, 67.
St. Mary, Isles of Scilly, 157.
St. Mawes, 135.
St. Olave, Exeter, 129.
St. Paul's Cathedral, 128.
St. Stephens' Fee, 123-4.
Sale of Estates, 135, 171-2.
Salisbury, Dean and Chapter of, 29, 35, 71.
Salisbury , Earl of, 142.
Saltash, 66, 113, 135-6.
Salters Hall, 150.
Samosata, Paul of, 82.
Sancroft, William, Archbishop of Canterbury, 18, 21, 29, 31, 40, 47-8, 64.
Sandhurst, Gloucestershire, Parish of, 46.
Samxay, Claudia, 129.
Saunder, Nichols, 12.
Sayer, Thomas, Archdeacon of Surrey, 140.
Scandalum Magnatum, 159.
Schism Act, 147, 149.
Sedgemoor, Battle of, 20.
Septennial Act, 136.
Seven Bishops, The, 24, 167; petition of, 47-8; trial of, 48-9.
Seymour, Sir Edward, 10, 100-1, 114, 122, 124.
Seymour, Sir Henry, M.P. for East Looe, 169.

197

198

9, 46;
Edward, 6;
Edward (uncle of Bishop), 13 note;
Edward (son of Bishop), 6, 58, 157-8;
Elizabeth (aunt of Bishop), 158;
Harry (son of Brigadier Henry), 157;
Sir Harry, 5th baronet, 99;
Brigadier-general Henry, 9, 12, 114, 121, 156;
Henry (son of Bishop), 157;
Hele (son of Bishop), 157-8, 175;
Sir John (of Altarnum), 5;
Sir John, 1st Baronet, 3, 4;
John (of Menheniot), 5;
John (uncle of Bishop), 11;
John (cousin of Bishop), 9;
John (eldest son of 2nd Baronet), 9, 16;
John, 4 Baronet, 12, 134, 146, 157, 171-2;
Sir Jonathan, 2nd Baronet, 4-5, 8, 11, 15-16, 115.
Trelawny, Sir Jonathan, 3rd Baronet, Bishop of Bristol (1685) Exeter (1689), Winchester (1707):
Ecclesiastical Career:
1675-85, Rector of St. Ives and South Hill, 15-19;
1685-88, Bishop of Bristol, 20-35;
anxious to do well, 21;
conducts visitations, 30, 32;
refuses to sign address to James II, 43-4;
intended for Exeter, 50;
one of the Seven Bishops, 49;
1689-1707, Bishop of Exeter, 65-83;
conducts Visitation, 65;
supports his clergy, 69-70;
firm disciplinarian, 65-9;
aids reform of cathedral, 73;
re-invigorates office of rural dean, 96-7;
visits Exeter College, 84-6;
legal battles, 89-90, 92;
attempts to relieve tax burden on clergy, 70;
supports revival of Convocation, 100-2;
1707-1721, Bishop of Winchester, 148-60;
conducts visitations, 141;
disciplines clergy and Fellows,

142-4;
strengthens Church in Channel Islands, 141;
Care of ordination, 141-2.
(2) Political Career:
devotion to Stuarts, 18, 20-1, 31;
opposes James II's religious policy, 44-9;
voting record in Convention, 57-8;
reasons for taking oath of loyalty, 58-9;
in opposition in William III's reign, 60, 68;
his opinion of leading Tories, 101-2;
attitude towards war with France, 128-9;
support for Marlborough and Godolphin, 128-33;
helps to secure Hanoverian Succession, 145-8;
opposes Jacobitism, 118-9, 148-9;
opposes concessions to Dissent, 149-51.
(3) Convocation Affairs:
his hopes for a sitting Convocation, 66, 99;
supports Atterbury, 100-1;
urges Lower House to proceed against heretical books, 105, 109;
grows disillusioned with leadership, 106-7;
draws up form of service, 108;
active in condemnation of Whiston, 108;
presides over opening sessions in 1714, 100.
(4) Cornish Parliamentary Affairs:
local government posts, 9, 12, 20;
named in borough charters, 19;
opposition to Earl of Bath, 115-8;
member of Stannary Parliament, 116;
electoral alliance with Godolphins, 117, 122, 128;
growing influence n parliamentary boroughs, 119-122;
loses control to Granville, 134-5.
(5) Financial Affairs:
inherits father's debts, 16;
contracts debts, 18, 20, 45, 51;
mortgages estates, 166, 169;
cost of law suits, 143, 167.

199